Marketing
with Seminars
and
Newsletters

Recent Titles from QUORUM BOOKS

MARKETING
WITH SEMINARS
AND
NEWSLETTERS

Herman Holtz

Q
Quorum Books
WESTPORT, CONNECTICUT · LONDON, ENGLAND

Library of Congress Cataloging-in-Publication Data

Holtz, Herman.
  Marketing with seminars and newsletters.

  Bibliography: p.
  Includes index.
  1. Marketing. 2. Seminars. 3. Newsletters.
I. Title.
HF5415.122.H65 1986   658.8   85–12304
ISBN 0–89930–099–5 (lib. bdg. : alk. paper)

Library of Congress Catalog Card Number: 85–12304
ISBN: 0–89930–099–5

First published in 1986 by Quorum Books

Greenwood Press
A division of Congressional Information Service, Inc.
88 Post Road West, Westport, Connecticut 06881

Printed in the United States of America

The paper used in this book complies with the
Permanent Paper Standard issued by the National
Information Standards Organization (Z39.48–1984).

10 9 8 7 6 5 4 3 2 1

Contents

Figures

Preface

Many modern marketers are finding to their dismay that their conventional and classic marketing methods are not working well for them today. The huckstering methods used for so long to sell shoes, automobiles, and breakfast cereal are simply not as effective as they once were.

That is not because those old reliables are worn out. It is because they are misused in many modern applications. The business climate is changing. We are rapidly departing from the era of the smokestack industries and are already almost hip deep in the information-industries era. Today's marketing problem is a different one from what it was, at least for many of our modern entrepreneurs. You cannot sell the products and services of the late twentieth—near twenty-first—century with nineteenth-century methods. You must learn and use twenty-first-century methods.

The evolution of more sophisticated products and services is only one cause of the need for new and different marketing methods. There are at least two other major factors that dictate the change.

One is the change in the customer base. The customer is different. Most people today are far more highly educated than our parents and grandparents were. Most of us are far more knowledgeable and aware of the world in general. Radio, television, satellite communications, and jet travel to all corners of the world have resulted in a far different customer. "Ring around the collar" advertising may work well for a laundry detergent, but it doesn't sell computers or automation systems to today's customer.

There has also been a great increase in the size of the average sale pursued by many of today's business ventures. Customers are being asked to spend many hundreds, even thousands, of dollars to buy goods and services. Catchy tunes and clever slogans won't do that job. In fact, no single sales presentation will produce sales, as a rule, for big-tag items. That kind of sale almost invariably requires repeated presentations, progressing through the several phases of identifying prospects, developing leads, making the presentation, and closing.

In fact, the high cost of conventional marketing is itself almost prohibitive today for the mass-marketing, hit-or-miss methods of yesterday. Increasingly, businesspeople are finding today that they cannot afford to spend their marketing dollars merely to make sales; they must direct their efforts toward creating customers.

One technique that overcomes many of the difficulties described and fits today's marketing needs is the use of newsletters and seminars as marketing tools. Used properly, these two methods overcome most of the problems in marketing today and offer all the attributes that modern marketing requires. They are, properly used, indeed a key to prospecting, developing leads, and creating customers.

Unfortunately, few businesspeople appear to be even fully aware of these two media, much less knowledgeable in how to employ them effectively. For example, as a result of a book I wrote to guide the reader in establishing a successful consulting practice, I continue to get frequent calls and letters from readers asking questions and usually seeking a bit of personal guidance. Most of the calls and letters verify a basic premise of that book—that is, independent consultants usually need help with their marketing much more than they need help with anything else in their pursuit of success. By far the majority of such inquiries from readers reflect their concerns with and frustrations in solving their marketing problems. They offer valuable services but are somehow unable to win contracts and create clients.

Many readers report their dismay at finding out that the brochures and sales letters they mail out do not bring results, and often do not bring a single inquiry or expression of interest, let alone an order for services. They cannot understand why a mailing of several hundred pieces, even of several thousand pieces, brings zero results. Naively, many tend to blame the failure on a variety of less important, sometimes even irrelevant, factors such as their own lack of professional writing skills and mailing lists of dubious quality. Many evidently believe that skilled copywriting and good mailing lists alone can sell anything one wishes to offer.

The problem is by no means confined to my readers nor to those engaged in new ventures but is a quite common one that is experienced by a great many established entrepreneurs, self-employed professionals, and small and not-so-small organizations. Even though the book referred to here is addressed to the independent consultant, the readership of the book is wider than that: The inquiries come from a rather wide range of practitioners and organizations because the term *consulting* is applied in a much broader sense than it once was. Today the term embraces the broad universe of technical and professional services that reflect the enormous proliferation of technology and other growing complexities of the industrial, business, and professional worlds of our society. In fact, many of those identified as consultants do not confine their offerings to services alone but also produce custom products for their clients.

This is the problem that many professionals have faced traditionally. Ethical codes alone have long made taboo even the hint of commercial advertising for lawyers, physicians, dentists, and many other professionals (i.e., "soliciting patients," as the ban on advertising by medical practitioners long ago expressed it). And even today, with the relaxation of such bans, few professionals use commercial advertising because they fear that the effect of "huckstering" will be adverse—that it will harm their professional image far more than it will benefit them. A large part of what the professional has to sell is what we have come to consider the professional image and professional dignity: an appearance of being above the necessity for actually asking for patients or clients. The public in general has been encouraged to believe that no professional worthy of the name need do this or should do this and that the act of advertising commercially—actually soliciting clients or patients—stamps the individual as unprofessional and, therefore, not one to inspire confidence.

It is this consideration, far more than any ethical or legal consideration, that has barred commercial advertising for many professionals, paraprofessionals, and entrepreneurs, even when law and ethical codes permit them to advertise commercially. Such advertising simply does not work well enough for many kinds of ventures, and for a rather simple reason: The sale of many kinds of services and/or products demands a large measure of customer trust as a prerequisite. The risk in retaining someone to defend a lawsuit, design a house, develop a custom computer program, or write an annual report is considerably less than that of authorizing a surgeon to remove one's gall bladder, but the difference is a matter of degree, not of kind: The patient/client/customer assesses the risk and tries earnestly to choose someone most likely to do the job at the lowest risk. Experience, skill, and dependability are prime concerns, usually somewhat more important than price. Buyers obviously do not order such services or products out of mail order catalogs or as the direct result of TV commercials and print advertisements.

The essence of this marketing problem is simple enough: Gaining the prospect's confidence is an absolute prerequisite to marketing success. This cannot be done by brochures, print advertising, sales letters, or any other traditional advertising method alone, although all of these can contribute to the goal, if they are discreetly and tastefully executed. The mistake is in believing that these things will of themselves produce orders or contracts.

None of this is to say that professionals and others with these special kinds of marketing requirements should not advertise. But the advertising required to cope with many of today's marketing problems must be different. It must be advertising that the prospect does not *perceive* as advertising, at least not in the heavy-handed sense of much of our typical advertising. It must be low-key and subdued, with special appeals in evidence, but subtle.

There is another important consideration. To sell a computer, an intercom system, a training program, special services, or virtually anything sold in business-to-business transactions, how will you reach the prospect? Television? Radio? Newspapers? Brochures? Sales letters? Personal calls?

All of these suffer the same handicaps: The prospect watches television and listens to radio as a consumer and is not receptive to such appeals. The other approaches are all interruptions to the executive's busy routine and are easily averted by being "out" to salespeople and by using the convenient trash basket for the mailing pieces.

Not so the properly conceived and executed newsletter and seminar. They reach the prospects as a benefit, not as an interruption.

Marketing
with Seminars
and
Newsletters

Chapter 1

A Fundamental Marketing Problem

There are many different types of professional and business ventures, and so there are many different kinds of marketing problems, especially for those which are not "one-call" businesses.

MARKETING CONCEPTS

Many people use the word *marketing* as a synonym for *sales*. A case can be made for distinguishing the two from each other, for they are not precisely the same. However, it is probably sufficient to examine marketing itself and not worry about sales, as a concept, for sales are the consequence of marketing. Effective marketing results in sales success, just as ineffective marketing results in an ineffective sales effort.

Overall, the task of marketing is to identify proper prospects—match the item to be sold with the prospects for the item, that is—the means for reaching those prospects with the sales messages, and the development of effective strategy to make sales success possible.

There are therefore several variables, especially the two variables of item to be sold and prospects to be sold to. Differences in this pair of variables alone result in the existence of many different marketing problems and situations, hence, a number of different marketing concepts. Like most things, marketing can be classified in a number of ways, and the classifications are useful to help us understand some of the rationales and principles that explain what marketing is all about.

Passive Versus Aggressive Marketing

One approach identifies two kinds of marketing, passive and aggressive. Passive marketing is practiced by many retail establishments, by opening the doors and waiting patiently for customers to enter and find what they want. On the other hand, aggressive marketing is best characterized by ventures who have salespeople out knocking on doors, actually calling on prospects, and pressing home sales presentations.

Those are the extremes. Actually, with only a few exceptions, all successful businesses have some elements of aggressiveness in their marketing, even if it is only running many sales, specials, contests, and other sales promotions.

Still, this does not change the basic nature of the difference between the venture in which marketing depends on somehow attracting the customer to the sale and the venture in which marketing is based on going to the customer. Those are the essential two shades, black and white, despite the several shades of gray between the extremes.

One-Call Versus Not-One-Call Businesses

Businesses are sometimes classified in terms of the basic marketing problem. For example, there is the one-call venture, in which marketing can be done successfully via aggressive advertising, hard selling, direct-response methods, and other tactics that produce sales directly as a result of the presentations and promotions. Television commercials, print advertising, direct mail, trade shows, in-store demonstrations, and traveling salespeople provide continuous examples of this kind of marketing, which is used to sell the vast preponderance of everyday commodities.

Despite the pervasiveness of this kind of marketing, there are many ventures which would rarely produce a sale via such methods but require subtlety, image building, and sundry indirect strategies and tactics to induce prospects to, finally, become customers or clients. Marketing for these enterprises is a far more complex problem, calling for relatively subtle and sophisticated methods.

The essential difference between these two marketing approaches is the nature of the marketing problem. In the second case there is usually the need to build up in the prospect a sense of confidence in the seller before the prospect can be induced to buy. It is that confidence which is essential to the sale of a great many services and even of some products. When the seller is a nationally known corporation of established reputation—General Motors, RCA, E.F. Hutton, or IBM, for example—a large part of the problem is solved because the public generally trusts the firm whose name is so well known. Not so the unknown firm who asks the prospect to spend a large sum of money or place his or her welfare into the hands of the seller. That firm must do something to build a sense of confidence in the prospect, which is necessarily done by indirect (for which you may substitute invisible or unseen) advertising and promotion and is often accomplished only gradually by successive advertising actions. But even those large, nationally known corporations had to build those impressive images, and most continue to spend large sums of money to keep their images polished, in what is generally referred to as institutional advertising.

ADVERTISING CONCEPTS

Advertising is one of our older professions. Like other functions in our society, it has advanced, grown, and changed steadily. Not too many years ago it was characterized principally by Burma Shave signs and billboards along the sides of the roads (not to mention signs painted on the sides of barns) and print advertising in newspapers and magazines. Today the latter kind of advertising remains, but the superhighways have all but ended the billboard era, and now the most pervasive medium of national advertising is undoubtedly the TV commercial.

Many books have been written about advertising; their authors usually offering their own theories about why and how advertising works and how to make it work. One of the typical and popular formulas reads:

1. A—(get) Attention
2. I—(arouse) Interest
3. D—(generate) Desire
4. A—(ask for) Action

The acronym is suspiciously neat and fortuitous. How convenient that it forms the easily remembered name of a popular opera! Still, there is a logic and even truth in the analysis: To be successful, advertising must first get the prospect's attention, of course; and to keep the prospect watching, listening, or reading, his or her interest must be aroused. A desire for whatever is being advertised is necessary to motivate the prospect, and, finally, the prospect must be asked to place the order or, at least, take whatever action is necessary next to the advertiser's purpose. Any careful observation of successful advertising, including TV commercials, will verify the truth of this acronym formula.

Although the four terms do describe the mechanics of what a successful advertisement does and is, unfortunately they do not provide the rationale—explain the fundamental strategy of advertising and sales motivational appeal. (The fundamental rationale is the same for both advertising and sales.) That is, the explanation does not demonstrate to anyone how to accomplish the effects called for and especially not how to arouse interest and generate desire. Moreover, it completely ignores one other critically important function that must be present in all advertising, but especially so in solving the problems of those not-one-call marketing needs we are addressing here.

That is the problem of credibility, of persuading the prospect to believe what you claim. That is perhaps not much of a problem in selling an item priced at a dollar or two; customers will venture that much to sample an unknown product or service. But when the price reaches higher levels, reaction changes, of course, and the prospect wants some assurance that the product or service is what it is represented to be.

Obviously, this is one of the situations in which the successful, nationally known corporation is at an advantage—where that institutional advertising helps greatly. But even so, it takes heavy selling because even the largest firm has competitors who are also large and well known. TV automobile commercials are one excellent example of how hard major manufacturers sell against competition, but many well-known corporations today make specific comparisons of their own products with competitive ones in the most direct and most aggressive campaigns to sell against competition.

This reflects another change in advertising, in a fundamental advertising and marketing philosophy. In fact, not too many years ago it was considered a strategic blunder to even mention a competitive product directly. (Sellers of oleomargarine, for example, referred to butter as "the high-priced spread.") Today advertisers rarely allude to competitors' goods and services by coded references but are totally uninhibited in identifying competitive products specifically by name in much of their advertising and sales presentations.

WHAT DO CUSTOMERS REALLY BUY?

Someone has wisely observed that customers do not buy quarter-inch drills; they buy quarter-inch holes. That is, of course, a fundamental truth, oversimplified to dramatize it and make the basic point clearly: Customers buy what things do, not what they are. Despite the fact that one can do other things with a quarter-inch drill than make quarter-inch holes, the message is clear enough: To sell effectively, you must understand what the customer really wants.

In advertising and marketing there are professionals who spend a great deal of time in something often referred to as "motivational analysis" which is the study of why customers buy. Of course, knowing what customers buy is most helpful in understanding why they buy. If they buy quarter-inch holes, that explains why they buy quarter-inch drills. But that still does not tell us how to sell the customers—how to persuade the customer to buy our quarter-inch drills rather than our competitor's quarter-inch drills.

That's one kind of selling: selling against competition, or filling a "felt need" for quarter-inch holes, to continue the metaphor, but filling it with our own product.

The other kind of selling requires creating the need—persuading the customer to want the quarter-inch holes—to begin with. And still this is the same problem, albeit somewhat more complex. This is why we must understand customer motivation. To persuade the customer to want quarter-inch holes, we must discover something else the customer wants that can be satisfied only by quarter-inch holes. Of course, some marketers do not even try to do this; they merely offer the quarter-inch drills to everyone who might conceivably be interested in quarter-inch holes, and wait patiently for orders in what is classically passive marketing. Others take a more aggressive approach through such measures as conducting demonstrations and suggesting reasons for wanting quarter-inch holes, in an effort to create the need. (The economy of do-it-yourself projects, the sense of accomplishment, or other appeals can be used.)

THE TWO MAJOR ELEMENTS: PROMISE AND PROOF

The basic appeal is to what the customer wants to achieve as a result of the purchase—to be able to make quarter-inch holes, to save money, to feel secure, to be loved, or whatever else really motivates the customer. Or, if selling against competition, the appeal may be that your quarter-inch drill is better than a competitor's quarter-inch drill—cheaper, easier to use, safer, more dependable, has a better guarantee, or is otherwise superior in some important ways.

That appeal is a promise you make, and if you make that promise properly, you will get the customer's attention and arouse his or her interest. Appealing to the what's-in-it-for-me concern in prospects is all but guaranteed to arouse interest. But that's not enough to generate the desire to buy—not with the sophisticated customer. Today's customer has some healthy skepticism and is not prepared to be persuaded by claims alone. There must be something more: proof. Prove that your claims are valid. The customer wants proof that your quarter-inch drill makes quarter-inch holes or that your quarter-inch drill makes better quarter-inch holes than someone else's quarter-inch drill or is superior to someone else's quarter-inch drill in some important way.

That is where logic must enter the advertising. The promise is an emotional one, something the customer wants to believe, and something that appeals to the emotions. For the enthusiastic mechanic, whether a professional or a handyman-hobbyist, there is actual pleasure (an emotion) in owning and using shiny new and thoroughly professional tools, in achieving workmanlike results, in being as good as any professional, and even pleasure in feeling a sharp new drill point boring crisply through wood or metal. Still, much as the mechanic wants to believe the promises, he wants proof that the seller can deliver on the promises, and that the purchase will produce the results promised.

What is Proof?

Just as there is more than one kind of truth, there is more than one kind of proof. There is the evidence normally accepted as proof in a court of law; there is the evidence accepted as proof by scientific observers; and there is the evidence accepted as proof by a troubleshooter analyzing an equipment malfunction, for example. But none of these is germane to our case. The only evidence to be considered here is that evidence accepted as proof by a customer. And that illustrates an important fact: In marketing, truth is exclusively what the customer accepts as truth. That is, marketing appeals must be based on customers' perceptions, and the success and failure of marketing is heavily dependent on how accurately the marketer has judged or shaped the customers' perceptions. But that leads us to another cogent marketing idea that has gained a great deal of currency and even become something of a "buzzword" in recent years: positioning.

WHAT IS POSITIONING?

The concept of positioning is credited to Al Ries and Jack Trout, New York City advertising executives and owners of their own agency, who created the concept some years ago, publicized the idea later (in 1972) with a widely quoted and often reprinted article series in the trade paper *Advertising Age*, and have since written a book on the subject (*Positioning: The Battle for Your Mind* New York: McGraw-Hill, 1981).

As Ries and Trout explain it, positioning is something the advertising strategist does to the customer's mind. It consists, in essence, of shaping the customers' perceptions to create a "position" in the market for a product, a service, or even a person or advertiser. For example, compelled by circumstance to be second in size to their rival Hertz, Avis turned their number-two ranking to advantage by positioning themselves in the customer's mind as the automobile renter who "tries harder" and, presumably, therefore gives better service and shows more concern for customers. That promise was implied at least, and the proof was the logic of their need to try harder. Obviously, it was successful: The customer accepted the argument as proof. The soft drink 7 Up was also in second place in its own industry but became the "uncola" with equal success. Alka Seltzer is what you take for stress or other causes of stomach upset; whereas Rolaids "spells relief." And Marlboro cigarettes became the rugged outdoorsman's smoke.

It's a useful idea in many other applications. Every candidate for the White House has a staff positioning him to be the friend of labor, the intellectual who can deal with our problems, the foreign-relations expert who can handle our enemies, the reformer who will straighten out our bloated bureaucracy, or whatever else the political strategists believe will be a winning position in the minds of the voters.

Organizations are also the subject of positioning strategies. For a long time, and even now, people in offices refer to "the IBM," rather than to the typewriter: "IBM" has become identical in meaning with typewriter. However, it has also come to mean computer, despite the fact that IBM manufactures and sells other products, so much so that one of its rival computer manufacturers has often referred to itself as "the other computer company."

Every product, every organization, and every public figure will assume a position, whether by design or by default: If you do not create a position, the public will do it for you, somehow inferring that position from whatever the circumstances appear to suggest. And once a position or public perception is firmly established, it is difficult to change it. If a product is identified by customers as being overpriced, for example, even drastic price cuts are likely to do little to change that perception. Conversely, if a product achieves a position of being cheap or shoddy, all the quality and price improvement in the world may have little effect in changing it.

There are exceptions, and sometimes a position can be changed. One of the oft-repeated marketing stories concerns hair spray, a chemical hair net, offering women a convenient replacement for the woven hair nets they had formerly used to preserve a coiffure. As a new product, hair sprays were relatively high priced at several dollars per container in the early days of their introduction to the market. But when a manufacturer marketed a new a hair spray for less than a dollar, the public shunned it. The low price apparently caused the customer to perceive the product as too cheap to be any good because the only standard the customer had as a guide was the price of competitive hair sprays. Raising the price to approximately double the original price solved the problem, probably because the manufacturer acted promptly enough to forestall the poor image from becoming firmly fixed in the customer's mind.

On the other hand, you do not have complete liberty to establish any position you wish. The customer is not so naive as to believe anything merely because you create a plausible rationale. You have to furnish that proof, and it must be convincing. But the way to do it is to search for and use whatever natural advantages you can find, rather than to try to weave a position from whole cloth. The position based in truth and in the customer's natural prejudices and preferences is far more effective than is one woven from whole cloth, regardless of the cleverness of any rationale manufactured to sell the image. Moreover, and as a corollary to this, the position you opt for had best not be one that asks the average prospect to abandon his or her prejudices or to make an unreasonable suspension of belief; that merely creates additional sales resistance, and no marketer needs to add obstacles to be overcome. That marketer of the underpriced hair spray, for example, might have opted to mount an entire campaign designed to prove that the product was of high quality, despite its low price, but it would have been an uphill battle with success very much in doubt. A much better, safer, and more profitable cure was readily at hand, and obviously it had also the advantage that it was a surer bet to surrender to the common prejudice that quality is related to price.

HOW LONG DOES IT TAKE TO ESTABLISH A POSITION?

That brings us to a key question, closely related to the subject of this entire book: How long will it take (usually) to establish the desired position? And by establish I mean established in the minds of the prospects. The marketer may establish the position in his or her own mind quickly, but that is not the same as establishing it in the minds of those who are the prospects. That can be accomplished almost immediately in one case but may require a great deal of time and effort in another case. And there are several factors that affect how readily prospects accept or resist accepting the position represented, but probably the principal one is that of risk, the risk that the prospect is asked to undertake in becoming a customer or client. But there are several kinds of risks represented:

Price. Price is one major risk, in the case of any product or service that can be classified as a big-tag item. The risk is small enough when the purchase calls for the commitment of only a few dollars, but it is a different matter when thousands or even hundreds of dollars are required as a consequence of placing the order.

Personal Safety or Health. If what is asked of the prospect appears to offer a possible health or safety hazard, resistance is in proportion to how great the prospect perceives that hazard to be.

Security. The security of the prospect's property, cash, or other assets is very much in the prospect's mind, when what is offered appears to offer a possible risk of such assets, and again the buyer resistance is in proportion to the perceived hazard.

Competition offers another obstacle, especially if by accepting the position you have targeted, the prospect is asked to abandon an existing perception. That is, if the prospect has already accepted something else as representing the best quality or the best value, and you are asking the prospect to now displace that perception by replacing it with your offering, you are trying to overcome an established prejudice, whether that prejudice is justified or not. It's always an uphill battle to fight established leaders on their own grounds, where they are strong, such as by trying to assume the position they are established in. Where someone is already clearly dominant in a market, it is necessary to seek a weakness, not a strength, to attack. And if a competitor dominates a market by virtue of a well-defined position, you are almost always far better advised to try to penetrate that market by basing your strategy on a different position than that of your dominant competitor. For example, seek out an area of that market the competitor is not serving well, for whatever reason, and position yourself for it. (More on this later.)

WHAT WILL IT TAKE TO DO THE JOB?

Xerox Corporation entered the still-new and fluid copier market with a system that was clearly superior to anything else available at the time. It was also much more convenient to use than most other copiers, was the only system copying on plain paper, and had extensive patent protection, so they effectively had little or no competition until their patents expired. But few entrepreneurs have the good fortune to have both a highly needed item and virtually no competition that can approach their item in quality and convenience. Most have to fight hard for their share of the market.

Unless you happen to be one of those fortunate few that can easily and swiftly dominate your chosen market, be prepared to mount a complete and ongoing campaign to build your image and establish a position. It will almost surely take appreciable time and effort to persuade prospects to perceive you or your offering as you want to be perceived—that is, to build the image you want and to have your chosen position accepted by your prospects.

THE MEDIA BLITZ

One way to mount the effort to establish your chosen position is to launch a major media campaign—radio, television, newspapers, and magazines, and perhaps even a direct-mail offering. The famous Publisher's Clearinghouse contest does this every year, and their exhortation is always to enter the contest ("Come on, send it in," urges the smiling commentator in their TV spots) because millions of recipients of the contest envelope throw it away without a second glance.

To do this the marketers find that they must battle the prejudices of many people that they have virtually no chance of winning. And there are even many who believe sincerely that no one wins. The position the marketer is working on here is one that promises anyone, even the humblest citizen, a real chance to win. And the evidence offered is the personal testimonial of a number of past winners, who are persuaded to appear on television flourishing their winnings.

A few years ago Esso, the trade name for Standard Oil's gasoline stations in the East (they used other trade names in other parts of the country), decided to change that trade name to Exxon and to use that same trade name throughout the country. (In an age of modern automobiles, superhighways, and people driving their cars all over the country, it was probably recognized as a marketing necessity to standardize their name on a national basis to make their logo recognizable everywhere, no matter where the customer came from.) The corporation mounted an extended media blitz, using all the media, to be sure that everyone learned that this new Exxon was not some Johnny-come-lately upstart seller of gasoline but was that same, good old Esso and could be found anywhere an automobile could travel.

Others use the media on a somewhat lesser scale but with the same philosophy. Sylvania TV works at establishing a position as the set with the best picture, targeting Sony especially in selling against competition. Maytag positions its appliances as being ultra-reliable, with its long-running and well-known lonely repairman commercials on television. Some computer manufacturers try to establish a different position for each model or class of machine they offer, and many try, with limited success, to compete with IBM's image as the computer for the business office. CompuServe, a public data base (subscription information service), says they don't care which computer you own; they can help you get the most out of it by building a position of service that fits everyone's needs and facilities. Kodak has gotten into the business of making and selling floppy diskettes for computers, shooting for a position of product reliability based on their established reputation and easily recognized persona as the leading seller of all things related to cameras and photography.

An Inherent Weakness in the Method

For the most part all these manufacturers who base their campaigns on media advertising depend on time and repetition—continuing exposure—to persuade prospects to accept the positions staked out. There is a basic weakness, however: All of the copy is paid advertising (although all also use news releases and try to gain a bit of free publicity too). With paid advertising the marketer has complete control over what the copy says, of course, which makes all the laudatory copy a little suspect. Prospects—readers, viewers, and listeners—take this into account with proverbial grain of salt when they evaluate what they see and hear.

OTHER CONSIDERATIONS

Obviously, the media blitz or even the use of the media for advertising on a somewhat lesser scale is costly. One reason for the media blitz and related large-scale use of the media for advertising is the need to cover a national or even international market. This is probably the most direct and surest way to blanket the entire country, and perhaps even the entire world, with a message. However, aside from the drawbacks already cited—the cynicism with which many people react to what is obviously paid advertising and the cost of the method—there is another inherent weakness in this method: It is highly inefficient because the advertiser pays for the total audience of viewers, listeners, and readers, but only a relatively small portion of that audience is of value to the advertiser. Esso managed to reach the ears and eyes of virtually every literate adult in the United States (not to mention the teenagers), and paid advertising rates are based on those figures. But only a fraction of those adults decide what gasoline to buy, and it was therefore only those for whom the message was intended and whom the advertiser really wanted to reach. Still, Esso had to pay to reach many elements of an audience which was of no interest to them. Advertising in mass-market media is a kind of package deal: You have the choice only of all or nothing at all.

This is an inevitable penalty in a great deal of media advertising, especially when you advertise in such general media as radio, television, newspapers, and other consumer publications. It is well known, of course, that a large portion of the national advertising dollar is wasted, much of the waste due to this factor alone.

SOME OTHER DISADVANTAGES

These are not the only problems and drawbacks to the methods of media saturation. There are also these handicaps:

It is extremely difficult to even estimate, much less actually measure results in terms of dollars invested in the campaign. The advertising agency responsible for an advertising campaign will try to credit any increase in sales to the campaign, of course, but it is virtually impossible to establish or prove a direct or causal relationship. A sales increase may be due to any of many other factors, such as seasonal fluctuations, changes in the economy generally, or some special event. So the difficulty in establishing the cause-effect relationship may even have advantages for the advertising agency but is a distinct drawback for the advertiser.

It is equally difficult to gauge the relative effectiveness or ineffectiveness of any given medium, advertising copy, or other variable, to determine what methods, media, mailing lists, or other variables produce the best results. At best, the advertiser can usually only make a best guess as to how well the whole campaign has produced results.

Even when special tests are devised to try to measure results, as much as they can be measured (and there are some ways to key advertising for the purpose of getting at least some useful feedback that can be used diagnostically), their usefulness is limited because of the great time lags usually involved in testing advertising in general media. Here's why:

Good advertising practice calls for making some tests to determine what copy works best and what media pull best. However, to test copy, one makes only one change at a time. Otherwise, it would be impossible to know which change in copy or in the offer produced which change in results.

Most advertising in general media takes a good bit of time to run. In fact, to place copy in a periodical, other than a newspaper, may mean that it cannot run until two or more months after being ordered. That means, in most cases, as much as three months to perceive or detect any results from such advertising and even more in many cases. If it takes three or more months to detect results and decide what to change for the next test, it is probably a year or more before the advertiser has determined what the best copy is and do the "roll out" (mount the main campaign). The result is that truly diagnostic tests are rather rare in this type of advertising, and such tests as are run—for some tests are run for major campaigns—are not as definitive or as diagnostic as you would really want them to be.

For example, one way used to test commercials is to run a preview of the commercial in a theater and ask the audience to fill out cards on which they register their interpretation of what the message is, what it means, how they react to it, and other such information. With this method it is not certain that what is being tested produces truly useful information. For one thing, whether the participant does or does not get the precise message intended is not necessarily descriptive of whether that participant would or would not buy the service or product offered, and that is the true and only sensible objective of the test.

Perhaps more important, however, is what has come to be called the Hawthorne effect, inspired by tests conducted in an electronics factory in Hawthorne, California. The test revealed that the results were distorted by the fact that it was a test, that the people knew they were part of a test. And probably this is also a manifestation of the Heisenberg uncertainty principle (postulated by Karl Werner Heisenberg, a German physicist) which points out that the fact of testing—of inserting the test instrument into the process—itself changes the process so that the results are less than totally accurate.

Such tests are therefore indirect and are certainly not the same as measuring actual results, although it is probably the best that can be done under the circumstances. It is far better, however, to test by observing and measuring results, which does not insert the test device into the process but is a direct and therefore more accurate method. It measures what you want to measure: to what degree your advertising produces sales.

There are many classic cases of expensive disasters in major advertising campaigns, which are largely due to these difficulties. Alka Seltzer, for example, spent a great deal of money on their famous "stomach" commercials. The commercials were amusing, even artistic, admired, and envied by many in the advertising business for these traits. Unfortunately, they were also a failure, for they did not sell the product. The less artistic and less amusing "plop-plop, fizz-fizz" commercials, however, did the job far more effectively. Nor is this the only such story; the advertising industry can relate many more, some even more disastrous and costly.

For these reasons, and especially because of the difficulties in measuring and evaluating the results of your advertising when using these foregoing methods, you have relatively little control, which is a distinct disadvantage and in some cases a fatal weakness.

ANOTHER APPROACH

Not every organization can afford this kind of investment in image and position. Fortunately, not every marketer needs to advertise and promote on this grand scale. There are other ways to build an image and establish a position, surely less costly and perhaps even more certain to produce the desired results. That is, there are other ways to approach the problem, especially when the target audience is somewhat specialized and somewhat restricted, when there is no compelling need to blanket the entire country with your message, and when you can identify the prospects or audience you want to reach at least in general terms. These other ways are basically through use of the marketing newsletters and seminars which are the main subject of this book. Here are just a few of the several advantages these offer as marketing tools:

Cost: Not only lower cost, but more controllable cost.

Measurability: Results can be made measurable rather easily, with these marketing tools.

Efficiency: If advertising in general media is a shotgun approach, one that blankets everyone, these methods are the rifle-shot approach, one that selects and aims at specific targets.

Accountability: Because the results are measurable, you can determine your return on investment—what your dollars have produced in results.

Speed: These methods are fast in terms of making tests, measuring results, and deciding on final copy for the roll out.

Control: All of these factors place in your hands a greater degree of control over your marketing and results than is possible with most other methods—a decisive advantage in itself.

In the pages to follow I will explore all these matters in greater depth and discuss not only marketing newsletters and seminars but also marketing and advertising principles as they can be used most effectively via newsletters and seminars.

Chapter 2

Newsletters and Seminars as Marketing Tools

Useful for any marketing application, newsletters and seminars are especially effective in solving certain rather difficult marketing problems.

THE MARKETING DEPARTMENT

David Voracek called his Alexandria, Virginia, company The Marketing Department, an effective suggestion to small-business prospects that he would function as *their* marketing departments. He has since started another company, which he calls The Design Department, because it serves clients by designing their offices and other physical facilities.

The first design assignment happened just by chance. The succeeding design assignments that compelled him to launch another enterprise he credits to the promotional newsletter he publishes (Figure 1). Mentioning that first design job in his newsletter brought those other design contracts and led to the founding of the new company.

That's not all Voracek has to say about his newsletter and the idea generally of publishing such a newsletter as a marketing medium. He reports that much of his marketing success is due to that little publication, and we'll be returning to the subject, for Voracek has been most generous in sharing his experience and giving permission to quote him. Among the wealth of ideas and information he offers in this newsletter, Voracek notes:

It is without question the best way I could spend my limited promotional funds. They say the best prospect for future business is a previous client . . . the newsletter technique is an ideal way to pull effortless business out of your reservoir of previous clients and contacts.

1.
Example of a Free Marketing Newsletter

Vol. 3 No. 1   A Newsletter for Friends of The Marketing & Design Departments

SEND IN THE POSTMEN

IBM interviewed 1,016 business managers and asked how they liked direct mail. 60% said they preferred to be informed about new equipment via direct mail, vs. only 25% who preferred a sales call. IBM tripled its direct mail budget.

BULK UP

Bulk rate mail goes up from 11¢ to 12.5¢ per piece on February 17. *(The "bulk rate" applies to mailings of 200 or more pieces)* Of course, with special "carrier route" sorting, you can get the postage cost way down to 8.3¢ each. Got questions? Give us a call.

PICKING THE BEST TRADE SHOWS

Which is the better use of your trade show dollars... a booth at the big, national shows, or attending the smaller regional/state shows?
According to a recent study by the Trade Show Bureau and the National Association of Expo Managers, regional trade shows have the higher percentage of first-time attendees. And more than 90% had *never* been contacted by the companies at the show. So you have a much better opportunity to open up virgin territory with a regional show.
One word of caution: more "top management" people attend the big national shows. But if you are after the real decision-influencers in middle management, you'll do OK at regional shows...if you "work" the crowd as hard, and take them as seriously, as you would the big national shows.

IN ROUND NUMBERS

Approximately 20% of your advertising budget will be spent to produce the ad materials you'll need for the media you select. Plus, in business campaigns, ads tend to have a longer shelf life usefulness.

HOW TO STIMULATE AD INQUIRIES

Regarding business-to-business advertising in trade journals, here are some of the recommendations from *Ogilvy on Advertising:*

- Always put a toll-free number in the ad, to make it easy to respond. Seven out of ten readers now use this method.
- Have *both* a coupon in the ad, as well as a bound-in reply card, and you're guaranteed the greatest number of responses.
- End your ad with a clear directive to "call for more information" or whatever. Don't be shy.
- Put captions under every photo in the ad, and make the copy *sell.*
- Try to devise (and picture) simple demonstrations which bring your competitive product advantage to life...and which the reader can easily demonstrate to himself.
- Talk *specifics* about percentages, time elapsed, dollars saved...

THE NEWSLETTER POPULATION

There are reportedly some 30,000 newsletters published in the United States today, and that may very well be a most conservative estimate; there is reason to believe that the number is even greater.

Theoretically, a newsletter covers some subject or addresses some interest that is so highly specialized that little coverage of the subject is ever offered by other media, although there are enough people interested in gaining the information to support a newsletter. In fact, that is not always true today. Many modern newsletters range widely in all respects, devoted to a broad variety of technical, business, professional, and consumer subjects and interests, some rather exotic or esoteric, others quite mundane.

Here is a small sample of newsletter topics, illustrating the diversity and fact that not all are devoted to weird and wonderful subjects: accounting, advertising, air conditioning, banking, beverages, building management, civil engineering, computers, drugs, economics, energy, entertainment, farming, geology, hospitals, insurance, jewelry, labor relations, libraries, machinery, medicine, mining, nursing, oceanography, office procedures, packaging, railroads, retirement, school management, securities, taxes, textiles, urban affairs, veterinary medicine, wine, and women.

Newsletters generally have relatively little in common with each other, and they differ from each other in more than topics and coverage. Some are published daily, some weekly, some monthly, and some on more extended schedules, such as bimonthly, quarterly, or even semi-annually. Some are quite elaborate, 24 and more pages, printed on glossy, calendared stock, with color photos and professional typesetting, while others are only two or four pages, composed by electric typewriter, and duplicated by office copier or mimeograph on inexpensive sulphite paper; and some are even published on newsprint, in typewriter-size or tabloid, although still represented to be newsletters. Some have circulations of many thousands, while others are limited to a few hundred, and to even less than a hundred in some cases. Some accept paid advertising, although most do not. Subscription costs vary from free to hundreds of dollars per year and are related to factors other than size and quality of printing and binding. (Some expensive and quite successful newsletters are composed on ancient manual typewriters and duplicated by inexpensive "quick copy" offset methods.) Some are produced by large and successful publishers of other periodicals, and some by individuals for whom the newsletter is a part-time venture. Some are published purely for profit, as a commercial venture, while others are published by non-profit groups for the public at large or for members of some association, and still others are published by industrial and business firms for employees and customers and customer prospects.

That last category is the one of greatest interest to us. It is what this book is about: using newsletters (and seminars) as marketing tools, which means that they are addressed to customers and, especially, to prospective customers (or clients, if you are in a calling that refers to your buyers as clients). Usually these are free newsletters, although there are exceptions to that; even newsletters that produce income through paid subscriptions and other exploitation are often used effectively as marketing tools.

SEMINARS

In the strictest sense of the word, a seminar is a group activity involving discussions and exchanges among a small number of individuals, usually addressing some advanced and highly specialized subject. However, like many terms, the definition has been broadened over the years and today is applied to any small-group session of people gathered to gain some useful, specialized information, usually delivered by one or more presenters from a lecture platform, and running from about one-half day to as many as five days. (Most commercial seminars offered today tend to be one-, two-, or three-day sessions.)

Seminars have been gaining in popularity for many years, inspired largely by the rapid expansion in technology, which has made us conscious of the need for special training. Like newsletters, their chief justification for existence, theoretically at least, is the need of many people for information not readily available elsewhere or the need for an environment in which questions, discussions, and other exchanges are possible, as they are not when one must learn solely by reading. Lawyers, for example, may attend a special seminar to learn the details of some new laws, such as those governing environmental control or product safety, and an engineer might attend a seminar to learn new technology, such as microminiaturization techniques or how to use new types of computer programs. On the other hand, some seminars promise employers to make their office staff more efficient, and some propose to teach executives how to cope successfully with stress and fatigue.

In fact, to demonstrate the diversity, here are just a few topics in which seminars are commonly offered: business writing, computer programming, consulting, contract administration, contract law, copywriting, data base management, direct-response marketing, energy auditing, federal procurement, general investments, integrated software, labor negotiation, mail order, management, marketing, new tax laws, office organization, proposal writing, real estate buying, sales techniques, speed reading, technical writing, understanding spread-sheets, value engineering, and word processing.

In many ways this list parallels the list offered to illustrate the typical subject matter of newsletters. Some cover little-known subjects or little-known aspects of common subjects, while others address quite common needs and interests, such as training office personnel in modern word processing methods.

As in the case of newsletters, seminars are distinguished more by their differences than by their similarities. Probably the single trait they have in common is that most tend to be extended lecture sessions, rather than group discussions or exchanges, although an occasional enlightened seminar leader does understand the need for and encourage the use of those elements of discussion and exchange. Beyond that, seminars differ widely. Some meet for a few hours or for as long as five days. (One organization conducts annual conferences and trade shows and offers a variety of three-hour seminars during the week-long conferences they hold in New York, Chicago, and San Francisco.) Some charge attendees approximately $100 per day, but an increasing number charge as much as $200 to $300 per day. On the other hand, some are conducted as adult education, are sponsored by local governments, and are offered at extremely modest rates, such as $35 to $75 per day. Some are purely lecture sessions, while others have discussions, participation, and are virtually workshops rather than seminars. Some are conducted entirely by a single lecturer or presenter, while others have a large staff of presenters, each of whom takes an hour or less for his or her own presentation. Some are sponsored by individual entrepreneurs who are often also the presenters, while others are offered by commercial organizations who strike agreements with college professors and other specialists to conduct the sessions, often for modest honoraria and the opportunity to gain some marketing exposure and possible consulting assignments or other such benefits.

Some seminars are presented on academic premises—in the classrooms of universities, for example—while many are presented in public auditoriums, but most are offered in commercial, rented facilities, such as hotel meeting rooms. And some are even presented in special environments, such as on cruise ships. Some are an element of a larger production, such as an annual convention or conference, but many are individual promotions, organized as commercial ventures. (One newsletter publisher in Washington, D.C., discovered that seminars were more profitable than his newsletters, and he created for his firm a multi-million-dollar market in seminars, but he is by no means unique in this. There are many others who made the same discovery and now make a profession or business of seminar presentations.)

Seminars are also offered by many entrepreneurs as custom, in-house presentations. In my own case, for example, I often present in-house seminars in proposal writing to the staffs of companies who pursue federal government contracts. But there are many others who offer seminars on a similar basis, especially inspirational-type presenters, such as Dave Yoho and Nido Qubein, who can offer thought-provoking concepts and inspire the sales staffs of many companies to extraordinary efforts or train corporate executives in the arts of leadership and inspiring followers to outstanding performance and achievement.

Many employ free seminars as marketing ploys, again as in the case of newsletters. The Evelyn Wood organization, teachers of speed reading, has long used free seminars as a marketing tool, for example, evidently with great success. And the Albert Lowry organization, teachers of the art of getting rich (on paper, at least) by buying real estate, has also used this as their principal marketing tool, again with evident success. And they even used a tri-level approach: newspaper advertising, a late-night TV program to inspire and encourage attendance at the free seminars, and the free seminars designed to inspire attendance at the paid seminars, which are the final objective of all the newspaper advertising and other promotion.

WHY NEWSLETTERS AND SEMINARS?

Advertising and promotion via newsletters and seminars offers both advantages and disadvantages, as do most things. There are two principal disadvantages:

- They require a relatively great amount of your time and labor to prepare and deliver.
- They require a great deal of skill to prepare them so that they do the job and exploit their advantages.

These are the advantages to be exploited:

- Newsletters and seminars are not obvious advertising and so can be made to appear to be objective and worth reading or attending for their content, thus escaping the stigma of "flackery."
- They can be advertised as "free" and thus become attractive and actually sought after.
- Because the prospects actually seek the newsletter or seminar—opt to send for it or attend it—you have their attention and do not have to fight for it.
- They are less costly, in general, than media advertising.
- They are highly flexible in virtually all respects.

THE APPROACH

The approach to the marketing newsletter and seminar is critical. You must disabuse yourself of any idea that either of these media can be 100 percent advertising matter and still do their job. That simply will not work for at least two reasons:

1. The material will be perceived as sheer advertising and will thus have none of the normal advantages over paid advertising, while having all the disadvantages.
2. The reader/attendee will feel deceived, even betrayed, and "turn off" entirely. You will thus lose that advantage of having the prospect's attention automatically without having to resort to special measures to command it.

The right approach, and your general philosophy or mind set, in fact, must be this: You will offer enough genuine inducement—useful information and other interesting content—to make it worthwhile for the prospect to send for and read or attend. You may consider this a kind of sugar coating for the pill of advertising-promotional content, if you wish, but it has to be present for the concept to work at all.

Generally, those who market through these tools are offering samples of what they sell, usually teasers that have some merit of usefulness in themselves but at the same time do not "give the store away." The idea is to stimulate the prospects' interest and work it up to a desire to buy, of course, and the strategy overall is to make it clear to the reader/attendee that while you are offering some worthwhile information or other goodies here, this is merely a sideshow, and there is far more to be seen and learned in the main tent.

Dave Voracek's newsletter (Figure 1) is an example. It always offers readers some useful information. But in each issue Voracek sends readers some kind of advertising message. One reason he started his newsletter, he says, was to combat being categorized, or "pigeonholed." Because his business is rather generalized, he had to combat the tendency of clients to consider him a specialist in only whatever task he had done for them. Here is his own explanation:

If I did a brochure for client A, he tended to think of me as a good brochure firm . . . if I did direct mail promotion for client B, he tended to think of me as a direct mail expert, and recommend me to others only as such. . . . So my objective was to find a way to "name drop" some of my other clients . . . so they could see that I worked for a variety of firms in a variety of industry categories. Plus I wanted to use this as a way to remind them that I do all the various marketing-related activities: a direct mail campaign for one firm, a new logo image for another, a trade show booth for yet another, a market research project for another.

The Albert Lowry seminar in real estate entrepreneurship, which I attended in gathering material for this book, was an excellent example of the method at work in this other medium, the seminar. It included all the classic elements of advertising and sales presentations and satisfied, also, my own rationale of promise and proof. It was an evening session of less than two hours conducted by a man who said that he had found this marvelous opportunity to be highly successful after spending years just getting by on barely acceptable wages. And while he didn't say so specifically, he implied rather plainly that he was a highly successful real estate entrepreneur now and could not for the life of him understand why everybody wasn't in on this bonanza in which all you needed was a little knowledge, a smidgin of alertness, and a lot of energy. The promise was plain: Anyone can do the same, and the Lowry weekend training seminar (the one prospects pay for, that is!) reveals and explains it all.

The speaker did give away a few valuable tips and clear up a few popular misconceptions, while simultaneously working up the excitement of the attendees by enriching the promise with such goodies as these:

- You can buy real estate without money or with the most nominal of down payments.
- You can trade up continuously, increasing your holdings steadily.
- You will learn what to do, what not to do, how to evaluate, and how to negotiate for financing as well as for real estate deals.
- The information in the exclusive seminar manual is not the same as in Lowry's published books and cannot be found anywhere else except by attending the seminar.

The presenter scribbled sets of figures on a projector, casting them on a large screen, to demonstrate leverage, profits, and all the other profitable maneuvers available to the knowledgeable real estate entrepreneur a la Albert Lowry.

It was a highly professional performance and presentation, although the handout was a flimsy and cheap-looking piece of printed matter with a prominent explanation that Lowry had been a butcher for years before becoming a wealthy real estate entrepreneur. The strategy was obviously to demonstrate that anyone, even a humble butcher, could do what Lowry had done, and anyone could learn his secrets of success in one weekend.

This is a strategy that may work but may also backfire; it may, in fact, actually discredit the expert because some readers may regard this as evidence of a lack of proper credentials. This is especially true in these days when experts are so often people who parade a string of academic credentials and extensive career experience as a top executive in some prestigious firm. However, that aside, I found that flimsy and cheaply printed handout a jarring note, especially when compared with such a highly polished and fluent presentation by a man who obviously knew what he was doing. If I had been seriously interested in learning how to wheel and deal in real estate, that amateur-looking handout alone would have given me pause and made me wonder why such an apparently successful operation could not afford a little better quality in the handout. (The cost differential between poor and good quality in printing is not that great.)

Nevertheless, except for that, all the marketing and advertising elements were there: the attention-getting general promise of a sure route to success and wealth; the interest-arousing clearing up of myths and misconceptions, especially those that add to the lure, such as no-money-down opportunities; the proofs and convincers, in the form of numerous anecdotes of others' successes and the figures showing the legerdemain of how to manipulate the dollars and extract the profits; the extra motivators in the claim of much exclusive, insider information in the seminar manual, which would not be available elsewhere or otherwise; and the call to action, in the form of the explanations of the weekend seminar, with certain price inducements; and the final exhortation to step over to any of the tables set up around the room and sign up for this once-in-a-lifetime opportunity.

Those who did not sign up on the spot for the weekend paid seminar received an exhortation in the mail shortly after, extending the "special price," which had been originally represented as available during the evening of the seminar only.

Inasmuch as this marketing seminar and the follow-up, paid-attendance seminars were regular occurrences in my area for some months, the marketing seminar was obviously a highly successful presentation, despite the weakness of the handout and what it said about Lowry's beginnings as a butcher, which I believe to be a risky strategy.

MAKING SALES VERSUS MAKING CUSTOMERS

Marketing is almost always aimed at achieving one of two possible results, depending entirely on what the marketer is selling. The aim is to make either a sale or a customer. The difference is highly significant in a great many respects, and it has an important bearing on marketing and advertising philosophy. It is extremely important to be conscious of the difference always. Confusion between the two objectives can be costly, if not disastrous.

The Lowry seminar was aimed at making a sale. It had to be, inevitably, because it had only one thing to sell, with extremely little probability of a second or follow-on sale to or through the original customer. The consequences of this simple goal are immediately apparent, and the chief one is that this single event, the marketing seminar, had to produce a direct profit to be worth doing and a profit large enough to be worth the effort, for there would be virtually no follow-on value in anything accomplished there otherwise.

In short, the seminar had to produce enough sales so that the costs of both the marketing seminars (Lowry held several free seminars for each paid one) and the paid seminar were covered and a profit still remained. There is no way that a loss could be recovered directly, since the entire cost of the marketing seminars had to be amortized over the sales of attendance at that one paid seminar.

The one slight fringe benefit gained from the free seminar was the mailing list of attendees. Lowry made little use of this, other than to mail a follow-up solicitation, which was also a rather simple and cheap-looking mailer, to those who had not signed up. Perhaps he could have made better use of those names, since he certainly had or could have compiled a long list from all those free seminars, which he ran in various locations in the United States. It is a good idea to ask attendees to register because the resultant mailing lists are always useful, if employed properly. For one thing, they can be brokered by list managers and produce income for the marketer in this manner. But they can also be used for other marketing promotions: Lists of interested prospects are always a valuable asset if used properly.

Aside from this, however, it is an obvious necessity, when you have only one thing to sell or, at least, are interested in selling only one thing, to base all calculations and plans on the premise that the sales resulting directly from the free seminar must produce enough income to defray all costs, including those of the free seminar, and leave a profit large enough to have been worth the effort.

There is one possible exception to this rule: In some circumstances, particularly in those big-tag enterprises that require more than one presentation or promotion to close sales, the free seminar may very well pay its way in ultimate sales benefits, although not directly and immediately. Still, there is a "profit" that must be calculated and measured to determine whether the free seminar was successful or not. That consists of at least two parts: the number and quality of prospects or leads generated, for those leads are the direct profits of the free seminar, if that was the purpose of presenting it, and the ultimate closes or actual sales resulting from the leads generated by the presentation. That takes some time to evaluate and measure, of course, but a good projection of that final result can usually be made by judging the quality of the leads.

In that connection, too, take note that while newsletters can be addressed to customers only or to both customers and prospects, free seminars are almost always used to address prospects, in an effort to make customers of them. Still, there are exceptions to this, too, for it is possible to use the free seminar as a valuable marketing tool addressing even current or former customers, in some cases. One such case occurs when you are introducing a new product or service. (Your own customers are obviously the best possible prospects, usually.)

There is, of course, one other alternative that would have been suitable for the Lowry marketing people, had they wished to pursue it, and that is to have something else to sell in addition to a paid seminar. That offers several possible additional benefits, while reducing the risk or "exposure." That is a management decision that each marketer must make, and I will discuss it in some depth later.

HARD SELL VERSUS SOFT SELL

The Lowry seminar was the example used for these observations, but the principles apply to both newsletters and seminars used for marketing. There is one major difference between the two, however, the consideration of which generally influences the marketer in making a choice between the media. That is the kind of sales effort required, for the two media are not equally well suited to all kinds of marketing and sales requirements.

In the case of such seminars used as the example here, the effort required to make sales has much more the characteristics of the hard sell than of the soft sell. That is, intense sales pressure is required to make the sale, because one of the factors dictating the need for hard-selling tactics is that the prospect will usually not come back, if once allowed to "escape." The professional sales expert would probably explain this as knowing when to close and closing at the proper time, pointing out the disastrous result of closing too early or too late. However, there are several general truths which help us understand this situation:

Where the item being sold is not truly exclusive or unique (despite claims made for exclusivity), the prospect inevitably weighs the cost of what you are selling against alternatives. At least some of the prospects attending the seminar cited were aware that there are many books on the subject of building a real estate fortune and that there have been other seminars and training courses held in my city. Weighed against the $400 to $500 cost of the seminar, alternatives often appear attractive, and the longer a prospect ponders the alternatives, the less likely it is that he or she will sign up for the expensive course or seminar. That explains, also, the weakness of the follow-up mailing: The marketer did not have high hopes, based on experience, for more than an occasional additional sale resulting and therefore did not believe it worthwhile to make a major investment in the direct-mail follow-up.

THE BENEFIT OF GROUP DYNAMICS

It is essential in this situation to urge the prospect to sign up immediately, while still enthralled or at least highly enthused by the presentation and the promises made. And if the seminar has attracted a large audience—preferably several hundred people—group dynamics are at work too. If the presenter succeeds in creating a pleasant mood and a wave of enthusiastic reception for what is presented, as most competent presenters can do, the enthusiasm becomes contagious.

Most of us have at least a little touch of insecurity. Urged to some action, we look around us to be sure that we are not alone. No one is eager to be the first to head for the table to sign up, but wants to be reassured by seeing others swarm to the registration table, and so is inspired to follow others. (That is why some marketers plant "shills" to start the march to the sign-up tables and thus encourage others to follow.)

Obviously, there are no effective group dynamics working for you with a newsletter. Hard-selling prospecting, especially for big-tag items, cannot normally be accomplished via a free newsletter, any more than it can be accomplished by a sales letter or brochure. Only direct, personal, face-to-face presentation can work effectively when there is much buyer resistance to overcome and hard-sell methods are required.

Another reason that the hard sell is required in such situations as these, however, is that the marketer feels it necessary to achieve one-call sales, when the price alone makes it difficult to do so because not too many prospects will spend several hundred dollars casually, without wanting to take at least a few days to think about it. And essentially, the sales the marketer is trying to make here are one-call sales, despite the preliminaries and pre-selling used to bring the prospects to the point of sale. Those preliminaries produce interested prospects, although they also produce a number of idle curiosity seekers for whom the seminar is merely a diversion and who have no true interest in becoming buyers. Merely to close with a single presentation a sale that normally requires at least an initial presentation and a follow-up sales effort itself mandates the need to sell hard, regardless of other considerations.

IS THE SALES SEMINAR A NEW IDEA?

It is not without reason that the French say that the more it changes the more it is the same—the Gallic equivalent of our own "there's nothing new under the sun." We may regard the sales seminar as a rather new idea, but it is in many respects something that has been with us for a very long time. In fact, it might be considered to be a modern version of what used to be called a pitch, in which a fast-talking and glib salesman gathered a group of people around his wagon, in horse-and-wagon days, or on the street or even in an empty store front, in Depression days, to sell some nostrum. Today, we refer jocularly to those people as "snake oil salesmen," nor have they vanished completely from the scene. Although much reduced in numbers, they can be found in carnivals, circuses, and in many other places yet, selling modern versions of snake oil.

One could hardly sell such nostrums on the street today or be quite so transparent with today's customers. The old-fashioned pitch must be modernized and made suitable for today's prospect, but the principles are the same: The successful presentation (seminar) attracts attendees because it is educational and even entertaining; the sales appeal is indirect; and the group dynamics are at work as effectively as ever, although the entire presentation is necessarily in modern dress.

On the other hand, it is a mistake to overdo the entertainment aspects of the public seminar. Attracting those who are not true prospects merely adds to your expense without contributing to your desired results. This is one effect of being excessively cryptic or general in wording your announcements. There are always those idle people who will send for samples and free literature simply out of boredom and the desire for some diversion. But there are also their counterparts who will attend a free seminar and occupy the seats you have paid for simply to pass some time or because they are curious. The idea is to attract *qualified* prospects, which in this case means those who appear to be genuinely interested in whatever it is you wish to sell. To achieve that, you must make the nature of your seminar quite clear in advance; you do not want the theme of the seminar to come to attendees as a total surprise.

SOME TYPICAL MARKETING PROBLEMS AND APPROACHES TO SOLUTIONS

The choice of which to use, seminar or newsletter, is rarely an arbitrary one. It is usually dictated by the nature of the marketing problem, determining which medium is necessary to carry out the marketing mission successfully. Of course, there are some situations in which both media may be used effectively, and newsletters may play a role even in situations that dictate hard-sell methods. In such cases the newsletter may be used as a medium to round up prospects and develop leads by using it to announce a seminar, do as much pre-selling as it is possible or useful to do, and urge attendance. There are many similarities between the two in how they can be applied and what they can accomplish. But there are also a great many different marketing needs and selling situations, and these influence and even dictate the choice as well as the mode of use in each application.

There is, as one example, the special marketing problem you may have as a professional person, if you are a doctor, lawyer, consultant, psychologist, professional lecturer, trainer, or in some other such profession. Aside from the inhibitions of ethical codes against blatant advertising in many professions, there is the simple fact that undisguised advertising simply does not work well—often, not at all—for professionals. The patient or client bases his or her choice of professional on matters other than advertising claims, generally revolving around the professional image. The buyer must always have some faith in you as the seller, but this sense of confidence is especially necessary when you provide some kind of professional service. And to inspire that confidence, you must build and maintain an image of dignity and reserve, to reflect calm self-confidence. But perhaps even more to the point, not only does conventional advertising generally fail to be at all effective in this case, but it has an adverse effect. It is disillusioning to the prospect, who must believe that you are above the need to advertise and, in any case, too dignified to become a huckster, and so it can do actual damage to your image. The newsletter offers a way to avoid advertising per se while achieving the benefit.

If you happen to be a professional or even a paraprofessional functioning as an independent entrepreneur, this poses a special problem for you in even making prospects aware of your existence and services, not to mention the additional difficulties of persuading prospects to patronize you.

You may have either of two marketing problems: If yours is a service for which patients or clients experience a felt need to seek out someone, your marketing task is to persuade prospects to patronize you, rather than a competitor. But there are services for which prospects do not feel the need to seek out someone but must be persuaded to try the service (or product, for that matter). Of course, you must recognize the difference between these two marketing challenges and approach your marketing appropriately.

For this application in general, both the newsletter and the seminar are practical approaches. Both can be undertaken in almost the guise of a public service, offered altruistically. Certainly, both can be done in a highly dignified way and avoid even the appearance of commercial huckstering, while establishing and promoting the proper image and delivering the message. You must recognize, however, one great difference between the two and take it into account: The seminar is a relatively large expense and is by its nature usually a "one shot" proposition. You either do or do not accomplish your purpose (make sales or generate good leads for sales) in that one session. It's almost impossible to go back and do it over, if you fail to carry out your mission in that session. (Of course, you can plan a series of seminars and learn from early mistakes, but that is a rather expensive proposition.)

The newsletter, on the other hand, can be produced rather inexpensively, has a continuing presence because it appears regularly before the prospect's eyes, and thus has a cumulative effect. This makes the cost of education—learning from early errors—relatively modest. And of course there is far less stress because the entire proposition of producing and sending out a newsletter is so much simpler in many ways than producing a seminar. It is, however, an obligation not to be undertaken lightly, especially if you wish to produce it as often as every month or even every other month. (Dave Voracek says that he began his newsletter as a monthly publication but found the burden of meeting each month's deadline too heavy and cut it back to once every two months. And he cautions against failing to produce it regularly, as promised, saying it will have an adverse effect, worse than if you had not begun it in the first place.)

The pros and cons, then, are obviously these: The newsletter is low stress, relatively easy and inexpensive to produce, keeps your name in front of the prospects, and enables you to send messages regularly and break down sales resistance through repetitive selling. (It is well known in direct-mail circles that with successive mailings to a given list, each mailing produces more than the previous mailing, and this may easily continue through several such cycles before reaching a peak and leveling out.) It is also better than a brochure and can, in fact, serve as a brochure. On the other hand, it becomes a harsh taskmaster—those deadlines come around regularly and press you to get to work. And if it is highly suitable to the type of sale that can be made only after repeated presentations and appeals, it is also slower to produce than the face-to-face effort of the seminar approach, where prospects can be signed up on the spot, in many cases.

Of course, the reverse is true for seminars. There is stress, expense, and a great deal of work to organize the session and turn prospects out for it. But it does not normally impose an obligation to continue offering sessions, and it does afford at least the prospect of faster closings of sales. It also produces a mailing list, which can have great value, and it offers a better vehicle for establishing your personal image, if that is one of your marketing goals, than does a newsletter.

In some cases, one or the other medium is clearly indicated as the right one for the job. If your objective is to sell low-priced items, such as books, reports, and other such items, the newsletter is almost sure to be a far better medium for you than the seminar is. But the reverse is also true: Ordinarily, seminars are too costly to produce and present to sell small-tag items. (However, many lecturers and presenters of seminars that include attendance fees do supplement their earnings by selling books and other literature to attendees.)

One weakness in many kinds of conventional advertising is in the dual difficulties of correlating results with effort and of getting those results with reasonable speed. Too often, it is many weeks and even months after an insertion order is placed before the advertising can be run. (Many magazines, for example, book advertising space several months ahead and sell certain key positions even farther in advance.) Copy you have devised in January, therefore, may not be put to the test before spring or summer, at best; and before you can utilize what you have learned from the advertising and run a second test, a full year may have passed. Moreover, it is often difficult to determine what portion of your sales resulted from your advertising when using conventional means.

Newsletters and seminars offer advantages in these respects because you can easily run small test mailings and small seminars to gauge results of an appeal on a small scale and almost overnight. This enables you to experiment with numerous ideas for copy and offers before you make a major commitment to a campaign.This advantage alone makes newsletters and seminars most valuable marketing tools. One of the cliches uttered frequently is the alleged quotation of an executive who is reported to have said, "I know that half of my advertising dollar is totally wasted, but I don't know which half." Judicious use of newsletter and seminar marketing can help you determine which half it is.

There is also a wide differential in costs. When you place an advertisement in a periodical, you pay to reach the entire circulation—all the alleged exposure of your advertising copy—even though much of that circulation consists of people who are not suitable prospects for you. With seminars and newsletters you can target your prospects much more precisely, hence, more efficiently. The result is a better use of your advertising budget generally.

In addition to that, there is this consideration: Newsletters and seminars give you nearly total control of your advertising. You can do as much or as little advertising as you wish to or believe necessary and justified. You can react rapidly to conditions of the moment, change copy, expand the marketing effort, expand the offer(s), or make other changes. And all of those are important considerations. Suppose, for example, that January is ordinarily a good month for orders, and you therefore increase your advertising budget in December and January. Or suppose that conventional wisdom in your industry suggests that you should do so. January may well turn out to be a good month. But it may not be. Last year's pattern and the buying patterns described under conventional wisdom are simply not dependable standards. When you have had to order your advertising months ahead, you may not be able to cancel it or cut it back when you find unexpected business conditions at a late hour. But with the control you have over these other two media, you can usually make rapid and sudden changes when you wish to.

These are not all the pros and cons or all the considerations, by any means, but are only general ones that are offered here for orientation. As I continue discussing different aspects of newsletter and seminar development and production, you will see many other applications to marketing and many special cases.

Chapter 3

Seminar Concepts and Promotion

As seminars go, this is a special one, with special rules.

WHAT IS A SEMINAR?

The question of what a seminar is concerns us here especially because the type of meeting and presentation which is the subject of these pages would not be considered a seminar by most seminar professionals. And that is true for more than one reason. Aside from the technical definitions of a seminar, most seminar producers seem to agree that anything more brief than a half day—three hours, in most seminar formats—is not a seminar at all but a speech or simple presentation.

It is unlikely that you will want to conduct a meeting and presentation of three hours. It would be difficult to hold your audience that long for a sales presentation (which is what it is, of course), even if you could fit such a program into an evening and still leave time to answer questions, from the rostrum or in private conversations, and sign people up or take orders. (Many seminar attendees prefer to ask questions of the presenter in a private, side discussion, after the formal presentation or during a break, rather than before the entire group, and sales are often consummated or initiated in these little side discussions.) Long before three hours had expired, attendees would begin to drift away. Such a presentation should not be longer than an hour or an hour and a half, ordinarily.

Despite this, *seminar* is by far the best term to use in describing the event. It has become a well-known term in recent years, as the frequency and diversity of seminar presentations has expanded. Moreover, it is recognized as something of value because seminar registrations are generally rather costly, so "free" has appeal, in this usage.

Therefore, although I use that term *seminar*, I am referring to the briefer presentations, as noted here.

WHAT THINGS ARE NECESSARY FOR SEMINAR SUCCESS?

There are two main concerns in the launching of a seminar enterprise: the content and the promotion. The first refers to the technical/professional success—valuable material, well organized, and effectively presented—and the second to commercial success—a well-attended and profitable venture. And that latter factor is itself largely, although not entirely, the direct result of the sales promotion and its effectiveness.

Both successes are important and both are necessary for overall seminar success, of course, although in many ways it is the sales promotion effort that is the more critical function. Good training and presentation materials for seminars and workshops are abundantly available, and there are professional presenters—even sales professionals who specialize in the "pitch" type of presentation—whom you can hire, but successful sales promotion of the seminar is another matter. Materials for achieving that are by no means abundantly available nor completely dependable. It is therefore not surprising that seminar producers generally consider sales promotion as the more important problem.

On the other hand, it may come as a surprise that essentially the same considerations apply to the free seminar. Despite the fact that it is free, prospects must be persuaded to attend, to "pay" with some of their free time, which is worth more than money to a great many hard-working people. It is not enough that the seminar is free; even that which is free must have some apparent value to attract applicants for it, especially when the applicants must make some special effort or be even slightly inconvenienced to take advantage of the free offer.

In short, you have a double selling job: Before you can use the seminar to make your sales presentations, you must sell prospects on attending the free seminar.

The two problems are not unrelated to each other. Obviously, if prospects attend your seminar in satisfyingly large numbers, it is because you have struck a responsive chord with your appeal. It is because enough people have found what you offer attractive and believe that you can and will deliver what you promise. Therefore, it is both the content per se and the way it is presented—the offer—that is the main factor in capturing or failing to capture the interest of the prospects.

The Offer

In my own lexicon of terms about advertising and marketing, I use the word *offer* in a special sense, synonymous with the sense in which I use the word *promise*. Offer is defined as what you promise to do for the prospect if the prospect buys what you are presenting. In that sense, it is not the free seminar that is the offer, but what (you promise) the seminar will do for the prospect who attends.

Suppose you wanted to persuade people to attend a course designed to help them quit smoking via hypnosis, and you chose the free seminar as a means for promoting this. Your offer, in its most basic terms, is a promise to help or make it possible for the attendee to quit smoking. But wait: The offer alone will arouse some interest because a great many people want to quit smoking, and your marketing problem here is not so much one of persuading prospects to develop a desire to quit smoking as it is to induce the prospect to (1) quit putting off the decision to stop smoking, and (2) take your course, rather than attempt to quit via some other method.

That latter objective is quite important. Sometimes an advertiser manages to achieve that first objective of inducing the prospect to finally act, but fails to meet that second objective and thus creates sales for competitors! In this case, you must sell against competition, even more than you must overcome buyer reluctance and procrastination. You must be sure to present some overpowering arguments for your own method. And that is an important part of the offer too.

It should be clear by now that your offer is something more than an offer to help the prospect quit smoking. Many others make that offer, and if you are to sell against your competition successfully, you must have some powerful (and preferably unique) inducement in your own offer. That is, you must find the right motivator. It could be any of several things. Some typical motivators are: low price, discounts, convenience, speedy results, no effort (of customer) required, guarantees, and special bonuses.

It is always necessary to examine what competitors offer (promise) and what appear to be the chief factors that make prospects reluctant to buy or, conversely, motivate them to buy. In the case of selling a program to help people abandon cigarettes, some special considerations should be taken into account. One is that a great many people really do not want to stop smoking but will yield to the mounting pressures to do so if it is painless enough for them. Another is that many people have tried to quit without help and have failed, so they are rather doubtful that they can, even with help. Another is that they tend to be skeptical about the promises made of painless withdrawal from smoking.

For this type of marketing goal, the seminar that offers a free "lesson" or demonstration of hypnosis will attract a great many people. It would probably not be difficult to gather a large audience. Converting those attendees into customers is another matter. Buyer resistance is likely to be rather strong, for all the reasons cited, and success in this enterprise probably depends heavily on the hard sell and signing people up to contracts, with payments (or at least substantial deposits) in advance. (Without that, a great many who sign up will "cool off" and fail to show up at the weekend program.)

One major objective of such a seminar must be to determine, as a result of the first few sessions, what the most effective motivators appear to be—that is, what is the offer that produces the best results? Price? Discounts? Guarantees? Evidence of effectiveness? Speed of results? Or something else? That determination is likely to be the main key to success for the entire program, and it will surely point the way to all the future marketing seminars in your campaign.

That is somewhat simplified as a statement, however. You need to find out what your offer should be to get the best results. You need to know, for example, what the right price is, what the guarantee should be, and how in general to structure your offer—what to promise—for greatest effectiveness.

That is another virtue of the seminar, and one that we touched on before: It enables you to test your offer quickly and to experiment, so that you can determine what offer prospects want. You must recognize that you cannot sell a prospect anything the prospect does not truly want, no matter what some overly enthusiastic sales specialists claim. You must either determine what the prospect really wants or find some effective way to make the prospect want what you wish to sell, which is much more difficult to do. Elmer Wheeler, who was often referred to as America's greatest salesman, remarked that if you wanted to sell lemonade, first you had to make the prospect thirsty. And how to do that, he had suggested much earlier, in his now-famous slogan, "Sell the sizzle, not the steak."

Of course, by that latter slogan he referred to basing the sales appeal on emotion rather than on reason, for we know that virtually all buying actions are based on emotional motivations rather than rational ones. The customer may decide rationally to buy new shoes because he or she has an absolute need for new shoes, but the decisions as to where to buy them and what specific shoes to buy are usually emotional, based on personal taste, willingness or reluctance to spend more than the minimum amount possible, and any of several other emotional factors.

Recognize, however, that while it is possible to persuade prospects to want something they did not want (or were not conscious of wanting) before you talked to them, it is much easier to motivate prospects to buy what they have a felt need for—what they had already decided they wanted. That means that it is better to find out what most prospects want and, if it is possible for you to do so and you are convinced that the prospects will indeed then buy, make that your offer.

But there are two offers involved here: the offer that will bring prospects to the free seminar, and the offer that will make the sale at the seminar or, subsequently, as a direct or indirect result of the seminar. And they are not necessarily the same offer, although they may well be. However, it is often advisable to reveal only part of the whole offer in inviting the public to the seminar.

With many seminars the two offers or promises are essentially the same—learn how to start a profitable business, launch a new career, or other such major benefit—and the announcements do not specify that there is a fee of perhaps several hundred dollars to attend a weekend seminar or sign up for training. (Of course, only the most naive attendee would fail to take it for granted that the free seminar is a sales presentation.) The presentation at the free seminar then elaborates by making it clear that some special training or equipment is required before the promised goals can be reached. Of course, the free seminar is a sales presentation, and at this free seminar the attendees will learn a bit of what is required of them next, if they are to achieve the success projected and promised in the advertising. For our free quit-smoking seminar, the offer that brings prospects to the lecture hall might be based on the goal of painless withdrawal from smoking, but the immediate offer might be a free lesson and demonstration, with no mention of the course that will be sold there. Otherwise it would probably be difficult to get people to the hall. But hypnosis does fascinate many people, and a free lesson in hypnosis would almost surely be an attraction for many, with a demonstration an even greater inducement to attend.

Motivation

The offer must include within itself some motivation to be effective as an offer. However, the offer itself is not always enough to do the job. A powerful motivator is needed, and it is best to build that into the offer, if possible. In the case of many seminars that promise to impart to attendees information on how to launch successful business ventures or make sound investments, an important key to motivation used quite often is the promise of little or no front money required. For those who are unfamiliar with investments, the fear that a great deal of cash is required is a major deterrent. Therefore, the promise that the prospect will learn how to begin investing or launch a venture with little or no cash is essential for selling these kinds of programs and even for selling the many books that have been published on the subject. Much as the prospect wants to believe that he or she can become a successful investor or entrepreneur, that fear that substantial front money is needed would prevent many from finding the promise a credible one and from identifying with or recognizing themselves as those to whom the offer is addressed. Therefore, the offer must explain that little or no money is necessary, where such is the case, and it is most effective when that motivator can be embodied in the basic title or headline announcing the program. That is exactly what was done in the case of Robert G. Allen's best-selling book on the subject, *Nothing Down: How to Buy Real Estate with Little or No Money*.

This rationale is true for most selling situations. There is usually a need for some motivator to propel that interest and desire to buy into a decision to sign up or place the order. It is relatively easy to arouse a great deal of interest and even desire (to buy) on the part of qualified prospects, but the final step of escalating that desire into a decision to buy is a giant step, comparatively. The desire costs the prospect nothing and thus comes easily. The decision to buy costs money and thus gives pause and requires much more powerful motivation to bring about.

Professionals in advertising and selling speak of selling benefits— desirable things the product or service does for the buyer—rather than the item itself. In fact, the benefit is not always what the product or service does but is often what it prevents or overcomes, as a kind of negative benefit. To put that another way, the two principal motivators are based on fear and desire for gain. And there is much evidence that fear is an even better motivator than is the desire for gain.

The well-known "ring around the collar" TV commercial is based on the fear motivation—the fear of being embarrassed. The benefit is the avoidance of such embarrassment. This is in stark contrast to the way other detergents are sold, because most claim to produce such direct and positive benefits as brighter colors, whiter clothes, and shinier dishes.

On the other hand, while it is possible in many cases to use either of these two motivations effectively, some products and services dictate the motivation strategy by their very nature. Insurance, fire-fighting equipment, alarms, locks, and many other items, for example, are designed to prevent, react to, or ameliorate disasters and misfortunes. That dictates the selling strategy. It is unlikely that any conceivable gain motivator would be as effective as a fear motivation in selling these kinds of products and services.

One writer, Howard Ruff, managed to incorporate both fear and the desire for gain in the title of his own best-selling book, *How to Prosper in the Coming Bad Years* (New York: Time Books, 1979), and it is reasonable to assume that the success of the book was at least partly the result of building both motivators clearly into that title.

PROMOTING THE SEMINAR

How you go about promoting the seminar—inducing people to attend—is another variable, depending on the nature of the subject and, more exactly, whom your proper prospects are—who should or would be interested, that is.

For example, if your seminar is of potential interest to virtually anyone and everyone, as in the case of the quit-smoking or real-estate-entrepreneurship seminars, you want to attract the public at large. You would therefore use advertising media that reaches the public generally—newspapers, radio, television, and possibly even magazines. "Possibly" magazines, that is, because most magazines are circulated nationally, and circulation outside your geographic area (within easy driving range of where you will stage the seminar) is of no use to you; it is a waste of advertising dollars. But you might want to use a magazine circulated only locally if the other conditions, such as lead time required for placement of advertising, are acceptable.

Choosing a Title

It is advantageous to choose a title for your seminar that is itself a good headline for your advertising. That title-headline ought to do two things: give a clear idea of what the seminar is all about, and sell it to the prospect. Gordon Burgett and Mike Frank, writing about public speaking and seminar presentations, titled their book *Speaking For Money* and explained on the cover, "If you're not earning $1,000 per speech or seminar, you need this book!" The implication of that blurb is plain enough, of course, that this book will teach the reader how to earn $1,000 or more per speech or seminar, and the authors deemed that message important enough to put it on the book cover in large print.

Obviously, these authors preferred to use a short and catchy title—and they succeeded admirably in doing that—although it did not give the reader more than a rather general idea of what the book was about. Certainly it did not really imply the benefit, which made it necessary to create the blurb to expand on the title. That's one of the drawbacks of the short, catchy title: It rarely permits you to get your entire message across.

On the other hand, Howard Shenson titled his own book on seminars *How to Create & Market a Successful Seminar or Workshop*. That title is a mouthful of words, but it does not require any supporting explanation. It tells its own story and incorporates the promise or offer. And in staging his own long and successful series of seminars on consulting, he titled them "How to Build and Maintain Your Own Part-Time/Full-Time CONSULTING Practice," with that capitalized word the biggest and boldest in the advertisement.

Another successful seminar producer, Frank Tennant, ran newspaper advertisements in which he announced as his seminar "How to Become a Successful FREE-LANCE CONSULTANT," running those latter words in the largest and most commanding type. And my own book and seminar on consulting are titled *How to Succeed as an Independent Consultant* (New York: John Wiley & Sons, Inc., 1983), with the seminar titled after the book to take advantage of the success and publicity the book has gained.

A highly successful seminar in proposal writing a few years ago was titled " 'Proposalmanship,' The Graduate Course in Winning Government Contracts through Strategy," again a long title but one that tells the whole story and includes the motivators. It drew an enthusiastic response.

Don't be dismayed by long titles. Ted Nicholas's *How to Form Your Own Corporation without a Lawyer for under $50.00* (Delaware: Enterprise Publishers, 1973) has sold over 200,000 copies and has been continuously in print for more than a decade. One way or the other, you must get your message across in the title, in title and subtitle, or in title and supporting blurb. There is something to be said for each approach, but my own preference is for the title that does the whole job, even if that does result in a long title.

The Appropriate Advertising Media

Not every seminar is of interest to the public at large. As a proposal consultant, my own appeal is not to the general public but to businesspeople, and even then mostly to those businesspeople who do or want to do business with the government. Experience has already demonstrated quite clearly that newspaper, radio, and TV advertising simply do not work well in reaching the clients described. Moreover, using those media means buying a great deal of circulation that is of no use, so they would be at best inefficient media to use even if they did produce good results.

The same consideration applies to the marketing of any product or service that is of interest only to rather highly specialized groups or prospects. These are usually products or services that are not classed normally as consumer items. That would be the case, for example, if you were an office-automation (OA) consultant selling your services to businesses for whom OA should be of interest.

There are two ways to reach your targets with an offer of a free seminar: via specialized periodicals, such as newsletters and magazines to the types of businesses you identify as your prospects, and via direct mail. In the typical case, you would probably be well advised to depend on the latter as your main medium and use periodicals, if at all, primarily to support and supplement your main campaign.

Mailing Lists

This is feasible because it is usually not too difficult to get suitable mailing lists of every type of business firm. Mailing lists, marketed by list brokers, can usually be ordered by any of a number of ways in which they can be categorized. You can get them usually sorted by type of business (banks, wholesale dry goods, appliance retailers, insurance brokers), by size (small, medium, large firms), or by other subdivisions, such as demographic characteristics or locales. Most list brokers today have their lists computerized and so can customize their lists for you in that manner.

Periodical publishers, mail order dealers, and others who do a great deal of their business by mail build up extensive mailing lists of customers, and many earn extra income by renting those names to others. But most owners of large mailing lists use the services of a firm that specializes in renting lists and handles the names as a broker, for a commission on each rental. These are the list brokers, of course, but in their advertising appeals to the owners of such lists they refer to themselves as list managers. (That latter word, *manager*, identifies an important function that is probably a more persuasive term to the list owners than the word *broker* is.) So while list brokers do own many of the names they rent out, a great many of the names they offer to rent are lists they are managing for someone else.

You ordinarily rent the lists for a one-time use only, although some brokers will make special arrangements with you. However, you become the owner of the names of those who buy from you or otherwise respond to your appeal.

Turning to list brokers is one way to find suitable mailing lists, but it is not the only way. Another way is to turn to associations. Many associations will make membership lists available on mailing labels or as directories from which you must copy names and addresses onto labels.

Many mailing lists are compiled from a variety of sources. In my own case, when advertising my proposal-writing seminars, I compiled my own mailing lists from a number of sources. (Rented lists did not work well for me, but that is my own, isolated case. Many others use rented lists successfully.) Probably the most fruitful source for me was the help-wanted advertising pages in the newspapers, especially those large display advertisements in the Sunday edition of the *New York Times*, the *Wall Street Journal*, and other such newspapers. Because I know the nature of the field I was addressing, I was able to judge which were the right companies to put on my lists.

Although that was my chief and probably my best source, I did use other sources of names and addresses, for example, association directories. I was able to buy a copy of the subscription list for the government's periodical *Commerce Business Daily* which was helpful. The Small Business Administration helped with some of its publications that included names and addresses of companies. And I gradually acquired names through my own sales, subscriptions (I published a newsletter, Government Marketing News), inquiries, and miscellaneous other sources.

There is still another way to build mailing lists—inquiry advertising. You have probably seen your fair share of such advertising, although you may not have recognized that it is a ploy for acquiring and compiling lists of qualified prospects.

One large mail order firm has for many years run small advertisements offering to sell those little name-and-address labels that people use to stick on their personal correspondence. You may have wondered how the company can sell these little labels so cheaply and still earn enough profit to pay for the advertising. The fact is that they do not worry about profit on this item. The profit comes later when they have mailed their catalogs to and won orders from these new customers who have now qualified themselves as mail order buyers!

A more common practice is to make a free offer—a free calendar, a free sample copy of a newsletter or magazine, a free booklet, or some other item that produces a name and address. Actually, the calendar is not the best idea, because anyone might want a free calendar, and ideally the inquiry should be one that qualifies the inquirer as a true prospect—that will draw a response only from those with a relevant interest. For example, only those with an interest in computers are likely to send for a booklet or sample copy of a newsletter on the subject.

This is a relatively inexpensive way to compile names because the advertisements can be small and inexpensive, and you are not asking for money but only for inquiries and requests for something free. You respond to the inquiries with whatever you promised, of course, plus all your promotional copy for the seminar.

Publicity

There is still another resource you can use: publicity. And you can combine the best features of print advertising and direct mail in using publicity. That is, you can persuade publishers of periodicals to publish information about your seminar and notices of your free offer to help you get inquiries and compile your mailing lists.

The newsletter publishers are probably the easiest ones to get help from in this respect, if you are careful to select those newsletters most appropriate and relevant to whatever your seminar is about. Advising readers about all events in their fields of interest, including seminars and free offers is news, in this case, and is therefore a legitimate function of the newsletter, despite the fact that it represents free advertising to you.

Newspapers and magazines are not usually as generous with free advertising-publicity for your seminars and inquiry-attracting giveaways, although it is possible to use them for publicity also. To do this effectively, however, you must work at it. That means giving the information some kind of "newsworthiness."

Achieving Newsworthiness

Strictly speaking, an item is newsworthy if and only if a news editor finds it to be news worth printing. However, the term has a considerably broadened meaning, as used here, and the item need not be important news in the literal sense. It can be any information or idea the editor believes will be of interest to his or her readers. It isn't exactly news that the local Lions Club or Rotary is holding its weekly luncheon meeting on Wednesday, but the meetings column of the local newspaper's financial section will carry that notice every week. And if the organization has persuaded the mayor or some other dignitary to address them, that might well command a special paragraph or two. And another section of the newspaper might carry special recipes for Easter, at the appropriate time of the year, and ideas for homemade costumes or even how-it-started feature stories for Halloween.

The way you get such stories into periodicals is usually via the news release or publicity release. Editors get releases daily in abundant quantity and manage to discard most of them with hardly more than a glance. And that is the key to writing successful releases: They must capture attention and arouse interest immediately, to become the exception rather than the rule.

If that sounds familiar, it is no coincidence. Getting your release used—or "picked up" as some newspaper people refer to it—is a selling job, and the principles of selling apply here as well as they do elsewhere. The editor reacts as everyone else does, with an unconscious "What's in it for me?" The editor is looking for usable material that can be fitted easily into whatever space is available and will be of interest to some significant portion of the readers. And those considerations dictate style and format of the release as well as its content.

The idea, then, is to avoid being too crassly commercial, although the editor knows, of course, that publicity is your objective, so focus on capturing interest before you broadcast your commercial message. Your release is competing with others; therefore, you must find some justification for the information in the release to be considered newsworthy—more newsworthy than the other releases with which it must compete for space.

Several classes of information make an item worth publishing. One is news, of course. If your seminar will deal with something that is new—a new idea about dieting, a new way to quit smoking, a new kind of computer application—stress the newness and the importance of the new idea. If it is news because it relates to something that has been prominent in the news, use that "handle." (Relate the seminar to that news.) If you cannot find a way to make the seminar or its topic newsworthy in some way, try another tack: Find something newsworthy to write about and mention the seminar as a follow-up idea or afterthought. For example, you might write a release that reports a record number of people quitting cigarettes or perhaps some new finding of the Public Health Service about cigarette smoking and its effects and then mention your quit-smoking seminar in that connection. But be sure to relate the two items so that the story is not complete without the mention of the seminar. Otherwise, the editor will cut that part.

Because your release must compete for space, try to avoid being literally too newsworthy so that the editor can save the story for another day, if there is no room in the current edition. The more durable the item is, in the sense of being still newsworthy if run a few days or even a week or two later, the more likely it is that the editor will save it and use it. Of course, this is especially true with regard to daily newspapers, but bear in mind, too, that if the release is truly hot news—useful only if printed at once—it is almost surely unsuitable for the weekly or monthly periodical such as a newsletter or magazine.

There are no true standards for releases, but there are some things that are considered to be good practice, especially since they simplify things for the editor and thus make it more likely that the editor will use the information. Figure 2 is a release that illustrates some of these

2.
Typical News/Publicity Release

CONTRACTOR PROFIT NEWS

FOR IMMEDIATE RELEASE

For more information:

Contact: Maryellen Mack

(617) 731-1913

EFFECTIVE PROJECT MANAGEMENT

<u>Brookline, MA - February 8, 1985</u> - CPN (Contractor Profit News) announces a special one-day seminar on Effective Project Management specifically tailored for the construction industry's project managers, principals and field supervisors schedule for six locations nationwide. "With the approaching busy season in the construction industry most companies will be getting more work. Pressure is on for project managers and field supervisors to expedite projects effectively", said Richard Garaffo, Editor of CPN. This one day program gives project managers and supervisors in the construction industry hundreds of exceptional tips to better manage projects, including:

    º How to make money on your next project.

    º How to define your project goals.

    º How to motivate your project team.

    º Techniques to bring the project in on time and under budget.

A primary cause of unsuccessful planning is.........................

(MORE)

Frank A. Stasiowski: Publisher
126 Harvard Street, Brookline MA 02146
(617) 731-1913

characteristics, exemplifying good practice in most respects: It has a release date, identifies the organization and place of origin, uses a headline that summarizes the story, and provides a contact, someone the editor can call to ask questions or get other details to expand the story. Be sure, however, to type the release double- or even triple-spaced because editors rarely use releases without editing and, usually, cutting.

There is mixed opinion about using headlines, with some writers on this subject advising against it because editors like to write their own headlines. However, the editors are still free to write their own headlines—they almost certainly will edit the copy anyway—and the headline you supply helps the editor evaluate the story at a glance, if the headline is well conceived to summarize the story. Those two advantages certainly appear to me to outweigh the possible disadvantage if, in fact, it is a disadvantage at all.

TIPS ON WRITING PROMOTIONAL COPY

Writing is more art than science, and that is probably especially true for persuasive writing such as sales copy. Still, there are some principles, tactics, and techniques that you should know about and which will be helpful in preparing your own promotional copy.

One of the first things to learn is to be extremely careful about which examples you emulate. A great many people are influenced by bad examples, which are abundantly in evidence: Even the most costly advertising, prepared by top agencies and top copywriters, is often well written but badly conceived. That is, it may be fluent, grammatical, polished writing but be completely ineffective as persuasive copy, usually because it violates some basic rule or principle of selling and advertising.

The principle this illustrates is that writing well has nothing to do directly with persuasive writing. Poorly conceived sales copy will not sell, no matter how fluently or skillfully it is written. And the reverse is true, also, because the effectiveness of the sales message is dependent primarily on the sales strategy employed. One highly successful sales message was criticized by many purists for its grammatical flaw in trumpeting that "Winston tastes good like a cigarette should." Grammatically, the copy should have read "as a cigarette should" but "like a cigarette should" worked very well; therefore, no one paid much attention to the critics. Message: Don't look to advertising and sales copy for examples of good grammar. The writing skills needed here are those of getting the message across as clearly and with as much impact as possible. (But first the message must be the right one.)

The urge to be clever is another enemy of good copy. Some copywriters have an irresistible urge to be clever and they succeed in being clever, but at the expense of the sales message. They get so clever that they forget to sell the product, they produce a weak sales message. For example, a chain of motels urged readers to "turn in" at their locations, sacrificing the most important element of the advertisement—the headline—to cleverness. In the body of the copy the advertiser mentioned a little bonus offered to every guest. That might have helped if the headline had persuaded the reader to get to the body copy. The headline, however, offered the reader no inducement to do so.

Another example of this need to be clever, rather than persuasive, is an advertisement for an electronic music keyboard, a miniature electronic organ, which is illustrated in the full-page copy. The headline reads, "How to strike a responsive chord"—again a pun (so many copywriters rely on puns for their cleverness) that offers the reader no inducement to get into the body copy where the pun is explained and the sales message is offered.

A Christmas advertisement features a photograph of a man wearing a shirt that is obviously too small and announces that the man's niece gave him a 14½ × 30 last year but will give him a more fitting gift this year—obviously referring to the bottle of whisky illustrated at the bottom of the page. (Again the inevitable puns.) This one has no other copy and so leaves it to the reader to infer the sales message, something that is not likely to happen.

There are three points to be made here:

1. The headline is by far the most important and most powerful element in sales copy.
2. Readers will not continue to read simply because you want them to; you must persuade them to read on by offering some inducement to do so.
3. Subtlety is also the enemy of good sales copy. It is risky to be subtle, and subtle messages almost always fail to make their point with prospects. You must be absolutely clear about your sales message.

The Headline

Advertising experts agree generally that if you do not capture your prospect with your headline, you have probably lost the battle already. They point out that if your headline is ineffective, even strong body copy will probably not save the day. (And the reverse is equally true: With a sufficiently strong headline, there is less burden on the body copy to do the job.) In fact, some put it even more simply by saying that if you don't sell it in the headline, you won't sell it at all.

Of course that's a slight exaggeration, expressed that way for emphasis. It takes more than the headline to make the sale. However, it is certainly true that if the headline does not draw the reader into the body copy, you can't present your complete offer and make your sales arguments. Failing that, you certainly can't make the sale.

The headline has a formidable job. It must do three things: (1) capture attention and arouse interest, (2) summarize the offer, and (3) persuade the reader to read on.

Some advertisers rely on other devices to get attention. They use photographs, line drawings, and cartoons. Some use humor or novelties, or other special devices. One print advertisement appearing in a current magazine, for example, features a drawing of Abraham Lincoln, and reproduces part of his Gettysburg Address in his own handwriting. The advertisement advises that this is a print that is available free of charge at stores handling the advertiser's product, which has only the sketchiest relationship to the drawing. (The advertiser is a software producer, featuring a word processing program.) On the other hand, an advertiser in a weekly business tabloid uses attention-getting art quite well, showing a person seated at a desk thinking hard, under the headline "Need an Idea?" And underneath the cartoon it says, "Send for a FREE Direct Response Format Idea Kit!" (This is an inquiry advertisement, of course, drawing inquiries from prospects to whom the advertiser will mail a package of sales literature, along with the free kit.)

The idea of all of these is to get attention so that the advertiser may present his or her headline and get on with the sales message. The problem is that it takes over only one task called out here for the headline, that of getting attention, but leaves the other two tasks still to be accomplished by the headline. If your headline does not summarize your offer and arouse interest, the reader will go on to something else, which does arouse his or her interest. So you really do not accomplish a great deal with these expensive devices unless you really get it all together—integrate the headline and art, as in that second example, where they support each other so well that neither illustration nor headline would be nearly as effective without the other. Unfortunately, this latter example is the exception, not the rule. Most non-headline attention getters have little to do with the sales message and contribute nothing to it.

This is not an argument against using illustrations. Quite the contrary, in many cases an illustration is a must because words alone can't do an effective job. But illustrations ought to be a proper part of the appeal, something that is necessary or at least makes a substantial and direct contribution to the appeal, not something dragged in as a diversion or simply to get attention.

Cryptic headlines are another no-no. Presumably, the idea is to arouse a reader's curiosity, if you can't arouse interest—much along the lines of the clever copy. But it produces the same result: The burden still rests on the headline after the gimmick has drawn attention. Getting attention has nothing to do with persuading a prospect to buy. It only has do with persuading the prospect to "listen" for a moment. And in that moment you must arouse some actual interest or you lose the prospect irretrievably.

Arousing Interest

There is no great secret about what it takes to arouse the interest of a prospect. The most reliable way of ensuring that the interest of the prospect is aroused is to answer the assumed question, "What's in it for me?" Whether the prospect formulates those words literally or not, the thought is there. Unless the prospect perceives an appeal to some personal concern, he or she will not linger long. Even aroused curiosity is soon satisfied, and if you have not somehow captured true interest in the interim, the prospect goes on to other things.

To put this another way, the headline ought to tell the prospect directly why he or she should buy whatever it is that the advertisement offers or, at the least, why he or she should read on and learn more. Here are some headlines that do that by stipulating the benefit:

"Now Ship Your Christmas Packages the Easy Way"

"Stylize Your Eyes with Aziza Silklining Pencils"

"You Can Get a Lot More Than Great Pictures Out of Konica Film"

Obviously, not everything can be so readily summarized in a brief line, desirable as it is to do so. Many advertisements require an illustration to go along with the headline to present the basic offer. In some cases, the headline must be followed with a subhead, as in the case of an advertisement for a ski resort, which headlines "5 of a million reasons why skiers love Butternut," and then lists the five reasons directly beneath the headline, numbering them individually.

At the opposite extreme are those headlines which talk about what the advertiser wants. One radio station broadcasts its own sales message, "We'd like to be your favorite radio station." Worse (and ironically) an advertiser who claims to be among the world's greatest experts in sales techniques headlines a print advertisement, "I want to train your sales force!" And Ford employed a popular entertainer a few years ago to tell TV viewers, after extolling the virtues of the Ford product, that "It's simple: Ford wants to be your car company."

These and many other similar headlines make the same mistake:

They talk about what the advertiser wants, and the prospect doesn't care about what the advertiser wants. Nor is that the only ineffective and self-serving message many misguided copywriters inflict on the public. Many headlines, and the complete copy for that matter, waste the time of readers, listeners, and viewers with claims and bragging that provide no concrete reasons for buying whatever the advertiser wants to sell. In fact, those statements are often not even evidence of superiority, much less an offer or a promise to do something for the prospect; they are merely unsupported claims.

That latter kind of copy falls into the subtle class too because it is evidently based on the assumption that the reader will interpret those claims of superiority as the reason for buying. Of course that rarely happens—prospects simply do not sell themselves very often—and the advertiser loses a great many sales to other advertisers, who give readers more specific reasons to buy.

Kinds of Media and Copy

You may have inferred that most of this discussion about headlines and copy was written with direct and primary reference to print advertisements. If so, that was entirely your inference, for it was not my intent to so suggest. Whatever was said here about headlines and writing copy applies equally to print advertisements, to radio and TV commercials, to news releases, to direct-mail packages, and to the seminar and the handouts too. The copy and the media may change, but the principles of selling and advertising do not. For example, sales letters almost always carry headlines, just as news releases do, and for the same reasons. Later, at a more appropriate time, we will discuss the complete direct-mail package. However, for the free seminar, you will not ordinarily make use of this, nor should you have to. But if you make use of the print and other public media—newspapers, newsletters, and newscasters—for publicity, you will need to understand these principles.

Some Words That Work

Certain words have proved to be effective over the years, and if you can work these into your headlines, so much the better. A few of those words whose appeal never seems to wear out are: "inside tips," "new," "exclusive," "inside information," "revealed" (for the first time), "free," "sale," "bargain," "never before," and "secret(s) of."

Most of these words are especially appropriate to selling a seminar presentation. Decide which ones apply fairly to what you plan to present in your seminar, use those terms, and get some of them into your headlines, if possible.

Using Radio and Television to Your Best Advantage

One possible result of sending news releases to TV and radio news-rooms is that you may be invited to be interviewed or invited to make comments on a news program, either via telephone or in person. Or you may engineer such appearances by selecting appropriate talk shows and offering to appear. I have found the publicity effect of these appearances, especially on television, is usually excellent. Television has enormous impact.

Of course you need not wait and hope that your releases will bring you an invitation. You are more likely to be invited to appear on a talk show or news show if you take the initiative and go after such appearances aggressively. Get in touch with the producer of each such show, not the host. It is the producer who arranges guest appearances, ordinarily.

Like the newspaper editor, the producer is aware that you seek publicity as a form of free advertising, and in turn the producer is interested in a quid pro quo—something for something. If you want a guest appearance, even a telephone interview, you must offer something of interest to the producer's audience. Decide what that is, send out your news release, and follow up with telephone call to producers of local talk shows, explaining what you can offer the audience.

Here are a few tips for maximizing your chances for getting on such shows:

· Stress that you are flexible and can make yourself available on short notice. Producers are plagued by unexpected cancellations of guests and will often turn to last-minute replacements. (That was how I got on one very successful TV show, with excellent results, which virtually compelled me to present a special series of profitable seminars.)

· Be prepared and willing to undergo a kind of advance interview-audition, especially for a TV talk show. The producer and host will want to be sure that you can handle yourself well on the air.

· Be persistent and keep calling periodically, pressing so that the producer does not forget or overlook you as a resource.

· Be sure to present your general credentials and express willingness to be part of a panel discussion or even part of the audience for an audience-participation show. (In fact, do go to such shows, if there are any in your area, and try to get on camera with your story.)

Persistence is important. Producers can be quite indifferent when they have no guest problems, but they will turn to you eagerly when they are stuck for a guest at the last minute. However, they will forget that you were in touch with them a month or two ago; you must keep reminding them, at least every week or two, of your availability and continuing interest.

One final observation: Some people hate to use the telephone and would rather write when making an inquiry. But probably a far greater number of people are of the opposite persuasion and would rather call than write. Bear this in mind in your advertising and public relations activities, and always provide a telephone number prospects may call for information. And have someone at that telephone number who can answer simple questions, but who is instructed to also get a name and address to which a brochure or sales letter can be addressed. Those names and addresses are valuable assets.

Chapter 4

Meeting-Room and Presentation Basics

> Modern as the idea of the public seminar is, a body of dos and don'ts has already sprung up and serves as a useful guide in planning and presenting business meetings.

ROOM AND SEATING ARRANGEMENTS

There are two basic room arrangements for seminars: classroom-style and theater-style. Like most things, each has its virtues and its faults.

Classroom-style means providing each attendee with desk or table space for writing, arranging materials, and otherwise working and participating actively during the session, as one would in a formal class. Theater-style is simply arranging the chairs in rows, as in a theater, for passive participation by attendees.

The classroom-style is appropriate for the regular seminar or workshop where the attendees are expected to take notes, participate in exercises, and otherwise do more than simply listen. However, even when the attendee is to do nothing but listen, the classroom-style is more informal and therefore more comfortable and relaxed. It is thus invariably appropriate for the lengthier sessions of formal seminars, which are typically all-day affairs and often of more than a single day's duration.

In the case of the marketing seminar, theater-style is usually more appropriate than classroom-style for at least two reasons: The session is generally short enough so that fatigue is not a factor, and theater-style is far more efficient than classroom-style in terms of utilizing the space. That is, a far greater number of people can be accommodated in any given room set up theater-style than if it were set up classroom-style. And since you ordinarily pay for a meeting room according to size of the room, as well as other factors, that is an important consideration.

The most often chosen places for seminars are hotel meeting rooms. Indeed, business meetings including seminars, workshops, luncheons, and other such events are a major part of the hotel business today. For many hotels (depending on certain variables) they are an even greater part of the overall business than are weddings, parties, and other social events. Therefore, hotels are geared especially to accommodate your needs, with respect to such meetings and gatherings.

Prices for the use of meeting rooms vary widely, and sometimes pricing structures in one hotel are the diametric opposite of those at another. For example, in many hotels a meeting room is far less expensive on a weekend than during the week. However, the opposite is true in other hotels. And the difference is the result of such factors as location. A hotel in a downtown business district is likely to have little meeting-related activity on non-business days and, therefore, offers far lower rates for its rooms on such days. On the other hand, a hotel in some neighborhoods is likely to be busy on weekends and holidays with parties, weddings, and other social events and so charges higher rates on non-working days.

In most cases, you must reserve the room far in advance, at least several weeks, both because you need the date firmly fixed before you begin your advertising and publicity and because hotels usually require advance reservation. However, when I called a popular hotel in McLean, Virginia, and tried to reserve a meeting room for a Saturday meeting to take place several weeks later, they refused to accept the reservation because, they explained, they booked many weddings, banquets, parties, and other such social events on weekends, frequently on short notice, and those are always more profitable than business meetings are, since the hotel usually serves food and drinks lavishly at such affairs. Thus, they were unwilling to commit and tie up a meeting room for a Saturday, except at a late date when they knew the room would not be wanted for one of those more profitable engagements.

Because of all this, never assume that what you find to be the case at any given hotel will be typical. The next hotel may have a totally different and even opposite policy. Check with several, at least, before making a choice, if you are going to use a hotel meeting room. You may also find that the hotel with the most reasonable room-rental rates has the highest prices for coffee and other refreshments and vice versa. The only way to know is to ask specifically about all these matters.

One difficulty you are likely to encounter is that of estimating the size of the room you will need. In some cases, you can make changes at the last minute because most hotel meeting rooms have movable partitions, which can be folded up or slid back to take in an adjoining room, thus enlarging the space. However, this is an option only if an adjoining room is not in use or if the hotel can move your meeting room at the last minute. To minimize this possibility, try to get advance registrations from attendees. Because you are not charging, you will get a larger than usual number of no-shows. (Even for seminars where attendees have paid in advance, you often get some no-shows.) However, with advance registrations, you will have at least a rough idea of the probable size of the attendance and can plan for it.

EQUIPMENT NEEDS

Hotels normally can supply blackboards, lecterns, and sometimes even projection screens and easels for charts, but most hotels resort to rental firms to supply projectors and other audiovisual equipment you need. However, it is usually possible to order anything you need as a package deal when reserving your meeting room, and the hotel will arrange to have it there. In fact, although you may bring your own projector, in many cases, many hotels insist that such equipment must be ordered through them. (And the same thing for food: Few hotels allow you to bring your own refreshments for meetings.)

Probably the most popular type of projector is the overhead projector, which is one that uses transparencies or view-graphs. In some ways, transparencies are less expensive, easier and faster to produce, and more flexible in use than slides are. Slides are generally mounted in a carousel, and it is quite inconvenient to change the sequence once set. However, with transparencies, it is simple to juggle them back and forth, to write directly on them while they are being projected, to cover part of them, to point to elements on them (rather than on the screen), and otherwise to use them informally. Moreover, they can be made on any common office copier.

Slides do have an advantage for some uses, of course, such as for supporting a lengthy and rather formal presentation. But for the give-and-take of the informal meeting, transparencies and an overhead projector are definitely more adaptable to spontaneous situations and more versatile as well.

One example of that versatility is the ability of the overhead projector to function as a large blackboard. For some uses, the blackboard is a good alternative, as is the easel and flipchart, especially if the room and gathering are small. However, in many cases, especially when the gathering is a large one in a large room, the blackboard is not too viable because attendees in the back of the room have difficulty in seeing what is on it. But the overhead projector and screen can function as an oversize blackboard if the presenter writes directly on the projector's glass image plate with a grease pencil or marking pen.

HANDOUTS

Most seminars include handouts of one sort or another, and there are at least three ways of issuing handouts: Some presenters have a complete seminar manual or portfolio of materials, which they hand out at the start of the session. Others distribute handouts periodically, as the session proceeds. And some combine the two methods, starting with a portfolio and handing out additions to it throughout the session.

There is something to be said for both methods. The issuance of a complete portfolio at the beginning of the session is more efficient, for some uses, but not for all. If the work of the session requires reference to materials handed out, time must be spent while the attendee searches for the right material, and the presentation must be interrupted during that period. However, handing out materials, even if done by an assistant rather than by the presenter, is also an interruption, so the advantage of one over the other is questionable, at least in this respect.

On the other hand, the distribution of handouts offers at least one major advantage from the viewpoint of presentation strategy. It helps to sustain interest by the change of pace and the anticipation it arouses. The seminar being discussed here is presumably a brief one, conducted entirely for marketing purposes, although in fact there may be other circumstances. (Even seminars for which registration fees are charged are often useful marketing tools, and at least some of what is said here might have valid application to such seminars.) The kinds of handout materials and the mode of presenting them to attendees is a variable that depends entirely on what it is you wish to accomplish in your seminar—that is, on the specific conditions and objectives.

From that viewpoint, let us consider several possible situations and objectives. There is the kind of situation discussed at some length earlier, calling for a hard sell or intensive and aggressive drive to make the presentation and the closes—to get the actual signed orders before the meeting ends. There is the situation designed to generate good leads for follow-up, possibly still calling for a hard sell but requiring follow-up sales efforts to close sales. There is the seminar designed to introduce a product or service, having an objective of developing leads but designed primarily to do the necessary advance work of building an image necessary to the successful selling of the product or service.

This latter situation is one that I have not discussed in detail, but it concerns a serious marketing problem for the independent (self-employed) professional trying to establish a practice, as it does for anyone trying to introduce a new product that is relatively expensive and serves a need not generally recognized by the public.

For these latter situations, where conventional advertising and sales tactics do not work well, a great deal of marketing evangelism is usually required. And in such situations, the purpose of the seminar is not to close sales on the spot, for it is not likely to be an achievable goal (although you will probably make an occasional sale on the spot). The purpose of the seminar in this case is to create an awareness of the product or service, to gain acceptance for it or pave the way for acceptance, and to build an image, with the development of leads a definite but secondary objective.

If your main objective is to close sales on the spot, it is probably not to your advantage to distribute any but the simplest handout. A portfolio and fat collection of brochures and other literature is more likely to slow the prospects' reactions than to speed them up. A sensible goal in such seminars is to hit hard a single, main idea and keep attendees' attention focused sharply on that idea. Anything that distracts from that is confusing and suggests to attendees the need for time to study your literature and think about things, especially about the side issues. That is what you wish to avoid, of course.

On the other hand, if you use the seminar to build leads, it is probably in your interest to make up a fat portfolio of good sales literature, for you want the attendees to carry away material they can study at their leisure. This is likely to make them better prospects for future sales.

That raises the question of what is good sales literature. Good sales literature is, of course, whatever does the job of making the sale or helping make the sale. But what is good for one application is not necessarily good for the next one. Again, the individual situation and needs dictate what is good. And again we are discussing those two situations of introducing the new product or service and building an image for a self-employed professional.

In many ways, although not in all, the needs of these two are similar. One goal common to both is that of gaining acceptance. And one kind of material that helps a great deal with that is the reprint of the favorable newspaper or magazine article written about the product, service, company, or individual. If you have these, by all means include them in the portfolio.

Any other literature of this general type is also useful, even if it is the formal professional paper or laboratory report that few lay people are hardy enough to wade through. But the mere fact of its existence is persuasive as an indicator of excellence. It's the parallel of the group dynamics effect mentioned earlier: It shows acceptance by others and thus encourages acceptance by your prospects.

Even more basic than this, however, are the brochures and other literature that provide the basic descriptions and explanations of what you offer. These should go into some detail in helping the reader understand exactly what that is. This literature also ought to demonstrate by rationale or whatever other means are available to you that your promises and claims are valid and that you can and will deliver what you promise. To help with this, any testimonials you have been able to get from current or former customers and clients are useful and should be reproduced and included in these handouts.

For some professionals, the seminar is an opportunity to provide a sample of the service. If you are a consultant, for example, you can probably offer a sample of your consulting services by answering specific questions and discussing attendees' individual problems, after your basic presentation. Remember always that you promised attendees something of value, and if your seminar is totally a sales presentation—if, that is, it offers nothing that is useful to attendees—you are deceiving the people who came to hear you, and you will probably defeat your own purpose. This is especially true if you are a consultant or other professional trying to establish a presence and build an image by demonstrating your capacity to help clients. They expect sincerity, not cynicism, in your presentation.

Another useful handout is a newsletter, if you have one, whether it is a free newsletter you publish strictly for marketing purposes or one for which you charge a subscription fee. Later, in discussing newsletters in greater depth, I'll pursue this further, but just as newsletters can be used to support the marketing of your seminars and other services and products, so can seminars be used to support other services and products. And in this case you may use the newsletter as an additional handout for marketing your main services or to help market anything else you wish to offer prospects.

In some cases, the handout material is itself a major inducement to prospects to attend the session. Many people attend seminars, even high-priced seminars, as much for the handouts as for anything else, when the handouts are exclusive items that cannot be gotten in any other way. If you believe that what you are handing out has that kind of value and appeal, you should feature it as an important reason to attend your seminar. Or you may find it worthwhile to devise some handout valuable enough to be such an inducement and feature it in all your advertising and promotion. But be sure to impart a value to it by stressing that the handout, whatever it is, will be given free to each attendee but is available only to attendees of your seminar.

THE PRESENTATION

Most hotel meeting rooms are wired for sound, propagated from a microphone mounted on the lectern. Typically, there is no dais in the small room, although some of the larger rooms designed for large audiences do have such a refinement. Many speakers are most comfortable standing behind a lectern during their entire presentation. On the other hand, some prefer to move about. That is one disadvantage of the lectern-mounted microphone. If you are speaking to a large group in a large room and feel the need for electronic amplification of your voice, you must either confine yourself to the lectern or arrange for a different kind of microphone—one you can carry with you as you move about.

Every speaker has his or her individual style. Some are more or less mechanical, delivering the presentation with unwavering and undeviating devotion to a prepared script, never changing a word or an inflection, no matter how often they deliver the presentation or speech. Others go to the opposite extreme of almost complete spontaneity, speaking only from general notes or a general outline, improvising, and reacting differently with each audience, never delivering the presentation or speech exactly the same way. And others have styles at various points along the spectrum between these extremes. Some even deliver carefully rehearsed and memorized presentations that sound and appear to be completely extemporaneous!

As in the case of writing, style is not something that you should affect or even work at developing deliberately. Style in speaking, as in writing, is something you should allow to develop and evolve spontaneously over a period of time and without conscious effort. Ultimately, you will develop a style all your own, and it will be far more of an asset to you than if it were a counterfeit of someone else's style.

At the same time, you should try to pursue certain standards in speaking and avoid the extremes. Of course, you should certainly have prepared a set of reasonably detailed notes and gone over your entire presentation mentally, but if you are truly the master of the subject you have chosen to speak on, you do not need a prepared script, and it is probably a mistake to use one. The use of a prepared script tends to make your presentation rather mechanical, hence, unconvincing, and if you need one, perhaps you are not yet ready to make the presentation. It is far better to have such mastery of the subject that you are completely confident about your ability to present it, to discuss it with listeners, and to answer any questions that arise. Then you will be comfortable with only a general outline of major points or some cue cards to guide you and remind you of the main points you wish to make.

Some professional public speakers recommend moving about and especially "invading" the territory of the audience by venturing a few feet into the aisles between rows of seats. However, virtually all recommend making eye contact with your audience.

Much advice is offered to beginners, much of it bad advice, even in this connection. Some speakers who ought to know better urge neophytes at public speaking to select someone in the audience and establish eye contact with him or her, maintaining it steadily. That's a good way to make that unfortunate individual quite self-conscious and uncomfortable and to persuade him or her to leave the audience as soon as possible. The right way to make eye contact is to move your eyes around and make eye contact with many people in your audience. But don't maintain it with any single individual for long. Go from one to another. You are speaking to *everyone* in that audience. Try to make eye contact with as many of the audience as possible and smile frequently, but at the right places.

Be as natural as you can. Don't worry about what to do with your hands. Don't even think about what to do with your hands. Do with them as you do when arguing with a friend or your spouse about politics, football, or Hollywood mores: Use them for emphasis, wave them about, spread them hopelessly, and gesture generally with them. They can be more expressive than all the words in the unabridged dictionary.

Do the same with the rest of your body. Raise an eyebrow, grin, sneer, frown, shout, whisper, as the occasion demands. Your expressions and gestures are extraordinarily eloquent, when used properly, and they work wonders at establishing a bond with your audience. Don't rehearse or memorize the gestures, any more than you would rehearse and memorize your words. They are effective only if they are natural and done without conscious effort.

Those dozens of listeners are also spectators. They came to see as well as to hear *you*. Don't stop at telling them. Show them too. Much of the key to success in public speaking is being a performer. Lose yourself in the part, as a skilled performer does. Talk to the audience, not at them. Reach out and embrace your audience with your words, with your eyes, with your movements and gestures. Do that, and they will not be able to resist you.

Chapter 5

A Few Basics of Newsletters

Newsletters have been the "secret weapon" behind many successful marketing campaigns, especially for highly professional and other soft-sell enterprises.

THE ESSENCE OF THE NEWSLETTER

There are many parallels between seminars and newsletters as well as many differences. More significant, however, is the fact that they happen to complement each other well for marketing applications: Each offers its own set of strengths. For on-the-spot hard selling, for example, the seminar is an excellent medium; whereas the newsletter is unsuited to this. But the seminar depends on inducing the prospect to take the time and go to the trouble of journeying to the meeting room and attending; whereas the newsletter goes to the prospect and does not even need to be bidden by the prospect to do so. Hence, we have the marriage of the two in these pages and, perhaps, in actual use for many applications, because in many cases the two can be combined into highly effective marketing ventures.

The term *newsletter* is something of a misnomer, for while some newsletters do deal in news, in most cases news is not the essence of the newsletter. The newsletter typically focuses on special interests that are not well covered by the newsstand type of periodical, nor even by those thick tabloids and slick-paper magazines referred to commonly as trade journals.

The reason for the lack of coverage by these types of periodicals is simple enough: Those periodicals require a relatively large circulation, at least in the multiple thousands, to be viable. They are expensive to produce and distribute, and subscription fees do not cover the costs. (In fact, many of the so-called controlled circulation periodicals are distributed without charge and earn no subscription fees at all.) They depend on paid advertising for income to cover costs and produce a profit, and that is simply not possible without circulation counting in the tens of thousands, normally.

Newsletters, on the other hand, with only a rare exception here and there, must cover costs and turn a profit from subscription fees alone because typical newsletter circulation is in the hundreds or, at best, in the low thousands. (There are exceptions, but these are relatively rare.) The reason for this is, of course, because the newsletter is addressed to that small group of people who want certain kinds of information which is not offered in the other periodicals.

The typical newsletter is four, eight, or more pages long but usually not more than 12. (Multiples of four, as a result of printing on an 11 × 17-inch sheet and folding it, is the common approach, although there are occasional newsletters of two pages, more than 12 pages, and of odd numbers of pages.) The page size is most often 8 ½ × 11 inches, the standard size of typewriter paper.

Subjects vary over an enormous range of business, technical, political, social, scientific, hobby, and other fields of interest. There are usually several newsletters offered in every industry, every wholesale and retail field, every profession, and every specialized consumer interest.

To illustrate that diversity, here are just a few newsletter titles selected at random from the pages of *The Newsletter Yearbook Directory*, third edition: Hospice Letter; Labor Relations Report; Chemical/Plastics; Fertilizer Newsletter; Media Law Reporter; and The Advice Business.

Not all newsletter titles are as clear as these in identifying what they are about. Here are a few others: The Hughes Report; Briefings; Followup File; Action Report; The Paper Plane; and The Hotline.

Claimed circulation for such newsletters as these ranges from a few hundred to several thousand, although most newsletter publishers are reluctant to reveal their circulation figures and are under no legal compulsion to do so, as publishers of controlled-circulation periodicals are. The Ruff Times, published by Howard Ruff, the author of a best-selling book, claims 150,000 circulation, but that is a definite exception to the rule. Extremely few newsletters even approach this circulation figure.

On the other hand, the *Directory* does report frequency of publication, subscription rates, and other information for most of the newsletters listed. And those range widely too, from purely nominal subscription fees, such as $5 per year, to several hundred dollars per year.

That brings up a relevant point: Whereas those newsletters charging substantial prices are primarily enterprises carried out as profit-

making ventures, newsletters asking for $5 or $10 a year are published as marketing media. The nominal subscription fees are intended to do little more than pay for mailing, and even that is not the
true reason for the small fee, in most cases. The true reason for
charging that nominal fee is often to offset or nullify the stigma of
being pure advertising matter, which being free implies. The fee imparts at least the suggestion of value to the newsletter. Free, to many,
means that the item is worthless, so even a nominal price imparts a
value to the newsletter. In fact, many newsletter publishers imprint
an annual subscription price even when the newsletter is distributed
free of charge to anyone who wants it, to lend the newsletter an apparent pecuniary value.

The essential value and appeal of many newsletters is that they cover
some rather highly specialized interest. For example, many investors
want more guidance than the daily newspapers offer and so subscribe
to one or more of the many investment tip sheets published by individuals who offer investment advice. Some of these generalize across
the entire securities market, while others specialize in high-tech stocks,
penny stocks, bonds, or some other special class of securities.

Specialized reporting, however, is only one possible appeal or orientation of a newsletter. There are others. One is as an advisory service, and many of these letters are to be found in the investment field,
counseling readers. Howard Ruff's The Ruff Times, mentioned earlier,
is one of these and not the only highly successful one. Another basis
on which many newsletters are founded is that of offering busy readers an abstract or condensation of all the important happenings, ideas,
and information published recently within the field of reader interest.
(The reader would have to find time to scan several dozen other periodicals to glean the information offered in many of these newsletters.) The well-known Boardroom Reports is a good example that abstracts a variety of items drawn from periodicals, books, newsletters,
and other sources, as well as publishes pieces written for them by experts in their respective fields.

THE FREE NEWSLETTER

The newsletter published as a marketing tool and given away without charge for that reason is a special case. Obviously it is going to
carry advertising, which is the reason for its existence. However, that
advertising is generally rather low-key, which is appropriate for marketing situations in which a newsletter is a useful tool.

Figure 3 illustrates such a newsletter published as a marketing tool
by a Washington-area computer retailer, Clinton Computer. The firm
publishes the Clinton Computer News, an unassuming name, on a

3.

Typical Free Newsletter Published as a Marketing Tool

Fall-Winter 1984-85
Frances D. Poling, Editor

277 South Washington Street, Alexandria, VA 22314
6443 Old Alex. Ferry Rd. at Branch Ave. (Rte. 5) Clinton, MD 20735

(703) 838-9700   M-F 10 - 8, Sat 10 - 5
(301) 856-2500   M-F 10 - 8, Sat 10 - 5

Clinton Computer Becomes Authorized IBM Dealer

Clinton Computer is pleased to announce that we have become an authorized IBM dealership. The IBM product line features the IBM PCjr, IBM PC, IBM XT, IBM AT, and the Portable PC. IBM computers offer a great deal of versatility due to the thousands of available software programs and peripherals.

The recent introduction of the IBM AT adds greater strength to the product line. This remarkable computer will run many of the programs written for the IBM PC, up to three times faster. The AT stands for Advanced Technology; it is based on the 80286 16-bit microprocessor. The AT will enable recalculations of large spreadsheets in seconds and it will retrieve files in a flash. The IBM AT is also available with

Clinton Computer owners Chuck Perilli, left, and Art Lundquist recently signed an Agreement with IBM to become an authorized dealer.

up to 3 million bytes of user memory for multiuser, multitasking operations.

At the other end of the spectrum, picture a computer under $1000 that runs many of the best programs written for the IBM PC—even Lotus 1-2-3. The PCjr has an advanced 16-bit microprocessor, plus a new typewriter-style keyboard. PCjr has been designed for the future, with a modular construction that is wide open for expansion.

Clinton Computer will be offering a variety of IBM packages, including training, service and support—all at an affordable price. The addition of IBM to our product line will allow us to serve even more microcomputer users. Please visit either of our retail locations for a demonstration and additional information.

Watch Out for Static Zap!

When it comes to your computer and your diskettes, static electricity can be a real hazard! Current integrated circuit technology has minimized the possibility of permanent damage. However, static electricity can still result in fits of "temporary insanity" from your computer.

The combination of cold weather and the use of hot (dry) air heating systems can be troublesome to your electronic equipment and your magnetic media. Even something as innocent as a kitty rubbing against your leg as you sit working at your computer can cause a discharge of static electricity.

Solutions?

1. Use a product such as "Static-Guard" on your carpet regularly. **2.** Discharge yourself on a metal object before touching your computer or diskettes. **3.** Use laundry and spray products that "reduce static cling" on your clothing. **4.** Keep kitty away from the computer. (One customer's feline decided that the top of the Lisa's terminal would be a nice warm place for a nap and proceeded to take a snooze. Lisa went berserk!) **5.** Inject moisture into your home/office's air with a humidifier.

Clinton Computer's Alexandria Learning Center features an entire classroom of IBM PC computers.

quarterly basis. This is a reasonably typical publishing schedule for a free newsletter. There is no real need to publish frequently, in most cases, and quarterly publication is probably far more often the case for these free newsletters than is monthly or bimonthly publication.

The newsletter illustrated here is printed on glossy paper and uses several halftones (printed photographs). The earlier editions were a typical four pages, but the current edition has grown to a less-typical six pages (printed on an 11 × 25 ½-inch signature, a sheet of two or more pages, folded down to page size). It is obviously fairly expensive to make up and print. Only by printing in quantity can the per-copy cost be brought down to some reasonable level.

That brings up another point: distribution volume. It is not a really viable idea to produce any newsletter, much less an expensive news-letter such as this, unless it can be distributed in some quantity, at least 5,000 to 10,000 copies. The publisher of the newsletter illus-trated here distributes about two-thirds of the copies by mailing, and the rest primarily by making it freely available in the two retail es-tablishments and related facilities operated by the firm. (This in-cludes learning centers at each location, where various computer courses are offered.)

As promotional items in these newsletters, this retailer offers dis-count coupons printed in the newsletter and advertises a learning center discount coupon book, among other notices. The tone of the let-ter is quiet and dignified, and the editor confirms that image building and promotion of confidence in the professionalism and integrity of the firm are among the objectives of the newsletter.

It is easily understandable that a large retailer of computers and related equipment is concerned with image and confidence building. Most computers represent a significant investment, usually several thousand dollars, for one thing. A large majority of those who buy personal computers are somewhat fearful, even apprehensive, and feel a need to be able to rely on the dealer for advice and help of various kinds. The more professional and "solid" the dealer appears to be, the more confidence the prospective customer feels in the dealer.

The computer business is not a one-call business. Customers rarely buy a computer the first time they look at one and the first time a salesperson makes a presentation. The sale of a computer is almost always the result of a series of exposures, demonstrations, presenta-tions, and other influences that ultimately result in the customer de-ciding what computer to buy and from whom to buy it.

Moreover, buying a computer is only the first step for the customer. The new computer owner will almost always buy other equipment, ac-cessories, and supplies. There are printers, modems, surge protectors, cables, connectors, switch boxes, programs, disks, disk files, paper, ribbons, and many other items the computer customer will buy. The computer dealer should not be merely making a sale; he or she should be making a customer.

All of this adds up to several excellent reasons for publishing a newsletter as a major marketing tool.

Only a small portion of the coverage in the newsletter cited here is unabashed advertising. The majority of the copy is either purely useful information or useful information which is indirect advertising for Clinton Computer. The inside pages of the edition illustrated here carry stories about computer usage in a local high school, illustrations and tips on minimizing eye strain in using computers, a story about California's former Governor Brown calling Clinton Computer for information, and several pieces of information about and schedules for courses offered at the company's learning centers.

This is an excellent balance of news, useful information, and advertising matter that gives the reader reasons to take the time to read the publication. (An excellent idea used by many newsletter publishers is to have the printer punch three holes in the margin, suggesting to the reader that the newsletter be bound and saved in a three-ring binder.)

GETTING INFORMATION

The gathering of useful information for a newsletter is a concern for many individuals who contemplate such a marketing effort. Actually, it is usually far less difficult than it at first appears to be. There are many different sources of "stories" (news and information items), depending on the industry the newsletter covers and the type of coverage on which it is to be based.

A first measure is to have yourself placed on the mailing lists of organizations who send out news releases that are relevant. A simple request to the public information or marketing offices of relevant organizations, explaining that you are publishing a newsletter, will soon bring you a volume of releases, memoranda, manuals, brochures, reports, and sundry other publications and documents. From these you can select whatever you believe appropriate and useful.

You need to read, too, always with an eye to potentially useful ideas and information. You cannot usually quote directly from others' copyrighted publications, but you can use the information offered. Copyright covers a given combination of words but does not convey any exclusive rights to the information or ideas presented by those words. You are free to use that information and those ideas, as long as you describe them in your own language.

On that subject, you can copyright your own publication, the newsletter, by the simple expedient of stating that the publication is copyrighted by you, giving the approximate date (year or month and year). This conveys common law copyright and is a legitimate copyright. It is not necessary to register this with the Copyright Office of the Library of Congress unless you get into litigation—if someone plagiarizes your material, thereby violating your copyright, and you wish to sue. Then the copyright must be registered with the Copyright Office.

Most publishers of free newsletters see no particular value in barring others from borrowing their information. Some copyright the publication and print a notice advising readers that they are free to copy and republish anything in the newsletter, as long as they credit the source. That kind of approved and authorized use of your material is, in fact, in your interest, giving you some free publicity for your newsletter and whatever it is that you are promoting. There is good reason to encourage that kind of borrowing of your words.

On the other hand, you may wish to use information that you are not sure you are legally free to use. Many of those organizations you send your request to will send you photographs, catalogs, drawings, and other useful items, including complete press kits. The implication that you are free to use these in your newsletter is plain enough, but few of those who send you that material will think to send you formal, written permission to do so. To be on the safe side in using these in your newsletter, it is wise to ask for a release, furnishing a form for the purpose.

I use such a form in gathering such materials for my own writing, and an example of one similar to the one I have used successfully for some years is reproduced in Figure 4. Modify and adapt this for your own use. (Some publishers use much more elaborate forms, but this has served me well.)

4.
Simple Permission Form

```
                              RELEASE

     Permission is hereby granted to Herman Holtz to reproduce and/or quote
     directly, with attribution, from material supplied herewith.


     _____      _____
     (Typed/printed name/title)            (Signature)


     _____      _____
     (Company/division)                    (Date)
```

Some respondents will want you to specify exactly how and where you will use their material, and some will demand the right to review and approve or disapprove the specific usage in the manuscript. In my own case, I refuse to agree to that because I pledge in my letter of request not to abuse their courtesy and criticize them, but only to report objectively. Moreover, few have made that demand on me, and I lose little by not using that material. And in some cases I have simply paraphrased, thus using the information in a manner that did not require anyone's permission or release of rights.

NEWSLETTER FORMATS

There are several terms used in newsletters that are jargon peculiar to the trade, but which you should know. One of these is *nameplate*, which identifies the title box, usually at the top of page 1, as in Figure 5, which is a bimonthly newsletter for the consulting profession.

In the case of this newsletter, it includes a *routing box* at the head of the leftmost column of page 1. This encourages the circulation of the newsletter within an organization it is sent to, thus adding to the distribution generally, if not to the number of copies sold. (This newsletter is a for-profit venture.)

Another item found in most newsletters (and also in newspapers and magazines) is the *masthead*. This is a single column, usually, listing the various principal functionaries of the publication. Usually this is somewhere on the inside pages of the newsletter, but in the case of the newsletter in Figure 6, another for-profit newsletter, it appears on page 1.

Note that while the first two newsletters cited here were typeset, this latest example is typed or "typeset" with a word-processor printer, many of which use the same kind of daisywheel printing element that many of today's typewriters do. But there are at least three other noteworthy features in the latter example:

The front page has a great deal of typeset material on it. In fact, it is printed up in quantity, and each month the publisher uses a copy as the first page, so that the type on page 1 need be set and printed only once.

The bulk mail indicia is printed on the front page, making this what is known as a self-mailer. That is, with a name and address label, it can be mailed as a "flat" or folded, without an envelope. (Most newsletters carry an address block on the back page to make the newsletter a self-mailer.)

This newsletter carries its copyright notice on the first page; whereas the newsletter illustrated in the previous figure has the copyright no-

5.

For-Profit Newsletter

CONSULTING OPPORTUNITIES JOURNAL

"America's Largest 'How-To' Marketing and Information Source
for the Independent Consultant"

| Vol. 4, No. 4 | January-February 1985 | ISSN: 0273-4613 |

ROUTE TO:

From the Other Side of the Desk . . .

WHY AND HOW CONSULTANTS GET HIRED — AGAIN

By Teresa Brown with Steve Lanning

TIPS ON SETTING FEES

*By Audrey Wyatt,
American Consultants League*

We get a number of inquiries from our members asking about how to set their daily consulting fees. Newcomers to the profession are concerned that they will price themselves out of the market or will grossly undervalue themselves. Old-timers are worried that, if they raise their fees, they will lose existing clients. All consultants, whether part-time or full-time, share the same dilemma: they have only their expertise and their time to sell. How then can they determine a fair but profitable hourly rate?

According to Howard Shenson in his book, *The Successful Consultants Guide to Fee Setting* (The Consultant's Library, 1980), the way to calculate your daily billing rate is to begin by estimating the gross salary you are able to earn as an employee. Divide that gross by the 261 working days in a year. That is your daily rate. To that, you must add your estimated daily overhead (business expenses) and then crank in a percentage for the profit factor (to cover the risk you take by being in business). His example:

Daily Labor Rate	$150
Overhead (110% of daily labor rate)	165
	$315
Profit (19% of $315)	60
Daily Billing Rate	$375

Herbert Bermont, considered to be the consultant's consultant, and a member of the American Consultants

(see **SETTING FEES**, pg. 2)

(Washington, D.C.) The saying is still true. You CAN sell just about anything to anybody — once. After that it is your reputation, your service after the sale, and your product that call for a repeat performance.

In COJ's quest to uncover and explore every profit-generating method for marketing professional services, we have found the views of the clients extremely helpful over the years. In this article we have put together recent comments by clients — and those consultants who hire other professionals.

While it is true that many consulting services are needed on a one-time only basis, developing your service with all the quality control and excellence you can muster is a must. After all, even one-shot service firms get referrals.

The Mark of a Good Consultant

High on everyone's list of qualities for the consulting professional is intelligence. But it was more than just gray matter that clients admired. That is, more than degrees or scholarship, and in many cases more than even making a good analysis of a client's situation.

Philip Caldwell, Chairman and CEO of Ford said that lateral vision is a must in those he hires. By this is meant the ability to "see" beyond one's own field of interest to the problems and opportunities of many if not all the fields affecting a professional's specialty.

We found this to be echoed with many others. They enjoyed that man or woman they hired as a consultant to tell them of things they uncovered in a situation in their own field of expertise.

This brings up another oft-repeated trait that clients speak of. Though it was expressed in different ways, the consultant who brought in the various

problems and/or opportunities from other areas showed that client his awareness. That is, aware of how the client's business functions, aware of the client's competitors, and aware of the client's products and services.

Robert McLean of IRM, Inc., a research firm in New York, noted that they have many opportunities for a one-shot contract. IRM's clients have situations where they require only a fast "fix-it" job. Accordingly, McLean mentions that consultants are frustrated as they don't get to use their full arsenal of talents — or even half of them — on many of their assignments.

Consequently, many consultants look the other way when IRM puts out a RFP (Request for Proposal). However, McLean sees cases where a "sharp consultant sees opportunity for us and our client in a related area while he is working on the assignment." The consultant then submits, after the initial job is completed, a proposal of how he could be used to exploit the opportunity uncovered in his initial job.

McLean states he has given assignments based on the consultant's follow-up proposal, after IRM's client sees the proposal and is open to doing it again. Although the opportunity for doing a follow-up proposal is definitely not present on every assignment, McLean keeps note of those consultants who have this "lateral vision" for follow-up on future work.

Straight-Talk on Assignments

One of the frustrating things clients have told us is when they have been sold by a consultant, perhaps the head of a firm, the job is handled by staffers from the consultant's office. The frustrating matter is that the clients were not informed of the who-handles-

(see **WHY AND HOW**, pg. 2)

6.
Newletter with Several Special Features

Volume 4   Number 1   February, 1985

☐ **YES**...I want to make my profitable

MAIL ORDER CONNECTION

...*The professional mail marketer's newsletter of effective response/profit techniques.*

published by:
STILSON & STILSON
P.O. Box 1075
Tarpon Springs, FL 34286-1075

BULK RATE
U.S.
POSTAGE PAID
Tarpon Springs
Florida
Permit No. 210

NAME: _____
COMPANY: _____
ADDRESS: _____
CITY/STATE/ZIP: _____

☐ Check here for info on how "MOC" subscribers save 25% on Galen Stilson's Consulting/Copywriting services.

THIS ISSUE ...

Split Test Variations ... Sales Within Sales ... How To Compute CPO For A 2-Step Promo ... Help Your Copywriter Help You ... How To Make Bonuses More Appealing ... And Much More.

MANAGING EDITOR

GALEN STILSON
Copywriter/Consultant
P.O. Box 1075
Tarpon Springs, FL 34286

ASSOCIATE EDITOR

JEAN STILSON
P.O. Box 1075
Tarpon Springs, FL 34286

CONSULTING EDITORS

RENE GNAM, President
Rene Gnam Consultation Corp.
Consultant/Copywriter
P.O. Box 6435
Clearwater, FL 33518

LUTHER BROCK, Ph.D.
"The Letter Doctor"
Consultant/Copywriter
2911 Nottingham
Denton, TX 76201

ED BURNETT, President
Ed Burnett Consultants, Inc.
Consultant/List Management
2 Park Avenue
New York, NY 10016

CRAIG HUEY, President
Infomat, Inc.
List Consultant/Full Service
25550 Hawthorne Blvd., Ste. 304
Torrence, CA 90505

ANDREW S. LINICK, Ph.D.
The Copyologist®, President
L.K. Advertising Agency
Seven Putter Building
Middle Island, NY 11953

WILLIAM COHEN, Ph.D.
Professor of Marketing
California State Univ., L.A.
5151 State University Drive
Los Angeles, CA 90032

PAUL ALEXANDER
Paul Alexander & Associates
Small Business Consultant
14504 Lanica Circle
Chantilly, VA 22021

COPYRIGHT 1984 by STILSON & STILSON

SOMETHING TO THINK ABOUT ...

"A direct mail letter often looks deceptively simple. Anybody can write a letter, can't they?

The fact is that an effective direct mail letter differs greatly from an ordinary letter. The purpose of most ordinary letters is simply to inform -- to communicate certain facts and/or ideas to the recipient. It's a one-on-one relationship, and if the writer's meaning is clear, the letter will be 100% effective.

The purpose of a direct mail letter, on the other hand, is to get action -- to make at least some of the recipients do what the advertiser wants. The writer must imagine what those who receive the letter are like, how much they already know of the subject, what their attitude toward it is, and so on.

... A direct mail letter must arouse emotion. It must make some of its readers want what is being offered enough to overcome their natural lethargy and their natural inclination not to part with their money. In fact, an effective direct mail letter is often, but not always, so strong that it would be offensive on a one-to-one basis.

It takes a distinct type of talent and personality to write a direct mail letter that pulls profitably -- someone who knows that people respond principally to appeals to their greed and to their fears, someone who can write clearly and logically, and who knows how to arouse emotion with facts.

That's one kind of expert an advertiser needs ..."

Alec Benn, from his book
THE 27 MOST COMMON MISTAKES IN ADVERTISING

"MAIL ORDER CONNECTION" ... the professional mail marketer's how-to newsletter of effective response/profit techniques ... is published monthly by Stilson & Stilson, P.O. Box 1075, Tarpon Springs, FL 34286-1075 (Phone. (813) 937-3480). Your subscription investment is only $64 per year. Quotes with complete attribution are permitted. Reprints require written permission. Reproduction is prohibited. News releases of direct interest to mail marketers is invited. Comments from subscribers are welcome.

tice inside, together with the masthead. It is a rather common practice throughout the periodical publishing industry to print the copyright notice near or in conjunction with the masthead. Note, too, that the newsletter of Figure 6 includes that idea mentioned earlier of bearing holes for mounting in a three-ring binder.

One of these latter newsletters advises readers on the front page what the subscription fee is. The other has the information tucked away inside its eight-page format. (Both are eight-page newsletters.) Both are printed on a good grade of heavy offset (not glossy) paper.

Note that most of the names listed on the masthead are of people referred to as consulting editors. That means that they are not employees of the publisher but are engaged elsewhere, usually in enterprises of their own, as the listings reveal. They contribute articles to the newsletter, some regularly, some occasionally, and usually without direct payment. The primary reason such individuals do so is that they get a certain amount of free advertising (publicity, that is) by being listed here and in the by-lines accompanying their contributions. It's quite a common practice, similar to that of inducing others to speak at seminars for the same reason. (The other newsletter referred to in this chapter also uses such contributors and carries their names on an inside page, giving them somewhat less prominence than does the newsletter in Figure 6.)

There is a divergence of opinion on whether a newsletter ought to be typed or typeset, and there are many examples of both practices to be found among published newsletters. Some publishers are firmly convinced that typeset newsletters look more polished and professional and command more respect from subscribers and prospective subscribers than do newsletters composed by electric typewriter. The other school believes that newsletter readers perceive typewriter-composed newsletters as more spontaneous and therefore offering fresher information than do typeset newsletters. Formal typesetting implies, they believe, that the copy has been polished, and burnished and is relatively old, as compared with typewritten copy.

There is, of course, some cost differential between the two approaches to newsletter composition. Formal typesetting varies widely in price but usually runs about $25 to $40 per page, depending on various factors.

It is a fact, and significant in this reference, that there is no apparent relationship between subscription costs and the method of composition, type of paper printed on, use of photographs, and other such matters. In fact, one of the most expensive (and successful) newsletters, The Gallagher Report, was still composed by typewriter the last time I saw a copy and contains nothing but solid text. However, a great many subscribers demonstrate their belief that the text is worth the price.

It is noteworthy that this newsletter began its existence a number of years ago as a free newsletter, launched entirely as a marketing tool by its business-brokerage entrepreneur to help market his services. The newsletter became so successful that Bernard Gallagher began to charge subscription fees for it and soon gave up his other business to devote his full time to the newsletter and, later, to another one he launched.

His is not the only free newsletter that became a profitable enterprise. There are many others, such as that of entrepreneur/writer Matthew Lesko, who launched his newsletter *The Information Report* to help promote the services of his firm, Washington Researchers, and later made a separate profit-making venture of the newsletter.

SHOULD IT BE FREE?

You can, of course, charge a nominal sum for your newsletter, such as $5 or $10 per year for four or six issues (quarterly or bimonthly, that is). That will defray basic costs—printing and mailing, at least—and will help establish in the reader's mind at least some image of a value to attach to your newsletter.

If you choose to do this, you may consider the advantages of assigning a larger nominal value to your newsletter—perhaps $36 or $48 per year—and offering a "special deal" for the lucky few who act promptly and can get a full year for only $5 or $10. It's a common tactic employed with frequent success.

There are other ways to add value. If your proper prospects are all businesspeople, you can require that requests be made on a company letterhead or with a business card accompanying them. If you solicit the general public, you may ask for the requestor to state age and occupation to demonstrate suitable qualifications.

Of course, every condition you attach to getting a free subscription or sample copy of your newsletter is a constraint that tends to reduce the effectiveness of your appeal—the number of people who respond to your appeal and request a copy. That's a trade-off, and you have to consider it. (Today, the postage is likely to cost more than the copy of the newsletter does).

GETTING CIRCULATION

You want circulation—numbers. It's largely a probability exercise: The more copies you get into circulation, presumably, the greater the results. But not necessarily. The circulation has to be the right circulation—those who are truly qualified prospects for whatever it is that you sell. Circulation to those who are not true prospects, no matter how great, is of no help, but is only an unnecessary expense.

There are other ways, and one is to rent or somehow acquire the use of suitable mailing lists, as discussed in an earlier chapter. If you have done a proper job of identifying and defining your prospects, you may very well be able to rent suitable mailing lists. Another is to run those inquiry advertisements mentioned earlier, inviting readers to request sample or free copies. Still another is to arrange to make help-yourself stacks of your newsletter available at appropriate trade shows, conventions, and other such convocations. Another is to offer producers of appropriate seminars quantities of your newsletter to include in their handout portfolios or to make them available otherwise to attendees.

You can also hand out copies yourself as you speak at seminars, attend meetings and conventions, and otherwise find opportunities. (Many of these seminars and meetings have literature tables in the back of the room or in the hall, and you can deposit copies there for attendees to pick up.)

Of course, you should also pursue all those publicity devices discussed in connection with seminars, to publicize your newsletter and encourage suitable prospects to request a sample.

With a little diligence, you will also find a number of public places where you can leave samples or circulars announcing the availability of samples and instructions for requesting them. If, for example, what you offer is of interest to the public at large and that is whom you are trying to reach, most public libraries have bulletin boards and literature tables. And most communities have centers of some sort, with bulletin boards, and cable-TV bulletin boards, too.

MUST YOU BECOME A JOURNALIST?

By now you may be a little dismayed at all the work involved in creating a newsletter, preparing the copy for each issue, getting it all together, and mailing it out even four times a year, much less on a more frequent schedule. In many ways it is even more complex and requires more time and effort than does the preparation of a seminar. At least it is or may appear to be so for the individual with no experience in or desire to become experienced in newsletter writing and related journalistic endeavors.

There are alternatives if you prefer not to do the actual work yourself. There are several alternatives, in fact, which permit you to do none of the work or only a portion of it, as you choose. That is, you can buy virtually any services you wish, which I will describe and discuss in greater detail in a later chapter. However, these are brief descriptions of the various options available to you:

Freelance writers and editorial consultants are available to do any part or all of creating a newsletter for you and preparing each issue for the printer. Such specialists are familiar with all aspects of the work and can guide you to any services you need for composition, makeup, artwork, printing, and mailing, or they can simply make arrangements for and manage all of these for you. Many of them have their favorite places to get necessary support services—vendors they have learned to use because those vendors are reliable, reasonable in their charges, and so forth. Many of the writers are also knowledgeable technically in some specialized subject area, so you can often find one who requires relatively little input from you to do the job of writing and editing the copy for your newsletter.

There are organizations who will handle one or more of the necessary major functions for you. Many of the larger ones have their own printing plants, typesetting facilities, art departments, and even mailing list services in a kind of "one-stop" service, and all know others who provide the companion services, and so can make appropriate recommendations or referrals for you.

The kinds of services described can be found in a variety of large firms. You will find some who consider themselves to be primarily printers but who have many other necessary facilities, such as those described, available to prepare your copy for printing and whatever else is needed to complete the job. However, similar facilities and services are available often in firms that are primarily mailers and fulfillment houses and in still other firms who are list managers or other types of relevant service firms.

If you do not know where to turn to find a freelance writer or editorial consultant (some sources will be suggested later) to help you, such firms as those just described often have rosters of such specialists and can help you find one that is suitable for you.

You can even get a ready-made newsletter on a kind of franchise basis. One firm, Cambridge Associates of Boston, offers two ready-made newsletters, Executives' Digest and Today's Executive, four-page monthly publications with your own firm name prominently displayed on page 1 and either half or all of page 4 for your direct advertisement. The publisher franchises the newsletters, and you can purchase from 50 copies to as many as you wish at a flat price based on the number of copies (starting at $27.95 per month for 50 copies, at this time), folded down for mailing in your own envelopes. (Of course, you can have your copies sent directly to your own mailing house, if you wish to have someone else handle your mailings.)

Obviously, all these services cost money; whereas you can produce and mail your own newsletter for far less cost, presumably, if you plan to mail to a small list. That's because the per-copy price is quite high to get the first copy off the press, but it declines sharply with quantity. You cannot produce 50 copies of your own four-page newsletter for $27.95, although you might be able to come in lower than $197 for 1,000 copies, but only if you do not charge for your own time and labor or pay for the services of others to do the job for you.

Of course, that newsletter you undertake as a kind of franchise is not uniquely yours, as your own newsletter would be, and since distribution is by mail, you may encounter some direct competition from another firm sending out the same newsletter. Moreover, this is a monthly obligation, and you face the chore and expense of mailing each month. You must therefore trade off those drawbacks, if they are drawbacks for you, against the convenience of getting out "your own" newsletter each month with little or no effort on your part.

There is still another factor to consider when weighing the ready-made newsletter against your own newsletter. In that franchised newsletter you are confined to the editorial copy the publisher prepares for each month's issue. Of course, you can use that back page for editorial copy of your own, instead of strictly advertising messages, but that is the extent of your own material in the newsletter. If you wished to insert a personal message of some kind, it would have to be on the back page.

And, again, while four pages is probably as much as you would want to use in a free (marketing) newsletter, you might wish to expand it. You would not be able to do so. Or you might wish to change the editorial philosophy, or type of coverage, but you would not be able to do that either. And if you wanted to start it as a free publication but convert it to a for-profit enterprise later, you might find some difficulties in doing that, too, for a variety of reasons.

Chapter 6

Some Special Seminar Ideas

Seminars are surprisingly flexible in the opportunities they offer enterprising individuals.

SPECIAL PLACES AND TYPES OF SEMINARS

Every year, early in December, *Training* magazine holds an annual week-long training and consulting conference and trade show in New York City. The program is filled with dozens of seminars, among other typical convention and trade show events. Most of the seminars are half-day—three hours long—and are presented by a number of companies and independent professionals who receive no pay for these presentations but who do get some benefits, such as travel reimbursement and per diem allotments for the days they speak. If you present a seminar there, you also get free registration for the conference, free admission to the other seminars (for which fees are charged by the sponsoring organization), and sometimes the sale of your books to be given out to seminar attendees. However, the chief reason most present these free seminars is for the advertising and sales promotion they are able to realize from the activity. For many, presenting the seminars free of charge is a marketing activity that produces worthwhile results for them. In fact, many of the presenters say that this conference is the most important marketing event of the year for them.

This annual convocation is sponsored and organized by a publisher, but it is fairly typical of many such conferences and conventions sponsored by various organizations. For example, the United Communications Group, a company that includes newsletter publishing, video production and on-line services (computerized public data base information system), also operates a seminar and conference group that organizes seminars and conferences and invites speakers to make presentations on the same basis: for the advertising and marketing exposure.

Many associations hold annual conferences and conventions and in many cases offer similar opportunities to qualified aspirants to present brief seminars or handle portions of a lengthier seminar.

Governments often sponsor such events. The Michigan Employment Training Institute, for example, has conducted seminar/training conferences for small business firms in Michigan to help the attendees learn how to market to federal government agencies successfully and invites speakers to handle portions of the presentation. And the federal government itself sponsors many conferences and symposia. For example, there have been several such events to discuss the energy problem alone, sponsored by the U.S. Department of Energy and before that by its predecessor agencies. And agencies within the sprawling Department of Health and Human Services have held many such events on drug and alcohol abuse, mental health problems, and other concerns.

Some Additional Benefits Are Possible

When you speak and offer presentations at such seminars and segments of seminars, you are not usually expected to do so entirely at your own expense, nor always without a fee of some kind. The sponsoring organization expects to reimburse speakers for the direct expenses in travel and per diem costs, of course, but in many cases the sponsoring organization has enough of a budget to pay at least a reasonable honorarium, if not a full speaking or consulting fee. And this does not diminish the potential marketing benefits of speaking before groups attending such events. As a speaker and presenter, you may earn a full fee and win sales or sales leads also, as a result.

Many seminar presenters have their own self-published books, manuals, cassette tapes, training programs, and other products to sell, and they can promote such sales both directly and indirectly at many of these events. For example, on a great many of these occasions there is a literature table, and you are free to deposit there your business cards, brochures, and literature presenting your offers. However, many also permit you to conduct back-of-the-room sales of such products, especially when you are not being paid a fee for your presentation. For some, this is icing on the cake, but for others, this alone makes the occasion worthwhile and even profitable.

Arranging to Speak at Such Occasions

In time, as you become well known in the appropriate circles, your telephone and mail will bring you invitations to speak at many such occasions, often with a query as to your fee, so that often the occasion is profitable in and of itself, as already noted. However, it does take a fairly long time before you become well enough known to draw more than a rare inquiry or invitation of that sort. But in the meanwhile you can take a few measures to encourage and accelerate the frequency of such occasions.

One of these measures is simply to call or write the sponsors of all relevant seminars—seminars that concern some area of your own field and are likely to attract attendees who would be likely prospects for your own services or products—and volunteer your services. Many will decline with thanks, of course, but many others will accept gratefully, if you make your presentation properly, concentrating on the benefits to the sponsors of the event.

You can learn of such events by watching for announcements in various trade magazines and even in the business and financial sections of major newspapers and news magazines. You can also ask friends to save any brochures they receive in the mail for such seminars and workshops. And in time you will begin to get a good many in the mail yourself, if you are not already receiving them.

Another measure is to make the same offer to the program manager in all relevant associations, setting yourself up to participate in their annual conventions. (Of course, you should be as active as possible in the associations to which you yourself belong and try to become a joiner, if you are not already one.)

INITIATING YOUR OWN PROGRAMS

It is not difficult to launch an entirely independent program of seminars and similar presentations, as an alternative to participating in others' events. There are many routes open to you for doing this. Here are a few examples:

Many companies offer speakers—advertise their own speakers bureau of various executives in the company—to whomever wants them, because it is good marketing to do so, and many organizations take advantage of the opportunity to get a free speaker at their meetings and other occasions. You can easily do the same thing, even if you are a small company and your speakers bureau consists of you alone. Make up a brochure or a form letter and send it to as many appropriate organizations in your area as you can find in the telephone directory and through other information sources such as the public library and the local Chamber of Commerce.

You can also ask to be listed by the local Chamber of Commerce and elsewhere as a speaker available free of charge. In many cases, local newspapers are pleased to carry such notices, and often city and county agencies will also list you in little publications of their own, if what you have to say is relevant to local government activities. Here in Montgomery County, Maryland, for example, we have a public building called the Care Center where meeting rooms, literature, and other kinds of support are available to many small, non-profit groups engaged in activities the county government believes the county should support. Among the groups that meet there regularly and get county support at least to the extent of free meeting rooms, literature, and publicity are one on alcoholism, another on drug abuse by youth, and another on dealing with and controlling rebellious juveniles. And some groups of this type are permitted the use of school buildings and other facilities for their meetings. These groups are glad to get speakers, and the local government is glad to provide the space and necessary facilities.

Many public libraries also have meeting rooms in which they conduct many free programs, including seminars of various kinds. One example is an evening seminar on small business principles and practices. You can, of course, offer your own little seminar or speech to the library system, which may sponsor you with a bit of publicity. Even if you do not need or want library sponsorship, you can often persuade the library authorities to allow you a rent-free room for your seminar.

Colleges, especially junior colleges and state colleges, conduct many adult education and extended education courses, some free, many for nominal fees, in a wide variety of subjects. You can get in touch with the people who organize these courses at your local universities and colleges and offer a course of your own. If they believe there will be some public interest in the course, they will be pleased to add it to the curricula offered.

On the other hand, if you want to organize and conduct an independent seminar open to the general public, you may be able to get a free meeting room at a local government installation, if you make the seminar one that is deemed to be in the public interest or educational in something considered to coincide with local government interests.

If your objectives and subject lend themselves to it—are almost universal in appeal—you can get a great deal of help and support. The hypothetical seminar I discussed earlier to promote something that will help people stop smoking would be such a subject. A great many organizations would want to support you, and many would want to invite you to speak. Anything that touches on some of today's greatest concerns—drugs, primary education, careers, unemployment, basic literacy, and the problems of the physically handicapped, for example—fits into that category. Whatever your topic, try to search out a direct connection to some concern such as these, and focus attention on that.

MAKING A SALES PRESENTATION INTO A SEMINAR

One exceptionally effective strategy that has been used only rarely offers a particularly advantageous way of making sales presentations directly to prospective clients, if the service or product being sold is a big-tag one that ordinarily requires one-on-one sales efforts—presentations to individual prospects. Of course, no executive ever has time to talk to a salesperson, and the tales of sales representatives sitting in outer offices for hours are legion. That's because by the very nature of selling, all sales representatives are perceived as people who want something from the prospect. Even when the sales representative insists that he or she is there to give, rather than get, the response is a cynical snort of disbelief.

Instead of making sales calls and sales presentations, the smart marketer can offer to present a free seminar not only to the targeted executive but to an assemblage of company executives for whom the seminar ought to be a significant and helpful event.

Of course, the whole approach must be handled with great care, for any offer of something free triggers that same cynical and skeptical response. Most executives are going to automatically perceive this offer as a thinly disguised sales presentation. It will take skill and planning to persuade any prospect to accept a bona fide offer of a bona fide seminar.

To accomplish this, it is necessary to offer assurances that no direct sales effort will be made during or following the presentation. You will admit, of course, if questioned, that the seminar is part of your company's marketing activity—that much is obvious, in any case—but it is a first stage, a purely educational process that you hope will lead eventually to business when the customer is ready to call on you for help. In the meanwhile, you want to do the pioneering and indoctrination effort because you cannot make sales until people are made aware of what you can do for them.

A detailed plan and outline of information to be delivered is essential. It is the proof that what you are offering is a true educational seminar and only indirectly a sales presentation. You should have an informal proposal made up for the occasion, and it would probably be far more effective if the proposal were not a slick brochure. That would be too suggestive of what you are trying to overcome: the conviction that it is just another trick to get a foot in the door and make a hard-sell sales presentation.

Of course, you should not go to the opposite extreme and produce a cheap or shabby-looking piece of paper either. You can prepare either a small brochure, neat and professional, but not gaudy, or a neatly typed sheaf of paper on standard typing paper of reasonably good quality.

There is more than one advantage to the latter approach. One is that your handout appears to be made up in limited quantity, as indeed it is, usually, prepared for a small and select group of fortunate recipients. That is the desirable impression to strive for, and the slicker the brochure or handout offered, the less likely it is that the prospect will believe that you are offering a seminar, rather than a straight sales presentation. However, there are other advantages:

Cost: It is the least expensive way yet easy to make neat and professional looking. In fact, you don't even have to go to the expense of offset printing, if you require only a handful, but can make copies up on any good office copier. Or, if you have a word processing system, you may even prefer to print out a number of originals, as you can do with such a system.

Flexibility: It is quite easy to revise, edit, add to, delete from, or scrap and redo entirely. And you can easily have more than one version, if you need more than one.

Time: You can make or remake it up and prepare as many copies as you need in a matter of a few hours; whereas, formally printed brochures generally require at least a few days and often a few weeks to have made up.

There should be no commercial messages at all in that initial piece of paper. Time enough exists for the verbal and written commercials after you have made the basic seminar presentation. But now you are still prospecting—trying to identify those who are truly interested and might reasonably be expected to become buyers. Therefore, that first handout must maximize the prospect's interest and motivate him or her to grant you the time to present your little seminar.

That means that the handout must be about the prospect's interests—the prospect's wants—and only about that. If your desire were to persuade prospects to retain you as a proposal consultant, to help write proposals for government contracts, as in my own case, your handout might open with a message along the following lines:

HOW TO WIN (MORE) GOVERNMENT CONTRACTS

Winning government contracts is a matter of writing winning proposals, and that is far more a matter of devising the right strategies than it is of writing skills (although the latter are useful enough). I can help you develop winning proposals, as I have helped many others.

That message addresses the prospect's real interest: winning contracts. In the way this is expressed, it addresses the wants of companies who have never before pursued government contracts, as well as those of companies who have done and do government business. (Everyone wants to do more business, of course.)

If you are addressing this to a proprietor or someone responsible for winning contracts, you are almost certain to get at least some attention, enough to elaborate on your offer. Address the prospect's principal interest at once, elaborate slightly on your basic message to explain your opening statement (you must demonstrate some believable rationale for your opening statement), and drop some hint of your credentials—some initial evidence that you can make good on your promise. (You'll describe these in more detail later.)

Now the stage is set. It's time to make your offer. Your brochure or handout might go on along these lines:

FREE SEMINAR

To help you understand how our services can help you win more government contracts, we offer you a free one-hour seminar—absolutely without obligation—to reveal a few of the insider tips that the most successful proposal writers use, revelations such as the following:

- How to *appear* to be the low bidder, even when you are not
- At least three ways to get inside information—marketing intelligence—that gives you a decisive advantage over competitors
- A simple technique for maximizing your technical rating
- "Worry items" tactics
- Our exclusive graphics-analysis technique for developing winning strategies

These are only a few of the priceless tips that will be revealed to you in this unprecedented one-hour giveaway of "trade secrets." You will learn more, much more, of why and how others are so successful in winning government business.

This seminar will be presented at your convenience in your own conference room or at any other site you wish. And we place no limit on how many of your staff may attend: Invite as many as you wish to share this information. And bring your questions along, too; we'll be pleased to answer them.

Of course, you may elaborate on that, perhaps include a more detailed outline and more arguments, but don't overdo it. Don't get carried away and try to make the sale of your service here. Remember that all you are trying to "sell" here is your free, private seminar, so focus on the benefits you can honestly promise. But do be absolutely scrupulous in *delivering* what you promise. That's extremely important. If you promise to reveal specific items of information in your free seminar, by all means do so, or you will generate indignation and jus-tifiable outrage, instead of sales. But don't go overboard in what you promise, either: No thinking person will expect more than a sampling of the goodies in a free seminar. If you appear to be promising too much—giving too much away, that is—the prospect is likely to be-come skeptical of your offer.

Even worse, you may very well confuse prospects so that they are not really sure what it is that you promise to deliver. It's important to achieve a sharp focus by stressing a few directly related points that address a single interest, such as how to quit smoking painlessly, how to use a personal computer, how to write a report, or another, well-defined benefit. Decide what the major promised benefit is to be and then be sure that all the things you promise to talk about relate di-rectly to that benefit.

THE RIGHT PROSPECTS

The type of presentation discussed here, the free seminar/sales pre-sentation, is probably especially appropriate to the larger business firms (if what you sell is something you sell to business firms, rather than to individual buyers) because they can assemble a reasonably large group—usually ten or more of the staff—to listen to your presenta-tion, and it is important to make this presentation to a group for more than one reason:

It maximizes the probability of winning a sale or two. (Even in the same company, it is often possible to make more than one sale, inas-much as department and division heads often buy independently for their own departments or divisions.)

It encourages some of those group dynamics effects referred to ear-lier. Even in the circumstance of all attendees being executives in the same organization, the approval of one encourages the approval by others. (On the other hand, the single attendee has a typical hesita-tion to act entirely on his or her own impressions, for fear of making a mistake. The reluctance of managers to make independent decisions is a general and well-known problem in management.)

It encourages questions and discussions, which you can turn to your advantage because that helps stimulate interest and lends the subject a definite aura of greater importance. A seminar, to be maximally ef-fective, must involve the attendees actively, for that and other rea-sons.

Therefore, you should certainly encourage and invite the atten-dance of as many people as possible, and when dealing with a large company, you may have to have several subsequent conversations to coordinate the seminar so that a maximum number may attend. But it's well worth your time and trouble to do so, in order to gather the largest group possible for your presentation.

The right prospects for this kind of presentation are, therefore, any who can assemble or help you assemble a reasonably large group to hear your free seminar. And, of course, companies are not the only possible targets for gathering groups together. In fact, some other types of prospects are even more appropriate targets for this technique, depending, of course, on what you sell and who are your typical buyers. However, don't be too quick to prejudge this, either. Here's why:

If you are selling that quit-smoking kind of service, for example, you might consider that your buyers are all individuals. Therefore, you would rule out companies and seek out associations and other such organizations as targets for your free seminar. And if your typical sales are to individuals and perhaps are relatively small sales, you would need the largest possible audience to make the whole thing viable for you, so you would approach sizable organizations.

However, you might be wrong in assuming that you cannot sell your service to companies and therefore should not waste time offering them your free seminar. The fact is that many employers are active in encouraging employees to quit smoking, lose weight, and otherwise act in the best interests of their health. Employers will often help finance programs for employees and provide a place to hold the seminar. (Actually, it is also in the company's interests, as it tends to reduce the cost of their health and insurance plans for employees.) Too, employers forced to lay off people often sponsor programs to help laid-off employees find new jobs.

Therefore, don't be too quick to assume that what you offer is something not suitable for employers.

Other than employers, a few types of organizations who are good targets for this kind of free seminar because they can help you assemble a large group of interested prospects are professional societies, trade associations, clubs, labor unions, community groups, and other sundry associations.

SEMINARS THAT PAY THEIR OWN WAY

So far we have stressed the free seminar as a marketing promotion device that, it is hoped, will lead to sales directly or indirectly. That is, it will either lead to sales made directly on the spot or will result in a superior prospect list—"hot leads"—that can be pursued with a high rate of resultant sales.

This latter idea is most appropriate to the big-tag sales that are usually completed only after several calls and presentations. In fact, that is the basic idea of using free seminars for marketing, because it is expensive to pursue a sale through several calls and presentations, and it is therefore essential that these efforts be directed toward prospects that are truly good prospects for eventual sales. That is what justifies using the expensive seminar method for prospecting leads.

That means that the seminar is generally too costly a marketing method to be worthwhile for the small-tag sales. Still, there are exceptions:

"BOR" Sales

One exception is the seminar that combines small-tag sales with the other general objectives by making on-the-spot sales of small items, such as books, tape cassettes, or other items that prospects might buy on impulse, in addition to pursuing the main objective of the seminar. This type of selling is known to speakers and seminar leaders, in fact, as back-of-the-room sales, and it is commonly practiced by full-time professional speakers, as explained by Gordon Burgett and Mike Frank in their book, *Speaking For Money*.

As Burgett explains it (he makes many seminar presentations every year), such sales are "usually books, tapes, manuals, pamphlets, reports, newsletters, anthologies, video cassettes," and other products. Burgett and others normally make these back-of-the-room or "BOR" sales in the course of presenting paid-attendance seminars, either their own productions or others' productions which they are paid to present. However, there is absolutely no reason for not making BOR sales as an adjunct to free seminars, too, and so defray the cost of the seminar and perhaps even produce a profit. (Professional speakers who sell their books, cassettes, and other items in BOR sales often remark that these sales, properly handled, produce a profit at least equal to their speaking fee. In fact, many say flatly that every public speaker should make such BOR sales and should always be able to realize at least as much from these sales as they do from the speaker's fee they earn.)

It is also possible to conduct free seminars solely to make those BOR sales, if you can make the economics viable. That means that you will have to assemble an adequately large group—it would be difficult to sell enough small-tag products to a small group to make a free seminar profitable—and if you are sponsored by some organization, you will need to have an understanding with them about it. That is, you will need to have their permission to permit you to make BOR sales. It would be unethical to surprise your host organization by selling items in the back of the room without first clearing it with them and might lead to embarrassing situations.

What to Offer in BOR Sales

Obviously, the products you offer for BOR sales must be of interest to the people you have managed to assemble for your seminar. That is, they must appeal to the same self-interest you identified as the main appeal for the seminar generally. On the other hand, you must give this some rather careful thought, for in the case of the free seminar in which the BOR sales are an adjunct and not the purpose of the seminar, there are possible hazards:

One hazard is that if you are offering a $25 book or $100 cassette program that the prospect perceives as an equal or alternative to the big-tag items you want to sell, you may defeat your own purpose. If you have written a commercially available book on the same subject as that for which you are trying to register seminar attendees paying substantial fees, you want to make it clear that the seminar and the handouts given there will cover many things not to be found in the book. It would be deadly to your purposes for attendees to believe that the book, readily available in bookstores, offers everything the seminar offers. Even if that is an obvious truth, your audience will not recognize that unless you tell them so.

For the most part, BOR sales are of information items, such as those already enumerated, because the events—speeches, seminars, and other presentations—are primarily and almost invariably information events, although they may include demonstrations of one sort or another. (For example, if you are a hypnotist, it is likely that you will ask for a volunteer and give a "live" demonstration.)

You may, of course, offer other items relevant to your lecture. If you are lecturing on diets and weight reduction, for example, you might offer books and tapes on the subject, but you might also offer appetite suppressants, exercising devices, and other relevant products.

In one case I was invited to be a guest at a seminar on consulting and public speaking presented by a rather well-known public speaker who happens also to be a skilled salesman (and, in fact, presents many training seminars on that very subject). He had a rather small group—probably not more than 30 people—but he was able to sell them several thousand dollars' worth of a cassette-book package for which he charged $250. (And they had paid to attend the session, too.) His technique, moreover, was to appear to offer the package as an afterthought, since he made no reference to it during his day-long main presentation. However, he was so persuasive that he virtually enthralled his audience. He only could have sold most of those orders then and there, while his listeners were all but spellbound by his fluent presentation. A follow-up appeal would probably have produced only a fraction of those sales because by then the spell of his mesmerizingly expert and smooth presentation would have long since worn off.

There is also the possible hazard that if you stress those BOR sales too much, you will distract attention from the real objective of your free seminar. You should not address the sale of those items at all during your main presentation, and when you do, at or near the close of your main presentation, make it quite clear that these are not an alternative to the main item you are trying to sell, but are helpful adjuncts.

There is an excellent possibility that many of those who do not sign up for your main marketing objective will patronize your BOR efforts. And if your primary seminar objective is the development of good leads for follow-up, the sale of BOR items will represent reinforcement of that objective, for those who purchase those items will indicate in so doing that they are, indeed, good prospects.

COST-CUTTING ALTERNATIVES

Recognizing that seminars are a relatively high-cost marketing approach (on the basis of cost per prospect, that is), anything you can do to reduce the cost of those free seminars is going to contribute to overall success. There are some ways not only to reduce the cost of these seminars but to increase their probable effectiveness at the same time.

The principal costs are usually in advertising to draw attendees, which includes some or all of the following: printing, mailing-list rental, postage, and space rates. However, there is also the cost of the handout materials, the hall or meeting room, and help, if you require help to handle the seminar, and especially if you require the help of a presenter on the platform.

Fortunately, it is possible to conduct cooperative seminars in which you share all these costs and so cut them in half for yourself. It is merely necessary to find someone else who addresses the same kinds of prospects but who is not directly competitive with you, nevertheless.

That task is less difficult than it appears at first, and the truth of that is easy to demonstrate. Every trade show is an example. The show appeals to some group of prospects, yet the majority of the exhibitors are not in direct competition with each other. Take a typical small-business trade show, for example. Virtually all the attendees will be individuals seeking ideas and opportunities for launching a small business of some sort. Among the many exhibitors will be franchisers of all kinds of businesses, publishers, equipment manufacturers, consultants, training-program marketers, and dozens of others offering business opportunities of every conceivable kind.

The two of you—and it could be three, four, or more—could thus share costs, mailing lists, printing, advertising, and the meeting room, and you would actually reinforce each other because the appeal of attending several presentations in a single free seminar is greater than that of hearing a single presentation. In fact, instead of sharing costs, you might want to simply pool your money and mount a much greater effort than any of you could manage alone. With a consortium of several of you cooperating in a large effort, you could assemble a virtual seminar/conference/trade show of your own and thus make a fairly major event of it.

PAID-ATTENDANCE SEMINARS

I have been discussing seminars on the assumption that I am talking about free seminars, and it is the free seminar that is most often used as a marketing tool. That, however, does not mandate that all marketing seminars be free ones, nor does it bar paid-attendance seminars conducted with a profit motive from serving as marketing tools. Quite the contrary, many paid-attendance seminars also serve well as devices to generate other business, even if the other business is a by-product of the seminar, rather than a direct objective of it. It is worth considering that before going on to other matters.

The seminar for which a registration or attendance fee is charged is rarely less than a half day and is more often one, two, or three days in length. It usually includes something reasonably substantial as a handout—a manual, reports, brochures, and often a collection of such items, assembled into a portfolio. And if the seminar presenter/producer has other products or services to sell, the portfolio includes suitable advertising materials, of course.

Obviously, the attendance at such a seminar is not likely to be as great as it would be for a free seminar. And yet such seminars often draw surprisingly large attendance and produce excellent results in terms of other business.

One reason for this latter result is that in most cases all attendees of the seminar are excellent prospects for any product or service directly related to that which drew the attendees to the seminar. The fact that each was willing to pay the attendance fee attests to their being more than idlers or curiosity seekers, of course, so it is possible that a paid-attendance seminar will produce even better results—more sales, if not greater attendance—than does the free seminar.

Virtually everything that has been said about free seminars and how they can be used in your marketing efforts applies equally to paid seminars. You can make back-of-the-room sales, you can try to sign up attendees for other items, you can build prospect lists, and you can do any or all of these. The fact of having been paid by attendees for the information and materials supplied in no way prevents or inhibits you from doing these other activities.

Chapter 7

Some Special Newsletter Ideas

Flexible and versatile as the seminar is, the newsletter is perhaps even more so. It is not a question of which to use but how to combine the two for greatest effect.

A FEW NOTES ON NEWSLETTER VERSATILITY

Newsletters and seminars were combined in this book because they are natural allies, with much in common, as already noted, and with a natural tendency toward symbiosis—each supporting the other's existence. And, as an earlier chapter pointed out, the two complement each other, too, each offering its own unique strength or advantage where it is most needed to complete the marketing plan.

In the previous chapter I discussed back-of-the-room sales. If your newsletter is one for which you charge a subscription fee, it is an excellent candidate for the BOR sale. On the other hand, if it is a free newsletter, the seminar is an excellent place to hand out sample copies and invite attendees to apply for free subscriptions.

But even before the seminar is presented, the newsletter can do its work of publicizing the event and inviting attendance. And it can do this indirectly, as well as directly, by using it for all relevant public relations (PR) purposes. For example, if your newsletter is free, it ought to include on the distribution list a wide selection of other relevant publications: newsletters, magazines, and newspapers. And if it is a newsletter to which you sell subscriptions, you should be offering complimentary subscriptions to those other publishers. In fact, used in this manner, your newsletter can be used as a press release. All you must do to accomplish this is to print a prominently placed notice to this general effect:

Permission is hereby granted to quote and/or reprint any content of this newsletter not otherwise specifically restricted by relevant notice, provided that full attribution is made.

You will find, when you offer complimentary subscriptions (or simply send copies) to other publishers, with or without formal agreement to do so, that you will in turn get many complimentary subscriptions to others' newsletters, often with the same general notice of permission to quote and reprint the content. This will help you keep informed, while it will also furnish you some useful material for your own newsletter. Too, you will soon be exchanging notices of various kinds—announcements of your seminars, for example—with others and thus getting some publicity that will result in business.

You can also furnish copies of your newsletter to other producers of seminars to use as handouts to attendees, where their seminars are in some way relevant to your own activities, thereby getting some added circulation for yourself. This is especially appropriate for paid-attendance seminars, where the other party is looking for low-cost or free material that is suitable to hand out to attendees.

Of course, if you are a guest speaker at others' seminars, especially if you are speaking without fee or for a nominal honorarium, you should have no trouble getting permission to distribute your free newsletter or solicitations to subscribe to your paid newsletter to attendees of those seminars.

THE SAMPLE NEWSLETTER

Many publishers of newsletters for which they charge subscription fees offer free sample copies in their inquiry advertisements and use sample copies as their principal mailing pieces in their direct-mail campaigns. Some use copies of their current issue or of whatever issue they happen to have in abundant surplus. Many, however, print a special issue which has a great deal of advertising copy in it, as well as a few samples of the regular features of the newsletter, and use that permanently as their sample issue.

There is something to be said for both approaches. Using whatever extra copies you have on hand of regular issues gives the recipient an authentic sample, whereas the special issue is not an authentic sampling. The special issue is heavier on advertising and sales copy, but that is not necessarily an advantage; it may be a serious disadvantage, in fact.

On the other hand, a newsletter publisher in California who makes a study of newsletter publishing and publishes results of his surveys and tests reports that the use of sample newsletters shows a generally poor return. He explains that by and large the advance advertising builds up respondents' expectations too high, so that when the respondent sees an actual sample, he or she is disappointed and feels let down.

This has some supporting evidence in the experience of many newsletter publishers trying to persuade readers to resubscribe. It proves to be an uphill battle in most cases, and newsletter publishers, like other periodical publishers, must resort to a great many different sales and advertising devices to persuade subscribers to renew.

This suggests rather strongly that these newsletters generally disappoint many of their subscribers and so foster a reluctance to renew their subscriptions. That must mean, also, that the newsletter was badly oversold in winning the original subscription. So it is logical enough that a sample newsletter that fails to live up to its advertising will disappoint the prospect and frustrate the sales effort.

The California publisher who advised readers that sending sample copies of their newsletter was a poor marketing tactic meant well. But he evidently failed to analyze the situation thoroughly and so drew the wrong conclusion. The problem is not in sending out sample copies, nor even in overselling the publication in advertising. The problem is in failing to live up to promises made—failure to produce a newsletter of the high quality and usefulness promised, that is. It is simply a problem of quality of the product.

There is clear enough evidence for this truth. The publisher of the Consulting Opportunities Journal (presented as Figure 5 in Chapter 5), for example, had the opposite experience: Sending sample copies of his publication was a most effective way of gaining new subscribers because the recipients liked the samples—found them helpful—and so agreed that this periodical was worth subscribing to. (This publisher sent sample copies of the current issue.)

All of this applies equally to the free newsletter, whether you ask prospects to "subscribe"—request their names on your regular mailing list—or simply mail out copies unsolicited, as you might any sales literature. Even the free newsletter serves no useful purpose but merely wastes marketing dollars if the recipient does not find it useful.

Figure 7 illustrates a fledgling newsletter published as a marketing tool by my office supplier. (The actual newsletter is printed principally in black ink, with a few headlines in red ink, on lightweight white paper.)

This little newsletter consists of four pages published monthly, and the principal means of distribution is by inclusion in orders going out. The back page is used for a form that always accompanied this firm's orders, in any case, so the newsletter serves a dual purpose. No doubt, it will grow in coverage eventually, as the editor is able to determine reader reactions and desires.

A New England motel chain publishes the free newsletter of Figure 8, a four-page publication printed on a rather heavy buff-colored

7.
Newly Launched Free Newsletter

THE

QUILL® PEN PAL

©Copyright 1985, Quill Corporation   *A friendly newsletter just for you!*   Vol. 1, No. 2   March, 1985

Dear Quill Pen Pal:

Communication has come a long way since the days of Paul Revere and the Pony Express. Today, the U.S. is in the midst of a full-scale communications revolution with satellite technology leading the way. While we haven't quite reached outer space yet here at Quill, we recently initiated a computer-to-computer communications system with a number of our suppliers.

In the months ahead, we'll be keeping you posted on all the steps we're taking to improve communications with both our customers and suppliers. For now, we want to remind you that placing your orders via telex is a fast, inexpensive, accurate way to communicate. It offers both the speed of a phone call and the hard copy accuracy of a mail order. Telexing your order is as simple as 1, 2, 3:

1. Enter Quill's Telex number, 46-7244

2. Enter your account name and number, shipping address, phone number, item and item numbers, and finally, your Telex number.

3. Your in-stock order will be on its way to you in a matter of hours.

Remember, at Quill, we always want to keep the lines of communication open.

Sincerely,

Marilyn Kier

Marilyn Kier, Editor

"DISK": A COMPUTER LANGUAGE YOU SHOULD KNOW!

Think fast. The last time you ordered disks for your computer or word processor, were they floppies, flexible, single- or double-sided, 8", 5¼" or 3½" disks? Chances are you can't come up with the answers off the top of your head.

But don't be intimidated by "disk" jargon. It's a language that's simple to understand and highly worth learning.

For example, "floppy" and "flexible" are two names for the same type of disk—the type that is removable. "Hard" disks, on the other hand, are rigid and generally non-removable.

Although all floppies have two sides, some are certified to record information on one side only. Hence the name "single-sided" disk. "Double-sided" disks can record information on both sides. This is an important distinction to note because some systems can use only single-sided disks while others can use only the double-sided.

A number of manufacturers say that single-sided disks can be used on double-sided systems, but we've found that it's really not a good idea. You not only run the risk of ruining your disk heads, but also take the chance of losing stored information.

As for size, we started with 8" disks and as a result of technology, have introduced 5¼" and 3½" sizes. Today, the typical 3½" disk can hold the equivalent of about 200 typed pages. Not bad for something you can put in your pocket!

We hope this information has been helpful.

TONER TRIVIA

Q: Why do some liquid copy machine toners get gummy?

A: Because you're probably not using your copy machine regularly. To help prevent gumminess, keep your toner in motion by running at least a few copies on your machine every day.

QUILL DESIGNS A CALCULATOR WITH KEY FEATURES THAT SCOOP THE MARKET

If we can't find a product already on the market that meets our standards, we'll work with a manufacturer to design a new one.

A perfect example is the new Quill® Desk Top Printing Calculator, a machine we designed specifically for fast operators. It's the first model on the market that combines the best operating characteristics of many top national brands. (Although we hear others are now on their way to market).

Features that provide maximum operating efficiency include a full-sized commercial keyboard with over-sized total, plus and "0" keys, a two-color ink cartridge with 2.5 line per second Epson-Seiko printhead, a single digit correction key for rapid corrections and a gross margins key for automatic markups or markdowns.

Other quality features include a four function memory, 12-digit display, a non-add key for dating or referencing tape items, and a print/non-print function for paper conservation.

It's no wonder that the Quill® Calculator, available exclusively from Quill for only

$69.88, has earned our "Best Buy" rating. It has key features that are hard to beat!

QUILL PRESENTS AN EFFECTIVE PRESENTATION PACKAGE

Did you know that using visual presentation techniques can significantly affect the outcome of your business meetings or training seminars? Psychological research has shown that using visual aids such as slides, overhead projectors and flip charts can influence audience perception, information retention and decision making. That's why more and more businesses are using these communication aids.

But, we discovered that no one was really servicing this field fully and that customers had to buy their supplies from a number of different sources. So, we decided to bring together more than 100 meeting/presentation/training/classroom supplies at famous Quill® discount prices, backed by our 8-32 hour delivery policy. We will be expanding our selection in the near future.

In fact, if you don't see what you need in our 4-page communications section inside, please let us know. We want to be your "one-stop shop" for all your meeting/classroom needs.

8.
Another Kind of Free Newsletter

🐨 KOALA INNSIDER

December, 1984   Volume III, Number II

Koala Inns Brings Historic Boston Hotel into the Future

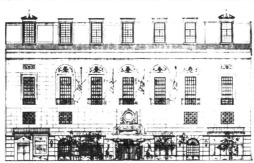

The old grandeur and charm of one of Boston's classic hotels will become a part of an exciting new future under the restoration and management efforts of Koala Inns of America Corporation. The historic Bradford Hotel, located in the heart of Boston's revitalized Theatre District, will begin a major renovation program in January and will eventually be renamed the Koala Grand Hotel.

As the first full-service Koala Hotel in a major metropolitan market, the new Koala Grand will also provide the City of Boston with its first downtown hotel to offer elegant accommodations at low to mid-range prices. "Our entry into the market is an exciting new venture for Koala Inns," says Robert S. Agnello, president of Koala Inns. "Our goal is to develop metropolitan hotels which can combine Koala's attractive rate structure with the luxury and convenience of a downtown full-service hotel. We

are selecting major cities throughout the Northeast United States whose locations will complement our other Koala Inn Properties."

Built in 1926, the design and interior decor of the Bradford Hotel are true vintage art deco. Koala will give special attention to maintaining this classic architectural style. Brass railings, marble floors and and ornate gold leaf ceiling designs in the building will be restored

to their original beauty. The multimillion dollar project, while focusing heavily on reviving the classic features of the hotel, will also provide modern comforts in its 300 guest quarters. All rooms and suites will be redecorated to create an "English continental" atmosphere. Many will be enlarged to provide suites for larger bedroom areas, and all rooms will feature period style furnishings. Walls will be completely resurfaced, windows will be trimmed in natural wood and marble will be added to the bedroom scheme. The entrance and lobby of the hotel will provide a preview of the luxury contained throughout, including Persian carpeting and ornate wood reception desk, custom made to enhance the hotel's early '20's period style. Furnishings will be plush and accented with dark navy and purple, or deep red, gold, and black in tones typical of the '20's era. The period style and grandeur of the hotel

Continued on page 2.

The Inn Crowd Newsletter

paper in black and a reddish-brown ink. It is distributed in the lobbies of the firm's own hostelries.

Note that the first example, the Quill Corporation newsletter of Figure 7, carries a copyright notice and a registered-trademark symbol beside the name. The Koala Inn newsletter carries neither. Some explanation and discussion of these appears to be in order here.

COPYRIGHT

Copyright is exactly what it says: a legal right to the specific copy. It establishes the owner's right to the specific wording, to the *copy*, and to that only. To print or publish material protected by copyright without the copyright owner's permission is *plagiarism*, theft, as illegal as any other kind of theft is. Technically it is an infringement that is actionable under federal law.

On the other hand, copyright confers no proprietorship over the information presented by the words. Anyone can use that information in any manner. Presumably, then, anyone can *rewrite* copyright material and copyright the rewritten material.

It's a bit tricky because a superficial editing or rewrite can easily be contested in court, and perhaps the court will decide that there was infringement, after all. It becomes a matter of degree, to some extent, as a judge and jury perceive whether the rewrite was a subterfuge to plagiarize or constituted a truly new and original work.

Fair usage is another gray area. Under copyright law one may quote briefly from a copyright work, as in the case of reviewing books or citing a source of information. How much one may quote under the fair-usage doctrine is difficult to establish, so in the event of serious conflict of opinion, resort to trial might be necessary to resolve the matter.

You can copyright your material by the simple expedient of using the copyright symbol © and/or the words *Copr* or *Copyright*, with the approximate date, which can be merely the year or may be more specific, and the name of the copyright owner. You can also register the copyright with the copyright office of the U.S. Library of Congress, and in the event of legal action it would be necessary to have the copyright so registered.

If you choose not to copyright your material, it becomes public domain material, which means that anyone can use it freely. (You can also copyright it and offer free usage to anyone who wants to use it, as long as they credit the source, as explained earlier.)

You cannot copyright titles. (Right now, for example, there are two books called *Getting Yours* in the bookstores, and they are in no way related to each other nor on subjects related to each other.) You can register them as trademarks, however, although few ever do because registering a trademark is almost as complicated and lengthy a process as getting a copyright is simple. Registering a trademark is done through the U.S. Patent Office, which is part of the U.S. Department of Commerce, and is almost as difficult as getting a patent issued. Few publishers apply for registration of titles, which is mostly practiced to protect trade names—special names of products or companies and other organizations. Lawsuits concerning copyright and trademarks are fairly infrequent, but there have been notable ones.

Of course, you can reproduce copyright material with the permission of the copyright owner, and that was the purpose of the release form in Figure 4, presented earlier. In most cases, if you want to quote or cite a brief passage from a copyrighted work, the owner of the copyright will grant permission, as long as you make attribution —acknowledge the source and give credit to the source by including a line such as "Reprinted by permission of _____" or "Courtesy of _____." However, sometimes you encounter someone who insists on knowing precisely what you will quote, how it will appear, and what remarks you will make in reference to the quotation. And some even demand the right to actually review and approve or disapprove of the specific manuscript passages affected. You can react to these conditions and demands as you see fit, but I have usually found such conditions and demands unacceptable and withdrawn my request in such cases.

NEWSLETTER CONTENT

Newspapers, especially those thick, big-city newspapers, address a very large reading public, often counted in hundreds of thousands. Obviously among such a large population of readers there will be a wide diversity of interests, hence the many sections and kinds of material found in the typical newspaper.

Magazines, even those of limited and specialized circulation, such as the free magazines found aboard the airplanes of the major airlines, also are rather diversified in their coverage, although the latter obviously envision and address two classes of travelers and their respective interests: the vacationer/tourist and the executive/business/professional. The kinds of articles published in those airline magazines reflect that orientation quite clearly.

Unlike newspapers and most popular magazines, newsletters do not have the space to carry diverse materials addressed to individuals with diverse interests. They are compelled to address narrow bands of interest. Moreover, they are in most cases compelled to be "strictly business": They have no space for crossword puzzles, cartoons, articles that are merely interesting rather than directly useful, or even photographs and other illustrations. Those that offer any of these kinds of material and features are in the minority and are far more the exception than the rule. Readers do not expect newsletters to be helpful in whiling away idle time. They expect newsletters to offer useful information as directly and as succinctly as possible. Witness those shown as examples so far:

The newsletter of Figure 1 offered ideas about marketing. That of Figure 3 discussed computers. Figure 5 illustrated a newsletter addressed to consultants, and Figure 6 illustrated one addressed to those in the mail order and other direct-response businesses. Figure 7 reproduced the front page of a newsletter oriented to buyers of office supplies and equipment, and Figure 8 reproduced one aimed at capturing the interest of travelers who stop at motels. Each of these addresses a narrow band of interests, but even that is variable: Some are even narrower in scope than are others.

For example, a newsletter that addresses readers in terms of their direct business or career interests is going to focus sharply on all matters related directly to that and only to that; whereas, a newsletter directed toward travelers as actual or potential hotel guests is probably going to be much broader. That's because the matter of where to spend the night or several nights is far less consuming an interest to the reader than are matters bearing directly on his or her business and career. This simply bears out the point made several times already about the need to address the prospect's direct self-interest.

The key to content is remembering that the newsletter is primarily a service medium. It exists to help the reader, and it cannot help the publisher if it does not first help the reader. Take note of the several items of the front page illustrated in Figure 7. All of it is designed to offer helpful, even how-to information to the reader (they are service articles), although two do manage to serve the publisher's own direct interests at the same time. But even then it is handled in a way that focuses on the reader's interests and potential benefits.

Figure 8 manages to do both also by devoting most of its four pages to pointing out where the firm's other establishments can be found and what amenities are offered in several of their inns and surrounding towns, as well as a column of recommendations for sensible practices when on the road on long trips.

Here are some of the kinds of articles or items found most commonly in such newsletters as these (bearing in mind that all these items relate to the field the newsletter covers):

New ideas or techniques applied successfully.

New products or equipment.

Answers to questions, often recommendations or solutions to stated problems.

New or pending legislation.

Personnel changes, especially of important figures.

Mergers, acquisitions, divestitures.

Guest articles by prominent figures (prominent in the field, that is).

"Think pieces" offering helpful philosophy, ideas, suggestions, techniques, tactics, etc.

Reviews of new products/services/materials.

Other news items, often those so specialized that they are not found in most newspapers or other periodicals.

SOURCES OF MATERIAL

One rich source of information has already been discussed. It is the morning mail, after you have managed to get your name on lists for press releases and other material as suggested earlier. Eventually you will begin to get so much material every morning that your problem will become one of what to do with it all, rather than where to get more. (Of course, much of it will be what is usually characterized as junk mail or otherwise not useful to you, but you'll soon learn to recognize that and dispose of it without wasting much time on it.)

You should do a great deal of reading, and you probably would do that anyway, for while the general press and even the trade journals often do not cover the same kinds of items newsletters do, they often furnish leads to or ideas for good articles.

You can publish notices in writer's magazines, such as the *Writer's Digest*, that venerable and most widely read writer's periodical, announcing your desire for contributions. (You may also get a listing in another publication of the same publisher, *Writer's Market*, a hardcover annual that is almost a bible of the freelance writing profession.)

You are expected to pay at least a modest sum for contributions from professional writers. On the other hand, many individuals, some notables in the field and even professional writers, will contribute material they have written without expecting a fee. Surprisingly, some of the most eminent and most successful figures are willing to devote their time and energies to making contributions without expecting payment.

Their motivations are several. Some want the "exposure" (publicity) the publication of their material gives them. Some simply enjoy seeing their names and thoughts in print. Some are sincerely eager to make contributions to their professional or business fields or feel some moral obligation to make such contributions. And undoubtedly, for many, all three considerations are motivators.

In any case, it is not difficult to persuade people to offer contributions, and you need not necessarily know all these people personally. You can publish open invitations to contribute in your own newsletter, and before long you will begin to get contributions. For many newsletters, this is the richest source of all. And even if you normally charge for your newsletter, instead of giving it away, it is a wise and almost standard practice to give complimentary subscriptions to those who contribute to your publication periodically. (Aside from being a courtesy that you should consider obligatory, that practice alone encourages contributions.)

Journalistic Style

Not everyone considers newsletter publishing and writing to be truly a part of the world of journalism, and in fact not all the principles and practices of journalism apply to newsletter writing and publishing. For one thing, few of the pieces in newsletters are true news items, yet some of the basic principles of journalism and newspaper publishing are useful.

Reporters are taught to write most stories in a pyramid style. That means to summarize the entire story in the first sentence (the top of the pyramid) and expand steadily from that point on, each succeeding sentence and each succeeding paragraph adding detail—broadening the base of the story pyramid. The purpose is to provide editorial flexibility such that the editor can cut the story to fit whatever space is available and still have a complete story, albeit without all the amplifying details.

That's a useful idea to apply to newsletters, where the need to cut stories to fit available space is even more acute than in the case of newspapers. Try to learn how to write your stories in this style.

Another useful idea is that of jumping stories. That term refers to the familiar practice of starting a story on page 1 and continuing it on (jumping it to) some interior page. This confers at least two immediate benefits: It permits a maximum number of stories (and their headlines) to be carried on the first page, increasing the probability that readers will find material of great interest to induce them to read on. It encourages readers to explore the interior pages (with their advertising, which is the lifeblood—income stream—of the newspaper).

Your newsletter will not carry advertising, presumably—few newsletters do—but it is in your interest to make your front page as interesting as possible. Therefore it is a good idea to start as many stories and print as many interesting headlines on your first page as possible by jumping your stories to later pages. (This is not a universal practice in newsletters, but it is unclear whether that is because many newsletter publishers are not trained journalists or because newsletter publishers do not perceive this as a useful technique.)

You must judge which stories are of greatest interest and appeal. Those are the ones that belong on the first page, and as in newspapers and magazines, you may decide to have a lead story—one that you feature on the first page and give the most extensive coverage as well as the most prominence. In that case you also usually provide a main headline that introduces the feature or lead story of the issue.

Another technique some use is to feature a different theme in each issue, with most of the coverage in that issue centered on that theme.

The choice of lead story or central theme is not always arbitrary. Circumstances may dictate it. For example, the occurrence of an annual national convention in a closely related association is an occasion for an issue bearing on a single theme or lead story, and an entire issue may be given over to matters concerning the convention.

But almost any significant event can set the theme or become the lead story: important new legislation affecting your readers' field(s) of interest; the appearance, disappearance, or merger of companies; prominent individuals entering, leaving, or moving about in the industry; or interesting new products or services appearing in the industry, to name just a few possibilities.

In the case of predictable events, such as national conventions and conferences, you can plan such issues well ahead because you know when the event will occur. But you can also plan special issues that are not based on events, predictable or unpredictable, but are based on useful ideas, available information, and careful planning. Here are just a few ideas for such special issues:

- Annual directory of companies and CEOs (chief executive officers) in the industry
- Annual "roundup" reports of important developments or changes in the industry during past year
- Fastest-rising young stars in the industry
- Year's new legislation affecting the industry
- Reported sales, other public financial data on companies in industry
- End-of-year or beginning-of-year interviews with prominent figures in the industry
- Results of an annual questionnaire sent to various organizations or individuals in the industry

INFORMATION-GATHERING USING NEWS RELEASES

A number of sources of information have been listed already, and they included news releases and other such information issued as PR activity by many organizations. (It's a rare day that I do not get at least a couple of news releases.) Theoretically, that release has been written to be directly usable, in toto or cut to fit whatever space you wish to give it. But that is not always the most effective method of using such releases. In fact, using the release in that manner may mean getting the minimum use from it, rather than the maximum use. Here's why:

You will recall that a properly prepared release includes a contact name and telephone number. That's because the release is usually only the bare bones of the story it covers. The story has been condensed and, presumably, slanted to the interests of the writers of the release. These are not necessarily your own interests, however; and it is often worth your while to see if there are other angles that make the story much more useful to you for your purposes. The contact name and number are supplied on any properly prepared release to help you get the rest of the story—the details and, perhaps, the story behind the story. That latter story may prove to be far more interesting and, more significantly, far more useful to you than the story offered in the release, as it is slanted.

One release on my desk is from the Contractor Profit News, a Brookline, Massachusetts, publisher, announcing a seminar titled "Computers in Construction." It describes the seminar as a half-day workshop and names one of three speakers. If you want to know who the others are, what the fees are, and many other details, you must call the contact. I am not interested in the construction industry, but I am interested in computers and their use, and I would like to know more about the proposed content of the workshop.

The Coalition for Common Sense in Government Procurement, a non-profit group in Washington, D.C., furnishes more information about their procurement conference, but it is still necessary to call the contact to get many of the important details. I am interested in knowing just who will conduct the conference and who some of the conferees are.

A release from the Metropolitan Transit Authority of Houston, Texas, reports the award of bonus payments to hourly employees, per an agreement with the labor union, and explains the basis for the awards in the briefest of terms. Again, one must call the contact to get more information about what is represented to be a unique plan in the transit industry or about any other aspect of the story.

INFORMATION-GATHERING USING GOVERNMENT PUBLICATIONS

Frequently, the best stories you get are the ones that result from calling contacts and getting the details behind the brief announcement of the release. (You may very well get an entirely new and different story than the release offers, in fact.) For example, many of the releases coming across my desk from government agencies in Washington, D.C., alert me to new legislation of interest and, quite often, to useful brochures, reports, and even more formal publications that I can get with a simple telephone call. (One useful report I got in this manner recently explained the government's new system and criteria for buying personal computers, for example, and it came at a time when that subject was of especial interest to me.) And many of those reports save me what would otherwise be many, many tiresome hours of research, which has already been done by the government and reported in their available publications. In fact, the government does so much information gathering and reporting that it is really foolish to embark on many kinds of information research without first making an effort to determine whether the information is already available from some government office. (And while there is a continuing trend in government to charge the public for things once given away freely and free of charge, in most cases the charges for the materials are modest enough, and there are still many publications and other documents made available free of charge.)

That points to another rich source of information and ideas: the government agencies, especially the federal agencies.

Most major cities have a federal office building or federal center which may comprise a number of office buildings, housing field offices of various federal agencies, and some agencies have offices in almost every city of even modest size. These are listed in local telephone directories, and so are not difficult to find. Among those which you are likely to find and which can often offer useful information, including brochures, pamphlets, and other publications, are the following agencies and their many offspring offices: Small Business Administration, Department of Commerce, General Services Administration, Department of Agriculture, Department of the Interior, and Government Printing Office (bookstore).

These are by no means all the agencies that are likely to prove useful. In fact, most government departments and administrations have numerous subordinate agencies within their structure, so even the handful of agency names indicated here actually comprises several dozen agencies.

Visit a Government Printing Office bookstore, if possible, and browse there. You will get a pleasant surprise, probably, at the wealth of material available, most of it at quite reasonable prices. Also get your name placed on the list of new publications the Government Printing Office sends out periodically. That will help you keep up with what is being published by that organization.

Most government publications are in the public domain, which means that they have no copyright protection but may be reprinted freely. However, there are exceptions, such as when a government agency gets permission to reprint copyrighted material from the holder of the copyright. That does not invalidate the copyright or give anyone else automatic permission to reprint it, so you must check before reprinting even government-published material to be sure that it is permissible to do so.

The limitation of space in a newsletter generally bars the reprinting of letters from readers, but you can include a question-and-answer column, reprinting readers' questions in summary form and answering them, probably in equally summary form. This is usually a popular feature and one that encourages readers to save their copies of the newsletter—an advantage from your viewpoint.

Guest articles and editorials are also useful pieces, especially if you can get well-known figures to contribute such pieces for your newsletter.

In time, after you have made conscious efforts to find materials and sources of material for your newsletter, you will find that you have developed an automatic, almost instinctive, "nose for news". That is, you will find yourself unconsciously alert at all times to the possible utilization of everything you read, hear, and see. It will become a conditioned reflex to react to all information, and you will not have the problem of finding enough material. Instead, you will have the problem of sifting a surfeit of material and trying to decide which is most useful.

Chapter 8

Production Methods For Newsletters and Seminars

There are many specific how-tos and dos and don'ts in newsletter publishing, as there are in all things.

THE CHOICES OPEN TO YOU

Publishing generally and newsletter publishing especially have their own jargon, methods, and tricks of the trade, as do all trades. Until now I have talked principally about the creative end of newsletter publishing—the kinds of coverage possible and desirable, the gathering of suitable materials, methods of using the newsletter in marketing, and other such aspects. But there is the practical side, too, known generally as production. That includes all those practical functions that are necessary to produce the physical product.

Of course, you can "vend" that work to firms or to individuals who do such work under contract, as mentioned earlier. However, there are some things to consider, pro and con, before making that decision:

1. You give up a headache or, at least, a potential headache, and thus relieve yourself of the everyday chores and problems involved in producing a newsletter.

2. However, you must still be involved and still make decisions, gather materials, and do much of the "front end" work, if the newsletter is to be what you want it to be. You can't escape that without giving up control totally, although you will inevitably relinquish some control. Of course, as the customer and payer of the bills, you have the right to dictate. But in practical terms you will have to compromise in many areas, as your vendor or consultant counsels you in some direction other than the one you think you ought to follow, so that you will find that many of your decisions are not made freely but are guided by someone else. That does not necessarily mean

that the decisions will be bad ones, but it is not always the alleged expert who has the right idea. Your own ideas may very well be better than those of the newsletter expert.

3. It will probably, although not necessarily, cost you more to have someone else handle most of the chores than to do it yourself, even if you are unfamiliar with the tasks and are learning by trial and error. Again, that is not necessarily bad, especially not if you can put your time to more gainful use at something else.

4. If you employ someone who does newsletters for others, your own newsletter may easily be less individual or distinctive than if you do it yourself because your contractor is almost inevitably influenced by the work he or she does for others. There is the potential hazard that your newsletter may resemble others' newsletters.

In short, this offers you the choice of the extremes: doing it yourself or having it done for you. However, there is a possible compromise course between these extremes: You can do some of the work yourself and vend whichever of the chores you decide you either cannot do as well as you want them done or which you prefer not to do yourself. Of course, to do that you first need to know just what the various chores and tasks are, and that is the major purpose of this chapter: In these pages you will discover just what those tasks entail so you can decide what you wish to do about them.

THE MAIN PHASES AND FUNCTIONS

Once material has been gathered and selected for publication, it must be suitably prepared, and then production can proceed. The major steps are these:

1. Designation and/or preparation of materials for publication in draft form.
2. Editing to prepare rough-draft materials and, when necessary, determine need for and direct rewriting/revision.
3. Composition of copy.
4. Preparation of illustrations, if any.
5. Copy fitting.
6. Preparation of mechanicals for printing.
7. Printing and binding.

There are substeps in each of these areas:

Rough Drafts

Rough draft is what you and others write for publication. The professional writer normally does some self-editing and revision of his or her rough draft and so offers the editor a second or possibly even third draft to review. However, if you use releases and other material you get in the mail, you consider that to be rough draft and treat it accordingly by cutting it to whatever size you want it and editing it suitably.

Editing

In some organizations, editing refers strictly to reviewing copy for adherence to grammatical and other rules of usage, and to general sense and organization—logical presentation. In others, the editorial responsibility goes well beyond this and extends to the performance of many chores necessary to preparing the copy for the printer. Whichever the case, editing means doing what is necessary to make the copy comply with both grammatical rules of usage and commonsense rules for presentation, and that includes asking the writer to rewrite and revise, if necessary.

Composition

Composition as discussed earlier, is simply typing or typesetting the copy for printing. (This will be discussed again in the next chapter.)

Illustrations

In many publications there is a significant element of graphic illustrations—photographs, drawings, charts, and other such material. Most newsletters, because of limited space, use little such material and usually none at all. However, illustrators who work on or with publications specialists generally handle some other chores, which are about to be discussed.

Copy Fitting

The daily newspaper and the weekly or monthly magazine is "open-ended." That is, it has no fixed number of pages but will produce each issue on the basis of need and expediency. Newsletters are not so flexible but are usually bound to some fixed number of pages and "column inches" of copy. Ergo, although copy fitting—making the copy fit the available space—is a necessary function on all publications, it is especially critical for newsletters. It thus entails some special functions and products known as laying out the copy and preparing plans referred to as *layouts*.

Layouts are rough drawings of the final published products, and they are usually made up by illustrators at two levels of detail: the rough layout, often referred to as simply a "rough," (Figure 9) and the more detailed comprehensive layout, referred to colloquially as the "comprehensive" (Figure 10).

9.
Rough Layout or "Rough"

10.
Comprehensive Layout or "Comprehensive"

NEW CEO TAKES OVER AT ABC MILLS

NOTICE:
FREE
REPORT

NEW SYNTHETIC
RUBBER DEVELOPED

BUDGET CHANGES

TRACKING
BUDGET
INCREASES
OVER FY

3

The rough, as the name itself indicates, is a generalized plan that defines the placement of the various materials or stories that make up the issue. It is a basis for making decisions about the placement of major elements, and when several people are involved in the process, the rough furnishes a basis for discussion and decision making. Of course, it is necessarily only a rough idea of the final layout at this time, however, because the copy is yet to be fitted to the space.

In the comprehensive the makeup of the issue is defined more clearly, and the next step is to make final decisions as to what the headlines will be, where they and the stories they identify will appear and be jumped to, how much space will be allocated to each story, where illustrations, if any, will appear, and other details that guide the actual copy fitting. It is still not cast in stone, however, and even the comprehensive may be used for discussion and decision making. However, the comprehensive is a guide for whomever is to do the makeup, or preparation of *mechanicals*, a jargon term for the actual copy—camera-ready copy—which will go to the print shop to be made into plates and printed.

Preparation of Mechanicals

Using the comprehensive for guidance, the materials are fitted to the space allocated for them. This can be a somewhat tricky job and is the reason for the journalistic pyramidal style, which permits whoever is doing the copy fitting a great deal of freedom in cutting each story to fit the allocated space.

From the practical viewpoint, this was done, classically, through the use of copy in the form of *galleys*. These are long strips of paper with the copy printed on them in a single-column form and which are literally cut and pasted up on paper forms being fitted in the process, to make up the issue. (You can fit copy by measuring and calculating, but this is not precise, although it does minimize the final cut-and-paste operation of physically fitting galley copy.) However, in today's world you can eliminate this messy operation entirely if you are using a modern word processor and do all that cutting and pasting electronically.

Printing and Binding

This final task is obviously one you will vend out to some print shop, unless you happen to be in the printing business yourself or have an in-house print shop, as some large firms do. And since you will have to make some decisions and give instructions to the printer you turn the job over to, you ought to know a few basics about printing and binding.

SOME BASICS OF PRINTING AND BINDING SERVICES

Printing today is done by what is referred to colloquially and informally as offset, or photo offset lithography to be more precise and technical. It is not necessary to know any of the details of the process, other than it is used today almost universally for printing and does not require raised metal type, as classical printing did for centuries—since Gutenberg, in fact. Modern lithography, to distinguish it from an older reproduction process used almost exclusively to reproduce works of art, is a process that utilizes photographic and xerographic methods to print virtually anything that can be photographed, creating a flat-surfaced printing plate. Hence, the term *camera-ready copy*, meaning simply copy that is ready to be photographed preparatory to printing.

That means that composition and typesetting no longer require metal type fonts. Offset printing can reproduce whatever copy you present to the printer, as long as it can be photographed. You can do typesetting yourself, using a typewriter, word processor and printer, or other equipment producing *cold type*, a term used to describe all such composition, distinguishing it from the type created from molten metal as in what are now old-fashioned linotype and monotype machines.

There is one other important point to understand here. Camera-ready refers to anything that is suitable to be photographed for printing and not only to the mechanicals you prepare for printing. That means that you can paste up material that is already suitable, such as clippings from other publications or material supplied to you in a suitable form (as long as you have the copyright owner's permission to do so, of course, or the material is in the public domain). Once you get yourself organized, you will get a surprisingly abundant supply of good materials that you can use in this manner.

There are several types of print shops, but they break down into only a few basic types. The neighborhood copy shop is a short-run shop, equipped to handle quick printing jobs requiring a limited number of copies—usually not more than a few hundred or a thousand or two at most—of relatively simple items. These shops are more labor-intensive than equipment-intensive because they specialize in simple printing jobs and short runs. They have simple offset presses that usually cannot print a sheet larger than 11 × 17 inches—twice the size of a standard sheet of paper. They cannot handle long runs—hundreds of thousands of copies—and complex jobs, such as thick magazines or tabloids.

The latter type of work is handled in a totally different kind of shop that has the equipment for complex jobs and long runs. They usually have large presses, often web presses such as those used in a newspaper plant, that can take blank paper from a roll at one end of the press and turn out printed and folded products at the other end. Such shops cannot handle short runs efficiently (unless they have a separate facility for short runs, as a few do) because short-run printing and long-run printing are so different from each other in what they demand for efficient operation.

There are also some specialty printers, equipped to turn out custom forms or specializing in a given field, such as magazines, newsletters, or similar publications. However, most of these also are long-run shops and handle only long runs efficiently because they are so equipped and organized.

Unless you have some reason to need a long run, you probably will want to use the services of a local offset shop or perhaps that of a mailing house that does the printing also. Many neighborhood shops, especially those franchised ones, have a scale of flat rates for each sheet per 100, 200, 500, or 1,000 copies. However, the larger offset shop, of the type which you will probably use, is more likely to calculate costs and prices on the following basis:

Platemaking: Printers make printing plates of the copy you supply. This is usually a charge per plate but varies according to each situation. If you do not want an especially long run—under 5,000 copies, say—the printer can usually use one of the less expensive plates, such as paper, plastic, or foil. However, photographs, which must be made into halftones, require metal plates, which are more expensive. And long runs of many thousands usually require metal plates as well. Moreover, those inexpensive plates are made directly from the camera-ready mechanicals; whereas metal plates must be made from negatives, so you have a negative cost for each plate, too.

Make-ready is the process and labor required for installing the plate on the press and making suitable adjustments until the press is ready to run off the copies from that plate. Each plate entails a make-ready charge.

Impressions: Most shops have some charge per 1,000 impressions or pages, which includes the cost of the paper, if you use ordinary offset paper, a sulphite bond that is relatively inexpensive. Of course, you can choose a more costly paper, if you prefer.

Folding: If you want your newsletter folded, ready for mailing, the printer will do so and charge for it, of course. (You can have some folded and some delivered to you flat, however, which is probably more useful.)

Binding: In most cases newsletter publishers print their newsletters on both sides of an 11 × 17-inch sheet, folded in the middle, creating a four-page newsletter, requiring no binding, of course. Even when the newsletter is six or eight pages, it is rarely bound. However, some publishers of newsletters of eight or more pages bind the pages, either with staples or mucilage. And some print their newsletters on both sides of 8 ½ × 11-inch sheets and bind them with a corner staple.

Drilling: You can have your newsletter three-hole punched (actually, the printer uses a paper drill, not a punch) for binding in a ring binder, at a modest cost.

Some typical costs will be explored in a later chapter, but in printing it is the first copy that costs the most. That is, the major cost is in the preparation—costs of platemaking and the many other tasks and functions necessary to print even a single copy. What that means in practical terms is that the per-copy cost is quite high for a short run and declines steadily with quantity, so that 5,000 copies tend to cost only a little more (relatively) than 1,000 copies.

For this reason it is usually wise to estimate your needs rather generously. The cost of going back to press to print a few more copies is high, compared with the additional cost of printing more copies than you need.

CHECKLIST FOR NEWSLETTER PLANNING

To assist you in drawing up a plan for your newsletter, a checklist is offered in Figure 11. Most of the items are self-explanatory, but a few require comment:

Your choice of paper is one of these. White offset paper is usually the least expensive, except for newsprint, which is generally used for newspapers and tabloids. However, there are many kinds and grades of paper, with book paper and laid paper stocks about in the mid-ranges, and glossy paper at the high end. But that is not only because the paper is itself costly. Glossy paper is much harder to print on because the ink is not readily absorbed and must be dried by special processes, such as by spraying a powder on it as it emerges from the impression roller or "blanket." That adds to the printing cost.

Printing in colors other than black also increases printing costs in more than one way: You must pay for a "wash" of the press for each color, because the press must be cleansed of whatever color was on it last before a new color can be employed. Also, each color requires a separate pass of each sheet through the press, multiplying the number of impressions and thus their cost. Too, you must make color separations of your camera-ready copy, adding to that cost, and each color requires a separate printing plate, running up the platemaking costs.

These can be sharp increases in costs if you are printing only a short run of about 1,000 copies. For longer runs the cost differential tends to shrink steadily, at least on a per-copy basis.

11.
Newsletter Planning Checklist

CHECKLIST FOR NEWSLETTER PLANNING

Check off those items you anticipate using/doing for your newsletter,
even if they represent only tentative decisions. They can always be
changed, and they represent preliminary planning, at least.

TITLE:_____

SUBSCRIPTION: [ ] Free   [ ] Nominal   [ ] Full fee   [ ] _____

NO. PAGES: [ ] 2   [ ]4   [ ] 8   [ ] _____

COMPOSITION: [ ] Typed   [ ] Typeset   [ ] Word processor [ ] _____

NO. COPIES: [ ] 1,000   [ ] 5,000   [ ] 10,000   [ ] _____

WRITING: [ ] Self   [ ] Consultant [ ] Freelance   [ ] _____

FEATURES: [ ] Photos   [ ] Drawings   [ ] Cartoons   [ ] _____

              [ ] Editorials   [ ] Guest articles/editorials

              [ ] Routing box   [ ] Monthly themes [ ] Masthead

              [ ] _____

PRODUCTION: [ ] Self   [ ] Consultant [ ] Freelance   [ ] _____

PAPER: [ ] Offset   [ ] Laid/book [ ] Glossy   [ ] _____

INK: [ ] Black   [ ] 1 color   [ ] 2 color   [ ] _____

OTHER: [ ] 3-hole   [ ] Bind   [ ] Fold   [ ] _____

MAILING: [ ] House   [ ] Contractor [ ] Vendor   [ ] _____

NOTES:_____

Most of the other items have been the subject of earlier discussions and need not be reviewed here again. Bear in mind that these are preliminary decisions, which you will almost surely amend and modify as you probe more deeply into what actually will be entailed in your newsletter venture.

Note the generous supply of blank spaces provided in the checklist, even to the extent of a space left for making notes. Feel free to use those blanks to write in your own options wherever you don't agree with any of the choices offered or wish to add items not provided.

In some cases you may find it appropriate to check more than one space under a given category. You might, for example, want to have your newsletter three-hole drilled, bound, and folded. Feel free in such cases to place your check mark in more than one box.

SEMINAR PRODUCTION

"Production," with regard to seminars, is much different from newsletters. It is primarily a matter of attending to those details mentioned earlier of finding the meeting room and arranging well in advance for using it and also arranging for whatever you need to make your presentations—handouts, projector, screen, blackboard, and anything else you may need. Some of the items commonly required for such presentations are listed in Figure 12, a checklist for seminars, following the same philosophy as in the checklist for newsletters: These are preliminary decisions, having as their chief value compelling you to think seriously about what you need or want to do. But the most important considerations are your main objective and the program itself. It is never too early to start thinking about that and planning it. And you would probably be well advised to study Figure 12 first, but do nothing about checking anything off until you have read the following discussion of key points.

The Main Objective

Suggested main objectives are provided, even to the extent of suggesting that you may want to opt for both the main suggestions, despite the caution earlier that it would probably be illogical in most cases to do so, since logically you ought to be in pursuit of one objective or the other, but not both. But this is not or should not be an arbitrary decision on your part. It is the logical result of what you are trying to sell and the circumstances surrounding the effort. If you are trying to sell something that normally requires extended and multiple sales presentations, you are probably setting yourself up for disappointment if you decide that you must close sales during or imme-

12.
Seminar Planning Checklist

CHECKLIST FOR SEMINAR PLANNING

Check off all relevant items, remembering that these are tentative and easily amended later.

OBJECTIVE: [ ] Close sales   [ ] Develop leads   [ ] Both

                [ ] Win clients   [ ] _____

REFRESHMENTS: [ ] Coffee   [ ] Cold drinks [ ] None   [ ] _____

DURATION: [ ] 1 hour   [ ] 90 minutes   [ ] _____

EQUIPMENT: [ ] Overhead projector and screen

                [ ] With transparencies

                [ ] Without transparencies

                [ ] Slide Projector and slides and screen

                [ ] Blackboard   [ ] Posters [ ] Flip chart

                [ ] Demonstration models [ ] _____

HANDOUTS: [ ] Manuals/brochures   [ ] Other printed literature

              [ ] Writing pads   [ ] _____

STAFF: [ ] Other presenter(s)   [ ] Assistants   [ ] _____

ADVERTISING: [ ] Newspaper   [ ] Radio/TV   [ ] _____

FOLLOW-UP: [ ] Mail   [ ] Telephone [ ] Personal call

              [ ] _____

NOTES: _____

diately after your presentation. And, in fact, if you try to close sales prematurely, you may very well foreclose your chances of making those sales at all by forcing the prospect to decide negatively on the spot. (This does not mean, of course, that you may not make a few sales nevertheless or that you should not make a modest effort to make whatever sales you can make at the seminar, but it does mean that you should be clear in your mind about what is a reasonable objective under the circumstances and do not press for immediate sales if the situation does not lend itself to this goal.)

Think carefully, then, about this, and do not attempt to plan seriously or even decide firmly to proceed with plans to stage a seminar until you have firmed up your decision about the objective and satisfied yourself that it is the right objective for what you want to accomplish ultimately.

The Program

If the objective is dictated by the nature of what you wish to sell and surrounding circumstances, the program is dictated by the objective. The program aimed at closing sales on the spot is not the same program as that aimed at generating leads for subsequent follow-up. However, whatever your objective, a list of attendees is always worth something, and you should never let the opportunity to gather that list slip away from you. In fact, you should try to get more than merely a list of names and addresses. As a minimum, you should get the name, address, and telephone number of each attendee, how or where the attendee learned of the session, and what he or she hopes to gain from the session (i.e. what the motivation for attendance was). This is important information for your future promotions but also provides useful input for your program.

Ideally, you should try to get even more information than this, and the best way to do it is to ask each attendee to fill out a little questionnaire which is among the materials you hand out to attendees. However, it is a mistake to simply make a blanket request and then leave it up to the attendees to follow through, for a great many will not do so if it is left to their initiative.

The most reliable way of getting this information is to ask the audience specifically to fill out the form, while you wait, and talk them through the items. Then collect the forms or have an assistant do so, if possible. (That's a preferable procedure because it has a great deal more favorable effect on the audience psychologically.)

Do not make the form too long. It would be self-defeating to make the questionnaire a chore to make out. (In fact, it is best to not even refer to it as a questionnaire.)

The form will vary from one case to another, naturally, according to individual circumstances, but Figure 13 offers some suggestions as to a few general questions or types of questions you might include.

13.
Typical Mini-Questionnaire for Seminars

INFORMATION REQUEST

_____(your business name) appreciate deeply the opportunity to tell you

about _____(whatever you are presenting). You can help us serve you

better by providing the following basic information:

Name:_____

Address:_____

City, State, Zip Code:_____

Telephone: (   )   -   [ ] Home   [ ] Office

Occupation:_____ Employer:_____

[ ] Single   [ ] Married   [ ] Rent   [ ] Own home

How did you hear of this seminar: [ ] Newspaper   [ ] Radio   [ ] TV

[ ] A friend [ ] Other_____

What do you hope to gain by attending? _____

_____

Remarks: _____

_____

Some presenters wait until the end of the presentation to ask attendees to fill out the forms, and they then invite them to make remarks reflecting their opinions of the presentation. There are two problems with this: Some people do not wait until the end, but "escape" earlier and thus usually do not leave a filled-out information form. And some of those who do stay for the entire session will bolt for the door at the end and not turn in the form.

This does not mean that some of these individuals may not be good prospects. Their names and addresses are worth having, for they are prospects, too. (They *did* attend the session, so they must have some interest.)

There are free marketing seminars that run for three hours or more, and their presenters apparently are able to hold their audiences for that long, but free seminars of more than 90 minutes are far more the exception than the rule. Even when attendees have paid as much as $200 for attending a full day's session, many show signs of fatigue and become restless as the day nears an end, and it is not at all unusual to observe several people leave the session an hour before it ends. You may imagine, then, that it is even more difficult to hold those who have paid nothing for their seats, if the session is long. For that reason alone it makes good sense to prepare the presentation carefully and edit it until you can include everything important without running over 90 minutes. (And it is even better if you can make all your points and get all your messages out in 60 minutes.)

One way to achieve this is by making generous use of graphic devices—transparencies, posters, flipcharts, and other such aids to presentation. Not only are these more efficient than words alone, and often the only really effective way to get some points across, but they capture the audience's attention more readily and are easier for an audience to follow and understand. Words require translation into images and concepts; graphic aids are the translations.

There is a kind of Murphy's Law operating: Anything that can be misunderstood will be. It is up to you to see to it that you cannot be misunderstood (although some will misunderstand you, no matter what you do). Keep checking to see if anyone has misunderstood. (I make it a practice to call frequently for questions and thus encourage listeners to stop me if I have failed to make some point entirely clear.)

Here are a few dos that ought to help guide you:

DO keep the presentation moving along briskly, without appearing to be in a hurry.

DO make eye contact with as many people in your audience as possible.

DO look pleasant, and smile whenever the occasion calls for it.

DO make points clearly, even dramatize them with gestures, raising your voice, repeating them, or by other means.

DO ask questions, at least rhetorically (that is, questions you answer yourself), but if possible try to involve the audience by asking them to volunteer answers. (You'll learn a great deal by listening to these questions.)

DO use your whole body to communicate—shrugs, gestures, the raised eyebrow, the upturned palms, and every other expressive movement. While it is not exactly show biz, you are on stage, and if you are natural and expressive with your whole body, your presentation is obviously far more interesting than if you deliver a monotonous lecture.

DO be overwhelmingly enthusiastic. Enthusiasm is highly contagious, and you can hardly expect your audience to get excited over your proposition if you don't lead the way by showing your own excitement.

DO respect your audience. They'll know it if you feel contempt for them.

On the other hand, there are a few don'ts too:

DON'T try to be Bob Hope. If your remarks are occasionally humorous *naturally* or you are a natural humorist, that's an asset, but don't try to drag comedy in by the ears. It won't fly at all and is likely to make you look foolish, which is deadly because you then lose the respect of your listeners.

DON'T lecture—that is, don't talk *at* your audience; talk *to* them. Be conversational and informal. Regard them, one and all, as your friends, and they will be.

DON'T fold your hands behind you, stare at the ceiling, fiddle with your ring, or look over the heads of your audience. You can't talk directly to people without looking directly into their eyes. And you certainly can't convince an audience if you refuse to look directly at them while speaking.

DON'T use $64 words. Use simple, everyday language that does not require anyone to work at understanding you or following your thought.

DON'T use four-letter words. Even in today's environment you lose dignity when you do this in a formal presentation. The language is rich enough for you to make any and all points as emphatically as you wish to make them without resorting to the four-letter monosyllables for emphasis.

Chapter 9

Using Word Processors to Help

Word processors can do a great deal more than the "gee-whiz" tricks for which they are so well known. In many ways they can, in fact, put small and not-so-small businesses on a par with large corporations, most notably in making you largely self-sufficient in a great many important ways.

THE TWENTIETH-CENTURY "INDUSTRIAL REVOLUTION"

Only once in a while does a single development have as profound an effect on the world as the computer has had. Much of what has happened in the past few decades depended, directly or indirectly, on the power of the modern digital computer.

But if we thought that the early computers, those expensive behemoths which have since come to be referred to as "mainframe" computers, had a great impact, we hadn't seen anything yet. The personal or desktop computer has in many ways had an even greater impact. Only the large organizations could afford to enjoy the direct benefits of in-house computers in earlier years. The appearance of microprocessors and the inexpensive personal computers changed that for all time: It is today a fairly rare business, large or small, that does not enjoy the benefits and convenience of the personal computer. In fact, many of those large corporations who already have one or more mainframe computers of their own have hundreds and even thousands of their smaller brethren on the desks of executives and others in their offices. The use of computers has indeed become personal.

WORD PROCESSING

All sources of information about the personal computer and its use agree that word processing is by far the most popular use and the most frequent reason for buying a personal computer. That has led to a great deal of publicity about word processing, so that almost everyone has today heard the term and has at least a general awareness of what it means. And that is probably what has led to the common practice of referring to the computer as a word processor. In fact, except for the relatively rare case of the "dedicated" word processor (a computer that is designed exclusively for word processing and is not readily adaptable to other uses), a word processor is not a machine at all but is the software program that can be installed in and used to "drive" any general-purpose computer with which it is compatible. (We'll discuss that matter of compatibility later.)

That is a significant point. It means that although you may buy a desktop computer for word processing only, in fact you have a general-purpose computer. And that means that you can use it for a great many other tasks, for anything a computer can do, within whatever are the capabilities of the model you bought. In addition to word processing, such capabilities include at least the following:

Any/all accounting functions

Inventory control/management

Record keeping and filing

Mailing list maintenance

Mailing support

Electronic mail and other communication

The application of word processing to newsletter publishing is, of course, obvious, and it is easy to perceive, also, that word processing is useful in preparing materials for seminars. Less obvious, perhaps, is the application of other software programs and their potential to newsletters and seminars. Consider, however, what some of these programs can do to help support these endeavors. (The following are introductory and are therefore only summary discussions; more detailed discussions will be offered later.)

Mailing List Maintenance

The computer is an invaluable tool for maintaining and managing mailing lists. With the right software, you can code your house lists so that you can make up and retrieve portions of them—specialized mailing lists, that is—in almost any fashion you wish—by zip codes, by age group, by occupation, or by other bases for selection. And, of course, you can keep adding new names and keep building the list, as well as eliminating duplicates and obsolete entries.

Mailing Support

Unless you plan to use a mailing house or some similar type of vendor to handle your mailings of your newsletters, literature announcing your seminars, and other related mailings, you will find that mailing by older methods can be almost unbearably tedious, as well as costly. The right software programs in your desktop computer can handle these chores for you, with minimal attention on your part. In fact, the convenience of being able to do this (not to mention the advantage of being able to do your mailing in-house and thus achieving independence) may itself be the decisive factor in choosing to do it in-house, rather than via a vendor service.

Electronic Mail and Other Communications

The desktop computer has made major, even revolutionary, contributions to modern communication. With even a modest desktop computer, a modem (a device to connect your computer to the telephone line), and the right software in your office, you have a window on the world. Your computer can talk to other computers anywhere; you can send and receive wires and cables to and from anywhere; and you can send electronic mail—messages—to others. This, as you will learn in this chapter, means not only do you have the ability to send and receive messages but also that you can have an enormous information-research capability and can do a great deal of—perhaps all—your research without leaving your office.

Record Keeping and Filing

Mailing list maintenance is only one type of record keeping and filing. You will find that you can use your computer to keep many other kinds of records and information that are useful for your newsletter and seminar activities, with many distinct advantages. One of these is space conservation. On my own desk are two diskette "trees," devices that hold twenty 5 ¼-inch floppy diskettes each. In my case, these diskettes can each hold up to about 100 single-spaced pages of text, so the filing capacity of these two diskette trees on my desk can go as high as 4,000 pages of single-spaced copy—the capacity of a good-sized filing cabinet. And it would not be difficult to find room for as many more diskette trees as I wish to use.

That's only one advantage. The other major advantage of filing your records on these little plastic diskettes or on the more expensive but higher-capacity hard disks is the ease and speed of access. My own diskette files are within arm's reach, and each diskette is labeled. I have one for purchase orders, another for general correspondence, another for articles, and so on. If I wish to look up an article, I simply select that diskette, insert it in the disk drive, and log on to that drive. The computer then presents me with a "command line," and I can call up a directory of whatever is on the diskette, if I cannot recall the exact name of the file I want. The computer screen then presents me with a directory such as that shown in Figure 14. For those not yet familiar with computers, this requires a brief explanation:

14.
Typical Diskette File Directory

DISK:B	FILES:14		ENTRIES:17	(175 LEFT)		SPACE USED:226K	(158K LEFT)	
CNSLTG	SEM	2K	HANDOUT	MTI	92K	RETURN	COM	2K	WSMSGS	OVR	28K
D	COM	2K	HANDOUT	UC	8K	TYPEWRIT	COM	4K	WSOVLY1	OVR	34K
D7	COM	4K	INKLING	1	10K	WC	COM	2K			
DELBR11A	COM	14K	PIP	COM	8K	WS	COM	16K			

Those file names ending in the suffixes "COM" and "OVR" are all programs stored on the diskette, and this directory is drawn up by the file shown as "D.COM." (The directory does not show the decimal point, but the file names in this system consist of two parts, the second part following a point, so that "HANDOUT UC" must be called from storage to memory by entering "HANDOUT.UC," as must all other files having a suffix.) Note that the file names are in alphabetical order, from top to bottom of each column, proceeding from the leftmost column to the rightmost. Other programs organize the files in a different manner (there are many other programs for organizing and presenting file directories, each designed according to the ideas of the writer of the program); I happen to like this program and the way it organizes and presents my files to me.

The other files are materials I have stored on this diskette, and I have assigned file names as I see fit (within the limits and rules of the system). "CNSLTG.SEM" is material used in my seminar on consulting. "HANDOUT.UC" is handout material for a seminar appearance I am to make to a seminar offered by an organization for whom "UC" is my designator, and "HANDOUT.MTI" is for still another seminar appearance, the sponsor designated as "MTI."

When material becomes ancient history and I do not expect to need it soon again, I "archive" or dead file it somewhere. And in some cases, where I am sure the material is of no further use to me and never will be again, I simply erase it from the diskette and use the space for more useful material. That ensures that I don't clutter up system with an evergrowing collection of files that are of absolutely no use to me.

AN OVERVIEW OF DESKTOP COMPUTERS

There has been a proliferation of desktop computers, in a market largely pioneered by Apple Computer Co., but now fairly well dominated by IBM with their original PC and their later XT, AT, and other spin-off models. Until IBM entered the market with the first IBM PC, by far the majority of popular desktop computers were of the CP/M variety. That is, they used the CP/M operating system, and a few words of orientation are necessary here to understand this jargon.

Early computers were the dullest of beasts. They had to be instructed in each step, no matter how often they performed those steps; they were incapable of learning anything, despite their unearned reputation for being great brains. We'll skip all the history of evolution and go directly to today's computers, all of which have operating systems. That is just a set of standard instructions for doing the routine, repetitive things that the computer must do continually—turn a disk drive on or off, transfer information, start the printer, clear the screen, load the program called for, among others. Some of the most basic instructions are permanently contained in the computer in a device referred to generically as "firmware" (because it is a type of software yet is permanently inscribed in a bit of hardware) and which you will see referred to as a "ROM," (for read-only memory) and partly contained on disk, which enters the information into the computer's memory at the beginning of operations. (These instructions are usually inscribed in the "system tracks" of every disk used in that computer, placed there by a program supplied with the computer for that purpose.)

CP/M today is regarded as standing for control program/ microcomputer but originally stood for control program/monitor because the forerunner of the operating system program was the control or monitor program, which was essentially the same thing: It monitored all operations in the computer.

The Apple computer emerged with its own operating system, Apple DOS (the latter for disk operating system, reflecting a prime function of the operating system, as well as a reference to where the main set of operating system instructions are normally stored).

The Tandy/Radio Shack TRS–80 computers had their own operating system too, TRS DOS, and TRS–80 computers were an early and major force in the desktop computer market.

Still, none achieved the popularity of CP/M until IBM emerged with its PC DOS, its own operating system, patterned after CP/M in many ways but still not compatible with CP/M. CP/M computers and PC DOS computers cannot run each other's programs (although conversion or translation software is now emerging to permit this). Such is the power of IBM, however, that it soon dominated the desktop computer market (winning approximately 35 percent of it quickly), with the result that almost everyone today produces computers running MS DOS, compatible (to some extent, if not totally) with IBM's PC DOS. In fact, the advertising of many of these computers features the claim "IBM compatible" as its principal attraction and proof of merit.

It is still possible to buy computers using CP/M, and there is such an abundance of CP/M software that was produced before IBM entered the market—they were slow to do so—that there is rarely any difficulty in finding adequate programs for CP/M machines. Still, many people are reluctant to buy CP/M computers, fearing early obsolescence, and, indeed, the market is so loaded with computers claiming to be "IBM compatible" that many believe that the CP/M computer is already moribund.

Many of the most popular software programs, such as the WordStar word processor and the Lotus 1, 2, 3 integrated spreadsheet program, are available in different versions so that you can probably buy a version that will run on your own machine, no matter whose model it is. But that is not true for a great many programs, so you have to be careful that you buy software suitable for your own machine.

IF YOU HAVE NOT YET BOUGHT YOUR SYSTEM

It is my presumption, a reasonable one for today, that if you do not yet have a desktop computer, you will eventually have one. Business is gearing itself rapidly to computer operation. Ergo, a few words of guidance may help:

It has become conventional wisdom in the computer business that software dictates hardware. That is to say that you should select first the software you wish to use and then seek the hardware that will run that software.

This is counsel you may have already heard, but it is rapidly becoming obsolete advice because conditions have changed. Originally there was a familiar pattern of an abundance of excellent hardware and a shortage of adequate software to install and run on the hardware. That has changed substantially and is true only for hardware—computers—using little-known and unpopular operating systems (usually the manufacturer's own operating system) for which little software has been or is being written. There are a few such operating systems still offered. Unfortunately, they place buyers of the machines almost completely at the mercy of the hardware manufacturers for software support. Commercial developers do not spend time and money developing programs for little-known and unpopular machines.

Early in the computer field, virtually all software was custom developed for the user. The desktop computer changed that. Hordes of software developers, many of them the tiniest "cottage-industry" type of ventures, poured out a surfeit of programs for the most popular machines. That is why there are today so many commercially available programs for Apple, TRS–80, CP/M, and PC or MS-DOS computers that there is little likelihood of being unable to find suitable programs for any of these machines. That is especially true for CP/M and PC or MS DOS machines. If you buy one of these, you are not likely to have any difficulties in finding suitable software.

If you have any doubts about this, you need merely look in one of the several directories of commercial software and review the programs available for any computer you wish to consider. Unless your needs are somewhat unusual, you will have no problems.

WORD PROCESSING SOFTWARE

Probably the greatest proliferation of types of programs has been in the field of accounting software: There is an overwhelming array of such programs. And probably the runner-up to those is word processing software: There have been an almost uncountable number of word processors developed and offered. But whether all are truly word processors is a matter of opinion. For there are two main functions in word processing, and while some programs do both, others do only one of the two, and it is necessary then to switch from one program to the other when using this latter genre. Hence, many experts distinguish between the two.

The two major functions in word processing are editing and formatting. Editing includes composing, punctuating, and correcting copy, organizing paragraphs, and sundry other tasks associated with actual text preparation. Formatting is associated with spacing, underlining, right justifying, and various other functions that determine how the copy is physically organized. (There is no clear demarcation between the two, for each software developer goes at the matter differently, but this is roughly the distinction.)

In what many purists consider to be a true word processor, both these functions or sets of capabilities are included in the basic instruction set of the program. On the other hand, some program "editors" and "formatters" permit one or the other of these sets of functions but not both within the same program. What this means is that you must first do your editing—write your copy—and then exit that program and load the formatting program to handle that set of operations. (That means erasing one program from the computer's memory so that the other program can be loaded into the memory.)

It's an awkward arrangement and thus leads to the conclusion that a true word processor is one that permits all these functions within the same program. That is therefore a guideline for you in selecting a word processor to run in your desktop computer. Be sure that it is a true word processor in which you can do all your editing and formatting.

The following are just a few of the basic functions and features, generally, that most word processors offer:

Word wrap: This is a feature that is a kind of automatic carriage return: You need not worry about getting to the end of a line and punching the return key or pushing the space-and-return lever; the handy-dandy little electron does it for you, automatically, when you write the word that goes over whatever you have set as the maximum line length. That maximum varies from one system to another, but for most writing you would set it at about 72 to 78 "columns," which is, for some mysterious reason, the term computer people use to describe the width of the image area—the maximum number of characters and spaces on a line. But type comes in different sizes, and if you are running your system at 12 pitch or 12 characters/spaces to the inch (elite type, in older typewriter terminology), 72 to 78 columns means a width of six to six and one-half inches. That's quite reasonable for a page that is eight and one-half inches wide: It allows margins of one to one and one-quarter inches. However, if you are running a 10-pitch type— 10 characters or columns to the inch (pica type, in typewriter jargon)—you might prefer to run a 65-column width to achieve the same result.

Some computers, especially the less costly home computers, provide a capability of only 40 columns—40 characters and spaces—and 16 lines. (That would be only eight lines in double-spaced copy.) Most "serious" word processors today offer 80-column width by 24 lines. And with standard typing running six lines to the inch (measured vertically), a full page of text is usually 50 to 55 lines, depending on the top and bottom margins. Therefore a "screen" (the display on the monitor) is usually slightly less than half a page.

Right justification: Most word processors allow you a choice of "ragged right" or "justified right" printing. Justified means that the right hand edge of all the lines of type are perfectly aligned, as the left-hand edge is (except for deliberate indentions).

Reform paragraphs: In most systems you can write in double-spaced, ragged right format and, after you have made all your corrections and revisions, have the program automatically reformat everything in single-spaced copy, with justified right-hand margins, if you wish. Or vice versa, for that matter.

Find/find and replace: Most programs will search out any special letter, symbol, word, or phrase, upon your command, and will find it each time it occurs in the file. And if you wish, you can have the program automatically replace the item with something else, so that you may have the program find every "Block" and replace it with "Bloch."

Move copy: You can in most programs have the system shift copy around, from one place to another and even from one file to another, delete material, add material, and otherwise manipulate copy in an entirely electronic cut-and-paste activity.

Copying: You can copy anything in any file in seconds. If you wish to reuse something you wrote previously, but modify it slightly, you can either go back to the original file and do the modification, or you can make a copy of that file and make your modifications to the copy, so that the original file is left undisturbed.

I use these latter two functions regularly in my own writing. I find it inconvenient to work with large files, and, in fact, the manuals that came with the system advise against it. However, in other respects it is convenient to assign each chapter of a book to a single file, even though some of those chapters can become rather lengthy. It is an anomaly, but I can have my cake and eat it too, in this manner: Each time I finish a small segment of a chapter, I add it—add a copy of it, that is—to the file holding the first segment, erase the recent segment in the working file, and write the next segment in it. I repeat this until the chapter is complete, and I then archive the completed chapter by copying it onto two other floppies. Then I erase the files on the working disk and begin the next chapter. So I keep my working disk always ready to accept more work—it can never get full, this way—while I have the insurance of two separate copies on two separate disks. (I also print out each segment, as I go, so I have a hard copy of finished work, too, as further insurance against loss.)

Graphics: Most word processors do not include graphics, although there are many graphics programs offered. Some are highly sophisticated and can be useful to engineers and designers to prepare quite complex and sophisticated drawings. Most designed for general business use, however, are able to convert figures into graphic representations such as charts and plots.

If your requirement does not often include a need to prepare such graphic aids, you may find it practicable to construct simple plots and charts with your word processor, for it is possible to do so, although far less convenient than having a software program do it for you. For example, Figure 15 shows a simple plot prepared on this system using the WordStar® word processing program. The plot is shown twice,

15.
Simple Graphic Illustration Constructed via Word Processor

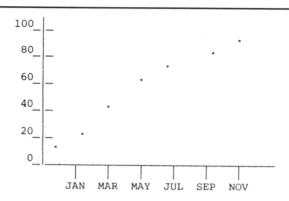

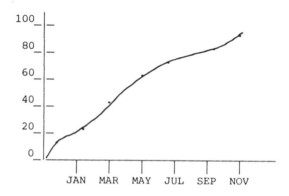

first as prepared by the program and printer, and then as completed by hand by drawing a line to connect the dots. (It would be possible but rather tedious to do the latter by machine.)

Of course I constructed the figure only once, which took about two minutes, and then copied it, which took about five seconds. And if I wanted to develop dozens of other plots, I could use this as a model, copying it over and over and just changing the numbers, months, or other designators each time to suit the new application.

Other simple graphics—bar charts, for example—can be constructed in the same manner. Some can be rather laborious to construct, but the most laborious part of the job need be done only once, if you design a suitably standardized model to be copied and adapted to each use. If, for example, you stored the simple plot of Figure 15 as a boilerplate file, you could easily change the scales or values of either or both the X and Y coordinates for different uses.

Tables and matrices: Of course, you can easily construct such tables and matrices as that shown in Figure 16 with a good word processor. Most word processors offer variable tab stops, as do typewriters, and many offer special features, such as automatic alignment of decimal points when presenting a list of items or table containing items with decimal points. Most also offer such printing refinements as underlining and boldface characters (as in the column heads of Figure 16), even with daisywheel (letter quality) printers. Dot matrix printers offer an even greater bag of tricks when it comes to printing, because of the inherently great flexibility of the dot matrix system.

16.
Typical Matrix or Table

MAKE/MODEL	OS	LANGUAGE	MEMORY (K)	LIST PRICE	NOTES
Victor 9000	MS/DOS, CP/M	BASIC	128/896	$4,995	2 600K disks
Wang PC	MS/DOS	BASIC	128/640	3,395	2 320K disks
Dynalogic	MS/DOS	BASIC	256	4,995	2 320K disks
Corvus Concept	Merlin	Pascal	256/512	8,000	1 1M disks
Osborne 1	CP/M	BASIC	64	1,795	2 102K disks
Atari 400	Atari DOS	N/A	16	299	4 88K disks
VIC 20	COMM DOS	BASIC	5/32	299	1 170K disk

Printing: Unless you are truly up-to-date on what is happening in computers (and the computer industry is so dynamic that anything that was on the market last year must be regarded as being already obsolescent), you should know what has been happening in the printer area of computer technology:

A short time ago a letter quality printer always printed characters from a daisywheel or other element, such as the "golf ball" of the IBM Selectrics. Dot matrix printing, accomplished by using a series of dots to create an approximation of alphanumeric characters, was much faster than letter quality printing, but far below it in quality.

That has changed. Dot matrix printers have been so improved (at a sacrifice in their speed, however) that they began to produce "near letter quality" printing and, more recently, what they call letter quality printing, which is so close to that standard that it is quite difficult to distinguish from daisywheel printing or its equivalent, even with the aid of a magnifying lens.

Dot matrix machines, at the same time, offer great flexibility because they create the alphanumeric characters spontaneously, rather than print preformed characters. Hence, they can offer mixed fonts, foreign characters, mixed type sizes, headlines, and rather sophisticated graphics.

Entirely new types of printers are also coming along rapidly, especially one that creates characters by spraying ink on the page and another that prints by laser and xerographic processes. (The laser beam, driven by the computer output, paints the copy on the copier drum for transfer to the page.) These latter types are much quieter in operation than the others, as is a new printer developed by IBM that uses a special electrothermal process.

Related Software

Some word processors include related subprograms as integral parts of the word processor, although they are more commonly offered as separate programs. However, they are closely related to word processing operations. One of these is the graphics software, already discussed. Another popular one is the spelling checker.

Spelling checkers: Spelling checkers are dictionaries contained on disks with several subprograms. The primary purpose and use of a spelling checker is to scan a file and verify the spelling of each word. When it encounters a word that either is not listed in the dictionary or is not spelled as in the dictionary, the program asks you for instructions. You can order the program to accept the word (it might be a person's name or some special term), or you can make a change. In most such programs you can also order the program to accept the word and "learn" it (add it to the dictionary). (My own speller was 36,000 words long originally but is now 44,000 words long, as a result of additions I have made to it.) You can also set up special auxiliary dictionaries in separate files, so that you can invoke them only in certain cases.

Such programs usually have a subprogram that enables you to look up any word in the dictionary, if you wish to check on its spelling. These are especially useful programs for proofreading copy because they detect typos that otherwise slip by even the sharpest human eye. However, they are not complete substitutes for proofreading by eye and brain because they cannot exercise judgment, of course. They are used most effectively to check a file in addition to checking by eye.

Grammar checkers: There are some grammar programs designed to help shore up any weaknesses you may have in grammatical practices. Again, they are a help, but you must not rely entirely on them; they can offer only limited help.

Word counters: Programs that count words are quite helpful and are sometimes found as integral parts of other programs because they are rather simple programs that require little space in memory. None are absolutely accurate in counting words as you would because their designers had to set arbitrary rules as to what constitutes a word. I have used three different word counters and done many comparisons. In general, the results differ by about 1 to 1.5 percent, but inconsistently because sometimes they are in total agreement, and when they are not, it is not always the same one that is higher than the others. (One of the programs permits me to decide what is the minimum number of characters that will be recognized as a word.)

Miscellaneous: There are programs designed to assist you in indexing, outlining, and sundry other tasks related to word processing.

Spooling

One great inconvenience many computer users encounter in using word processors is the temporary loss of the computer while it is printing. Electronic circuits operate almost instantaneously, as the speedy electrons swarm around the chips and other electronic components. Mechanical devices are slowly lumbering beasts by comparison. When you press the keys on your keyboard, each letter appears on the screen before you can lift your finger. When you load a program from a disk, you wait several seconds for the disk drive to scan the disk, find the program, and transfer it to computer memory.

When you order a file printed, the computer must wait for the printer. The computer can pass the entire file to the printer in a relatively few seconds, but the printer handles the data at a speed set by its mechanical devices. Even the fastest printer can't accept data from the computer as fast as the computer sends it. Therefore, the computer waits and spoon-feeds the data to the printer, ignoring all your demands for attention meanwhile. This can easily keep your computer tied up for a half hour or more while a file is being printed and you twiddle your thumbs in frustration.

The way out of this dilemma is to relieve the computer of the data—store it temporarily ("buffer" it, in computer jargon) somewhere where it can be sent on to the printer at the printer's speed, leaving the computer free to do other work. And while there are hardware devices called *buffers* that are designed especially to do this, there are also software solutions to the problem. In fact, I use one of these software solutions myself. It's called a *spooler*. (The terms *spooler* and *buffer* are used interchangeably by many, but traditionally the buffer is a hardware device, while the spooler is a software program.)

In the case of my own system, I use a spooler program to solve the problem. This program intercepts the data on its way to the printer and stores it on one of my disks. The computer then believes the printing is completed, since it has gotten rid of the data for the printer, and is available to do other work, while the spooler program takes over the task of running the printer.

Each method, the hardware method and the software method, has its own advantages and disadvantages. The software method is less expensive, generally, but the hardware method offers a number of features you don't get with the software method. But both get the job done so that you do not have to find other things to do while you are printing out files.

FREE SOFTWARE AND FREEWARE

Commercial software is expensive, although there has begun a trend downward in software prices as a result of increasing competition. Especially, there has been great competition from the smallest software development firms (it requires little capital to launch such a venture, and there are many tiny firms in the business) and from public domain (free) software and a species of software called *freeware*. The latter two are not quite the same.

The personal computer phenomenon in the United States has no known counterpart except, perhaps, that of ham radio operators of years ago, in the infancy of radio. Many of the hobbyists and enthusiasts (many of whom are referred to as *hackers*) in computers are at least as expert as are the professionals in the industry. (The Apple computer was the creation of two such hobbyists or hackers.) These people have written a great many programs, usually for their own use, and then generously donated the programs to the public domain so that anyone could use them without charge. Frequently they copyright the software but grant everyone permission to make personal use of it as long as they do not attempt to sell it.

Others have made their software programs available free of charge but request voluntary donations, for which they offer services, and this genre of software has come to be called freeware. While most public domain software includes instruction manuals on the disk, which the user reads on screen or prints out, much of this kind of documentation is sketchy and not very helpful. With freeware, there is usually little or no such documentation on disk, but if the user makes the requested donation, the writer of the program will furnish a printed manual and "support" the software. That means that he or she will answer specific questions and will supply all revisions, corrections, updates, or other changes or improvements to the original program. And many will also share the profit by paying a commission to anyone who passes on the software to someone else who then makes the requested donation.

There are several ways to acquire public domain software and freeware:

Computer clubs: One of the several common activities of computer clubs is to help members acquire free software. Usually, someone in the club is responsible for gathering free software, generally by *downloading* (transferring) it via modem and telephone from electronic bulletin boards, and copying it onto disks. Members are charged nominal sums, usually $4 or $5 per disk, which pays for the disk itself and helps the club maintain a treasury.

Direct downloading: You can do your own downloading by calling up one of these bulletin boards—there are thousands of them throughout the country—and requesting it.

Purchase: There are services, sometimes run by the computer clubs themselves for the general public (as distinct from a service to members), offering these public domain programs on disks (usually disks containing several related types of programs), generally at about $12 per disk. The charge is for the service and for the disk itself, of course, and not for the software.

Rental: There is another kind of service in which the firm rents disks full of software to be copied. You must return the disk after you have copied everything on it (or everything that you want).

Of course, not all free software is useful or even good software. Much of it is not useful in any given case. On the other hand, some of it is superior to commercial products. Since I acquired my "d7" file manipulator and "d" file-listing program, I rarely use the ones supplied with the original commercial software that came bundled with my machine: I find these free programs to be far superior. But I have also acquired much free software that may or may not be well designed and well documented but is simply not useful to me.

Most of these latter services sell a catalog, often in a disk format, rather than on paper. In the case of the bulletin boards, you can get their directories of software programs downloaded, and a typical one appears in Figure 17. Each of these listings identifies the file, the disk area (A0, A1, A2, etc.), and the size of the file in K (for kilobytes). Note the top listings of three columns in the first directory, listing catalogs. (The operator of this bulletin board is a vendor of computer-related merchandise and wins business in this manner.) The file names are cryptic because the CP/M system limits you to a maximum of eight characters for the forename and three for the suffix, following the dec-

17.
Directories of Free Programs Available for Downloading

```
A0>dir
--STRIP .MAP     4k    -DISKETT.CAT     4k    -SMART   .CAT     4k    -SOFTWAR.CAT     8k
-SPECIAL.         4k    -STAR    .CAT     4k    -UNIFORM.CAT     4k    CERTIFY  .OBJ    16k
COMEXEC .AQM     8k    CPMBUGS .LBR     8k    CRC-50   .LBR     8k    DIRF31-S.LBR    32k
DRVU400 .BQS     4k    DUINSTAL.LBR    36k    FRONT41  .LBR    28k    FU12     .LBR    60k
INTEREST.LBR    20k    KAMASD1 .LBR    88k    KP-DB19  .LBR    68k    KPFBAD58.LBR    32k
KPHPCALC.LBR    16k    LOGON-UD.LBR    16k    MEMDUMP  .PQS     4k    MEMWRK   .LBR    32k
MEMWRKA .LBR    12k    MLOAD23 .LBR    28k    MLOAD24  .OBJ     4k    NEWBASE6.LBR    12k
NULU11  .LBR    56k    PATCH17 .LBR    60k    PTYPE    .LBR    12k    PW-CHG   .LBR    48k
ROS25   .LBR    56k    RS232CBL.LBR    16k    SD94KP   .LBR     8k    SD97     .LBR    80k
SETOKI2 .LBR    28k    SFF-12  .LBR    28k    TRGRAFIC.LBR    16k    TURBOREF.LBR     8k

A1>dir
BANNER  .LBR    12k    DBL-PRT .LBR    12k    DIRCHK   .LBR     4k    DIRLABEL.LBR     8k
DISPLAY .LBR     4k    EPSON80 .LBR     8k    EX14     .LBR     8k    FINDBD54.LBR     4k
FIX     .LBR    40k    GEMIN10X.LBR    24k    GRAFTOOL.LBR    32k    K4TIME11.LBR     4k
KP-COLD .LBR     4k    MAKE    .LBR    12k    MAKE15   .LBR    16k    MT180L   .LBR    12k
NECPRTR .LBR    12k    OKI92   .LBR    44k    PRO-SYMB.LBR    24k    PROBE    .LBR    48k
PUBPATCH.LBR    16k    SPRINT  .LBR    28k    SUPERSUB.LBR     8k    TXT42    .LBR    16k

A2>dir
APPEND  .LBR     4k    BROWSE  .LBR    16k    COMPARE  .LBR     4k    CONCAT2  .LBR    12k
D       .LBR     8k    EDFILE  .LBR    24k    FILE14   .LBR     4k    FIND     .LBR     8k
LISTT   .LBR     8k    LSWEEP13.LBR    24k    LU300    .DOC    36k    LU300    .LBR   112k
LU300   .OBJ    20k    LUX12A  .LBR    64k    NSWEEP2  .LBR    32k    RENAME   .LBR     4k
SAPX    .LBR     4k    SQ110B  .OBJ     8k    SQUSQFLS.LBR    40k    USQ119   .OBJ     4k
USQ119N .LBR    16k    USQBASE .LBR    12k    VLIST    .LBR     4k

A3>dir
ANIMATE .LBR     4k    ANYCODE .LBR    16k    CHEKBOOK.LBR    16k    D2MENU   .LBR     8k
DATASTAR.DQC     4k    DB/CAT  .LBR    36k    DB/GRAPH.LBR    24k    DB/HELP  .LBR    36k
DB/MAST .LBR    12k    DB/NOTES.LBR    12k    DB/SQRT  .LBR     4k    DB2-CMD  .LBR    28k
DCAT    .LBR    12k    DIR     .CMD    12k    ENSOFT   .LBR    12k    FTNOTE14.LBR    36k
INDEX   .LBR    28k    KP-DB18 .LBR    40k    MAILLIST.LBR    20k    MORTGAGE.LBR    20k
OUTLINE .LBR    16k    PERFIN  .LBR    28k    POKE1    .LBR     4k    PRETTY   .LBR    28k
PRINTEXT.LBR    16k    PW-SWAP3.LBR    28k    QUIKGRAF.LBR    52k    SHRINK   .CMD     4k
TAXES   .LBR     8k    WCOUNT  .LBR     8k    WS-USER  .AQM     8k    WS2260PT.AQM    12k
WS330PT .DQC    12k    WSFAST17.LBR    12k    WSLSTKP  .ASM     4k

A4>dir
BAUD+   .LBR    12k    BYEK10Z .AQM    36k    INTTERM  .MQC    12k    KP-RCPM2.LBR    28k
KPM720  .OQJ    16k    KPVT100 .LBR    12k    LOCKER   .LBR    28k    M7XXKP   .AQM     8k
MBYE-33 .AQM    68k    MEX-OVR .LBR   120k    MEX112   .LBR   136k    MXO-KP41.AQM    28k
NEWCHAT1.AQM    16k    NUCHAT+ .LBR    28k    PROMODEM.LBR    20k    PROTOCOL.TQT    16k
RUNOBJ10.AQM     8k    SMODEMK .LBR    76k    SPLIT10  .LBR     4k    XMTIME   .LBR     4k

A5>dir
CASM    .LBR    64k    ENCRYPT .LBR    16k    FORTH    .LBR   164k    FORTHTUT.LBR    40k
LASM3   .LBR    16k    PMAKE2  .LBR    44k    RATFOR   .LBR    80k    RESOURCE.LBR    52k
TURBLOAD.LBR     8k    XLISP   .LBR    84k    XLT105   .LBR    80k    XREF241  .LBR    56k
Z80     .LBR    16k    ZM      .LBR    48k    ZTRANS   .LBR     8k
```

imal. However, in time you learn to decipher much of this and feel more comfortable with it. Certain words, in fact, are direct clues: For example, the word "MODEM" in a file name tells you that it is a communications program for using a modem. An "UNSPOOL" file is connected with buffering and printing. An "UNERA" file is for unerasing or recovering erased files. And "TYPEWRIT.COM" is a special program that enables you to use your computer and printer like a typewriter.

One of the inconveniences of computer usage is that many of us get completely out of the habit of using a typewriter and turn to the typewriter only with great reluctance, forced to do so to type labels, write a brief note, or address an occasional envelope. The "TYPEWRIT" program (the name lacks a final *e* because the rules allow only eight letters before the decimal point) solves that neatly. It permits you to type one line at a time and prints that line when you press the return or enter key on your keyboard (which is a carriage return). So you can easily type labels and notes this way.

The three-letter suffixes all have meaning, to help classify files in some sensible and logical manner, for there is a huge abundance in types of programs, as well as in specific programs. And even then, many programs are neither fish nor fowl, while others are both. But the following represent a few of the suffixes fairly well recognized as standards.

CAT: Catalog data.

COM: Command file for CP/M 80 computers.

LBR: Library file, which means that there are several programs bundled together in a single file, which must be "delibraried" when you get it to separate the various programs. (You can get free programs to do this.)

OBJ: Object file, usually a designator for COM file that is downloaded, often as part of a library file. (OBJ files must be renamed COM before they can be used.)

ASM: Assembly program, used to "assemble" and/or "install" a program in a given computer.

DOC: Documentation file, a text file, usually instructions for assembling, installing, and/or using a program.

DIR: Directory file, as in Al>dir, A2>dir, etc. in Figure 17. (Most CP/M programs do not distinguish between upper-case and lower-case letters.)

BBS: Bulletin board system file.

TXT: Text file.

You may note that certain of those suffixes listed in Figure 17 have a *Q* as the center letter. That indicates a "squeezed" file. Squeezing is a technique that reduces the size of the file to shorten the time required to transmit it. Squeezed files must be unsqueezed before they can be used, and free programs are available for that purpose only. Thus AQM is a squeezed ASM file, DQC is a squeezed DOC file, and TQT is a squeezed TXT file. (Programs that unsqueeze them rename them accordingly.)

GENERAL COMPUTER COMMUNICATION

Obviously a personal computer enables you to do a great many things better—faster, more conveniently, and more efficiently—than you could do them before. But it also enables you to do things you could not do before. For example, it is actually possible to do almost everything necessary to prepare a newsletter or a seminar program without leaving your desk. Today, you can call another computer on the telephone and exchange complete texts. But that applies to other individuals, such as yourself, who have personal computers. That is, any personal computer equipped with a modem and the proper software can transmit files to another computer or terminal—upload them, that is, which is the opposite of downloading them.

An individual in Florida, with whom I contemplate a possible collaboration on a specialized book, recently sent me a draft manuscript he had written. But he sent it over the telephone! It arrived in a slightly different CP/M format than the one my own system uses, but fortunately I have programs that convert one CP/M format to another. That enabled me to translate his disk to one of my own and so I was able to read the material.

It is to be expected that soon there will be few firms or other organizations, even the smallest ones, that will not have their own personal computers and will not expect to find others without such computers. There is the problem of compatibility, of course. Relatively few computers of different manufacturers (and even different models turned out by the same manufacturers) are completely compatible with each other. Today, even those machines that tout themselves as being "IBM compatible" are not entirely so.

That will change. Although we will probably not get complete standardization, we will get software and perhaps hardware, too, that will provide the compatibility by acting as translators between systems—something that exists already on a small scale and must inevitably grow. (We hear constant complaints that there is a lack of standardization in the computer industry. The true problem is not a lack of standards; it is a surfeit of standards, for a great many people have created their own standards and tried to impress them on others. And even IBM, powerful and dominant in the market as it is, has not been able to force more than partial adoption of its standards.)

Already it is possible to send your copy via telephone to a typesetting house, which will then convert it to formal type for you. Or you can send your camera-ready type to the print shop, although you will still have to physically deliver illustrations, unless they are computer generated and can thus be transmitted over the wire. At least two of my books have been typeset from my own WordStar disks in this manner.

There is no denying that the personal computer will be as commonplace tomorrow as the electric typewriter has been for many years. One might as well try to turn out a newsletter or other materials with a quill pen as to try to ignore the personal computer.

Chapter 10

Costs

The cost centers and the cost options available should be the greatest concerns.

THE FACTORS THAT AFFECT COSTS

These are times not only of varying degrees of inflation but of rapidly changing technology, both of which appear to have become a way of life that will not soon change. Both make it exceedingly difficult to forecast costs. Inflation tends to drive costs up. But in some cases technology drives them in the opposite direction. Printing costs, for example, dropped sharply as the newer offset systems began to replace the letterpress methods, for two reasons. One was that before offset became virtually the only printing method practiced widely, typesetting was generally considered to be part of the printing costs; the typical customer had little choice, except to ask the printer to attend to the typesetting chore. So even small print shops often included a costly linotype machine in their standard shop equipment, alongside the traditional and inevitable California Case for those small printing jobs that had to have the type set by hand. Second, printing itself became less costly, with the lower costs for platemaking, especially when the copy included illustrations of various kinds, and with many automatic features added to printing presses, reducing the amount of manual labor required.

Today many print shops and even neighborhood copy shops have photo-typesetting equipment—for setting cold type, that is—but by far the majority of small print shops do not set type because relatively few of their customers ask for the service. Instead, many customers do their own typesetting via typewriters and word processing systems. (However, most small printers do know typesetters to whom they turn to for typesetting, when customers want their copy typeset.)

The major expense for most seminars is advertising, and that may include media and mailing costs, depending on how you choose to advertise. The latter entails list rental, printing, and postage, of course, as well as the labor of preparing the mailing. Printing costs are still changing, as new technology continues to affect the processes and equipment used; postage costs have continued to increase; and most other costs have continued to rise. Still, you have alternatives today you did not have only a few years ago, such as the freedom to do much of your own mailing-list management, and even much of your own mailing automation, if you have a small computer, and thereby reduce some of your costs.

What these things cost today, as this is being written, is therefore of relatively little importance. But that is only partly because costs are changing and today's costs may have little relevancy for you when you undertake a seminar or newsletter project. It is also because you have a great many choices open to you, and you will almost surely have an even greater array of choices in the future.

This chapter will not therefore attempt to forecast the costs that you are likely to encounter, although it will generalize to furnish some rough idea of typical costs. But even that is not the real purpose or the real significance of what will be offered in this chapter. What is far more important than the figures is an awareness of the various and sundry cost centers involved in producing newsletters and seminars, and what the several alternatives are in each case—what options you have available and how they affect costs.

SEMINAR COST CENTERS

It has already been pointed out in this chapter that advertising—creating an awareness of the seminar and inducing prospects to attend—is normally the major cost of seminars. The other typical costs and cost centers are these:

Meeting room: Depending on size of room, location, day used, and other surrounding circumstances, a meeting room can run from as little as $25 to as much as several hundred dollars, even for a couple of hours' use. It pays to shop around a bit, if you want to get the best price. You can generally arrange with the hotel for equipment rental, if you want an overhead projector or need anything other than a blackboard. The rental fee will be on the order of $15 to $25, probably, for the projector, with no charge for the blackboard.

Refreshments: Hotels tend to charge from about $15 to $25 per gallon for coffee, and this is a rough guide to the cost of cold drinks, too. And hotels generally forbid you to bring in your own refreshments.

Clerical support: This is highly variable, of course, depending on how much help you require to manage the details and may be less than a hundred dollars, or it may be several hundred.

Handout materials: Again, this is highly variable, depending on what you hand out, but it is usually less than $50 for a typical session of 50 to 100 attendees.

Transparencies: Transparencies for the overhead projector are quite inexpensive to make or have made for you. In fact, they can be made on any good office copier and generally do not cost more than about $1.50 each to have them made in a typical copy shop. However, preparation of the original copy from which the transparency is to be made is another matter, and this is again highly variable, depending on whether the original is simply typed material or costly original artwork.

These "other" costs, therefore, rarely amount to more than a few hundred dollars, at most, and they can often be kept under that figure if you can minimize the use of special labor or special services.

On the other hand, advertising and other promotion costs tend to run a great deal more, and properly so, in a sense, for they have a great deal more to do with the success or failure of the event.

ADVERTISING AND PROMOTION

No factor has quite as much to do with the overall success or failure of your seminar as your advertising and promotion does, perhaps not even your presentation and program. The reason for this is simple: Most advertising and promotion depends to a large degree on the size of the total audience and the "rightness" of the audience as suitable or qualified prospects for what is offered. And that is the consequence of the advertising and promotion, of course, which determine who and how many respond to the appeals and show up at the seminar.

To appreciate this fully, let us look at it from another perspective: There is no denying that even with a huge turnout, a poorly conceived and poorly presented program will not produce much in the way of satisfactory results. Still, even the best program cannot produce results if it is presented to the wrong prospects or to too few prospects.

In fact, advertising is so inexact a science (and probably far more an art than a science) that it is quite difficult to really know what is a good program, except in retrospect (20/20 hindsight, that is!). The advertising industry tends to evaluate and judge advertising in terms of creative and artistic merit, but sales professionals judge merit in terms of total sales volume. And while we are aware of certain basic truths and principles that appear to work in creating effective advertising and sales presentations, the end result—sales—is the only measure of quality that finally has any great significance for the marketer. For what appears to be well-written advertising that follows all the "rules" faithfully may fail miserably to produce good results, while a presentation that violates all those "truths" and is judged to be poorly executed may produce excellent results. It happens constantly.

What all of this adds up to, then, is that regardless of the quality or presumed quality of the program (since we've no way of knowing in advance whether the quality is high or low), the nature and size of the attendance is the chief controlling factor that determines success or failure. And it is therefore justifiably the area on which you should lavish the most tender, loving care and whatever dollars it takes to do that well. And these are the principal cost centers for that:

Media advertising: In print media your most likely vehicles are newspapers, since magazine publishing schedules do not lend themselves well to this kind of advertising, although there are a few exceptions to this. (Some magazines, such as *Training*, run special sections for seminars and similar events and may be useful for advertising your own seminars.)

Costs tend to be high in these mass media because they reach so many people. A relatively small announcement in the daily newspaper can easily cost you several hundred dollars each time you run it, and in many newspapers and other periodicals there are different rates for different days and for different sections of the publication. That, however, is an advantage because you probably want to reach a certain kind of audience and therefore want to consider what section of the newspaper is best for you.

If you want to reach women generally, for example, the sports pages are the wrong place, for relatively few women read the sports pages. But if you want to reach people in the business world, the financial pages or business section of the newspaper is likely to be helpful. There are, however, many other sections in any large city newspaper, and you should consider all, in terms of your targeted audience.

There are a number of weekly and monthly (and even a few daily) newsprint periodicals, tabloids, that reach specialized audiences in various trades and professions. You should research these to try to find one suitable for your own purposes.

Bear in mind that advertising space rates in periodicals are based on total circulation or readership, and in most general-circulation periodicals, such as a city newspaper, relatively few are likely to be good prospects for you. You must weigh that against the cost.

But even the specialized periodicals present a similar problem of wasted advertising dollars because you are paying for their national distribution, in most cases, although your message is addressed primarily to those in the local area.

Ergo, unless you do want to reach the general public or you think that reaching people all over the country serves your purposes, you may wish to consider whether print advertising will work for you at all.

Broadcast media—radio and television—offer another choice. These can be used on a local basis, although that presents the same problem of being addressed to the public at large. You can target audiences to some extent, however, by choosing time and station. Radio messages broadcast during rush hours will reach a large audience in automobiles, traveling to and from work, so you will be reaching people who work at jobs. Broadcasting on late-night television ensures that few children will be watching. You can also choose spots such as during commercial breaks in news broadcasts.

But there is another way to use media advertising, as inquiry advertising, and we'll discuss that shortly in connection with another way of advertising, using direct-mail methods.

Direct-mail advertising: As in all things, direct mail has advantages and disadvantages. Its principal disadvantage is that it is a great deal of work, even when you use contracted services for much of the work. But it has more than one major advantage:

• It can be aimed—you can target audiences with great precision.
• It is far easier to measure results with precision, to determine not only what works and what does not work, but how well it works and, with enough intelligent effort, even why it works or does not.
• It is highly controllable: You can decide how many people to reach, exactly when to reach them, and what the follow-up is to be.

In terms of costs, the major cost factors are mailing lists, printing, and postage. We have discussed printing already, so there is no point in pursuing that further. Postage is another matter. At this moment, first-class postage is 22 cents for the first ounce. There are several methods for reducing postage costs, however: pre-sorting first-class mail, which requires using the nine-digit zip code, reduces its cost somewhat, and using bulk mail reduces it by nearly half. However, in a practical sense those are useful methods only if you mail in large quantity.

Mailing lists can be rented, although they vary in cost quite widely, from lows of about $35 per 1,000 names to as much as $100 per 1,000 names for premium lists. Most major list brokers will specify a minimum quantity you can order, usually 3,000 or 5,000 names.

Normally you rent these lists for a single use, but some brokers will make special arrangements with you for multiple use, and some will allow you to have unrestricted use of the names for a period of time. (However, the names of any who respond to your mailings become "your" names and can be added to your own house lists, to be used as often as you wish.)

You can get lists sorted by any of many possible parameters, such as the following, which represent only a few of the possible categories to illustrate the wide range possible: mail order buyers, professionals, engineers, bank presidents, male executives, buyers of last three months, seminar registrants, book buyers, executives, comptrollers, housewives, female executives, buyers of items over $100, and credit card mail order buyers.

Major list brokers will usually supply a printed catalog of their lists, explaining the categories by which you may order, the numbers in each category, and often also offering to make up special lists for you. Frequently their lists are so coded that their computers can retrieve names and make up lists of categories other than those listed.

When you add up the postage, printing, and cost of names, you arrive at something on the order of $300 to $400 per 1,000 names. It is possible to reduce that somewhat, with quantity mailings, but you are not likely to be able to get far below this range.

In practice, if you are mailing only 2,000 to 5,000 pieces, you can probably handle it in-house without great difficulty, especially if you have the assistance of a computer and proper software to support mailing activity. (Today, you can probably get most major list brokers to supply mailing lists in electronic media [instead of on labels of one type or another] that can be copied onto one of your own disks and used in your own computer.) If you are going to go to heavier mailings, however, you would probably be well advised to consider using a professional mailing house to handle the whole thing for you.

INQUIRY ADVERTISING METHODS

Renting mailing lists from list brokers is only one of several ways to acquire mailing lists. Inquiry advertising is another. Inquiry advertising is an excellent answer to the problem of using mass media—newspapers, magazines, radio, and television efficiently and effectively. By using some or all of these media to draw inquiries, you accomplish three things at once: You overcome the high cost of media advertising, of which so much is wasted, because inquiry advertising usually requires only small, inexpensive advertisements; you can be highly selective, through wording your advertisements properly, and so draw inquiries principally from the prospects you want; and you build mailing lists for direct-mail campaigns.

That latter consideration is an important one. Often you can gather the lists of names less expensively in this manner than you could rent them, but even if they cost you more, they really cost you less because they are your own lists, and you can use them as often as you wish. Moreover, they are often far better lists than you could rent from anyone, in the sense that they are targeted better, that is. And, finally, you have the potential of ultimately renting these lists to others and earning income from them yourself. Most important, however, is that you have complete control of the entire process, as well as of the lists you have built up in this manner.

You can compile lists from a variety of sources. In my own case, the display help-wanted advertisements in the financial pages of such major newspapers as the *Wall Street Journal* and the Sunday editions of the *New York Times* and the *Washington Post* were one major source of names of employers I wanted to reach. (This was before the *Wall Street Journal* and others began to publish weekly tabloid compilations of such employment opportunities. Today, I would use these publications as a principal source for compiling my lists, which would be far more efficient.) Membership directories of trade associations and other such organizations were another resource. (It is not always possible to get these, but with a little resourcefulness you can gather a few of them.) Federal government agencies were a help, too, furnishing such directories as one that listed several thousand minority-owned firms and another of contractors to the U.S. Navy. And I was able at the time to buy a copy of the 29,000-name subscription list for the Commerce Department's periodical, the *Commerce Business Daily*, which was another major resource, in itself a major mailing list.

Often you can find other entrepreneurs in ventures not competitive with yours but addressed to the same kinds of prospects. Frequently these other entrepreneurs also do advertising by direct mail and will be glad to trade names with you, which enables you to double your store of names quite swiftly! On one occasion I traded lists with three different entrepreneurs, quadrupling my total store of mailing lists, even after "cleaning" them, which means eliminating duplicates and "nixies" (those returned as incorrect addresses, deceased, moved or otherwise undeliverable).

The most effective way to draw inquiries is to offer readers and listeners (in the case of radio and TV commercials) something that is not too costly to you but is likely to have enough value for and appeal to those readers whom you consider to be good prospects to induce them to make requests for the item. For that reason alone it is usually unproductive to offer things that are useful to and would therefore appeal to everyone, such as a calendar or memo pad. Such an offer would produce inquiries from many people who are not prospects, such as school children, for one.

This is one way to marry the free newsletter—or even if it is not free, a sample copy of your newsletter—to your seminar promotion.

But if you do not have a free newsletter to offer, you might develop and offer a special report, a useful brochure, or a reprint of something you have written earlier. Here are examples of such small advertisements:

U.S. GOVERNMENT OFFICIAL REPORT on smoking hazards and best methods for quitting. Copy available FREE, on request. Call, write: (Address/telephone number.)

FREE COPY OF *Government Marketing News* to help small business win government contracts. Call/write: (Address/telephone number.)

A more direct way is to use your direct-mail package itself as the free offer by wording your notice properly. You can ask readers to send for your direct-mail package by explaining summarily what free information is to be offered in your seminar, without mentioning at this time that you are talking about a seminar, and offering details to any who write or call. Your direct-mail package will then elaborate on this by explaining that you are offering a free seminar and making the appeal. Here are some examples of how you can do this with small notices, even with classified advertisements:

LEARN HOW TO WIN GOVERNMENT CONTRACTS. It takes know-*how*, rather than know-*who*. FREE information. (Address and/or telephone number.)

STOP SMOKING THE EASY WAY. New, painless method, no withdrawal agony. FREE demonstration. For details: (Address, telephone number.)

Of course, these are terse messages, and they do not attempt to present details or sell hard. They shouldn't have to, if your offer is tempting enough. Your objective is to run small, inexpensive advertisements, asking nothing from readers except a telephone call or postcard requesting the information and relying on widespread circulation for results. That is, you should run as many of these little advertisements as possible—run them for as long as possible in as many periodicals as possible or with as many radio/TV spots as possible.

Everyone operates within a budget, and presumably you will set an advertising budget for this. Keeping your copy sparse will help you maximize the number of advertisements you can afford to run. And in terms of money, here are several factors that affect how many notices you can run—how much each notice will cost you, that is:

1. Rates of the media you choose
2. Size of the advertisement

3. Position/time chosen
4. Number of times run
5. Number of media used

All of these affect costs, of course, and most of them have something to do, directly or indirectly, with the results you are likely to get. However, those most likely to be critical in terms of results are usually those numbered here as 4 and 5. That is, assuming that you have selected media that reach those whom you wish to reach, you will probably get the best results per dollar invested by maximizing the number of media in which your copy runs and the number of times you run them. For example, if there are a half-dozen journals which are suitable for your purposes, use them all but run the notice at least three or four times.

KEYING AND TESTING YOUR ADVERTISEMENTS

One thing you want to know in such campaigns as these is where your advertising dollars are doing the best job for you by producing the maximum results. It's not difficult to determine that, if you key your advertisements, so that you are able to measure the results of each advertisement.

There are many ways to key advertisements and even direct-mail copy so that you can tell from the response which advertisement or which mailing (or which list of names) brought you the best results. You will recognize these as methods widely used by others:

· Add a suffix letter to your post office box number, suite number, address, or other address designation. (Of course, you change this for different media, different days or months, different appeals, etc.)
· Add a "Dept." number or other designation to your address.
· Give the giveaway item a distinctive name and instruct the respondent to "ask for _____."
· Add a prefix or middle initial to your name, if you operate under your own name. Or, if you have some generic name, such as Ajax Merchandise Associates, make some change in the name, while keeping the main identifier, such as Ajax Marketing Associates.
· To key the telephone calls, instruct readers to ask for "Mr. Kelly," for the "Stop-smoking package," or otherwise identify the advertisement to which they are responding.

You collect the information on a form, such as that of Figure 18, which aids you in analyzing results. You can thus determine where and how to get the most out of each of your advertising dollars, as all

18.
Suggested Data Form for Evaluating Responses

Key:_____ Medium:_____ Day:_____ Cost: $_____

DATE	NO. CALLS	NO. CARDS/LTRS	NOTES
TOTALS:			COST PER INQUIRY: $_____
			COST PER ATTENDEE: $_____

the professionals in the field do, by breaking it down into a cost per response or inquiry. However, what you really want to know is how much it cost you in terms of attendees, since the rate of response is necessarily proportional to the rate of attendance. After you have run the seminar, you can analyze the attendance records and determine what the follow-up or attendance rate was, again in terms of cost per attendee.

Even that is not truly the end of the trail, for the real objective is closes, and you need to know what percentage of attendees from each category finally became customers or clients. And you may want to determine this in terms of number of orders or dollar value of business, depending on the circumstances of your enterprise. Moreover, you may be able to determine this immediately, if you are making direct sales at your seminar, or it may be a matter of some time before you can determine this. In either case, you should make the effort, for if you do this and do it well, your success ratio will climb steadily to some peak before it levels off.

You are, therefore, really testing your advertisements to see which work and which do not. But you are also testing the various media and the various days, and you will almost surely get a few surprises: You will find it most difficult—actually impossible, in most cases—to guess which media, which wording, which free offer, which days produce best, and you will learn to collect and study these data very carefully, for your final success depends to a large extent on this.

It is necessary to keep data for each and every advertisement you have keyed, to determine whether there are differences and, if so, what they are in media, days, seasons, kinds of copy, and other factors.

NEWSLETTER COSTS

Newsletters and their costs are quite a different proposition, of course. Still, the cost centers are analogous. The production costs are preparation—research, writing, editorial work, and typesetting—and printing. The principal variables here are the preparation costs, since the printing is the same, whether you do all your own editorial work or hire someone to do all or part of it. (Some newsletter publishers gather the materials to go into each issue but hire a freelance writer/editor or consultant to do all the work of getting the copy ready for the printer.)

Printing costs vary as much as do other costs today, but even within any given situation there are the variables mentioned earlier of paper, colored inks, platemaking, etc. However, for purposes of getting a rough or ballpark idea, assume that printing a modest number of about 1,000 copies of a four-page newsletter should result in a per-copy cost on the order of 15 to 25 cents per copy, and that will drop to less than half that with an appreciable increase in the print order (number of copies printed). Depending on the size of your venture and the number of prospects you want to reach, you may want to go to many thousands of copies, but for even a modest effort, you probably ought to print at least 5,000 copies, since you need not distribute these all at once and may want to make each issue last for three months before creating another one. It is not necessary to distribute a free newsletter on a frequent basis, and quarterly publication is quite reasonable.

Hiring a specialist to help you is one of those purchases you should not make hastily. For one thing, costs will vary widely: They can run as little as $100 to $200 per day or as much as $500 or more per day. Unfortunately, the capability of the individual and the resultant quality of the work has no direct relationship to what the service costs you. So it is best to ask around, interview more than one individual, and even ask for proposals, with samples of the individual's work.

You can ask friends and associates for suggestions. Or if you find a large print shop, especially one that specializes in newsletters or what are called more generically "company publications," you can probably get useful referrals to capable newsletter specialists.

There is also a newsletter called the Newsletter on Newsletters and a newsletter association, about which information will be provided later.

The biggest cost in a newsletter is, usually, the distribution costs. When the newsletter is one for which you charge a subscription fee, distribution means marketing, and you have the same situations as just described for drawing attendance to a seminar. But even a free newsletter needs to be mailed out, and that costs postage and mailing labor, even if you do it yourself.

One way to keep that part of the cost down is to mail the newsletter as a self-mailer. That means mailing it without an envelope by using a mailing label on it, with or without a mailing block, which is a special area on an outside page especially designed to bear the label, return address, and postage. You can mail the newsletter unfolded, as a "flat," or folded to business-envelope size.

One advantage of the latter approach is that you can easily carry a supply of newsletters around with you in an inside pocket, purse, or brief case and use them as brochures, thereby adding to your circulation. And, of course, you can always deposit a supply of them in convenient places where the right people are likely to see them and pick up a copy. You can do both, having some folded and some delivered flat, as mentioned earlier in another connection.

One way to maximize the benefits of the newsletter is to make a rather large initial printing and mailing—several times the quantity you would otherwise send out—using mailing lists you have rented or built up and asking recipients to request continuation of the newsletter, if they wish to continue to receive it. (Print that as a notice in the newsletter.) But require them to send a business card or make the request on a business letterhead so that you can verify that they are legitimate prospects for business, worth sending free newsletters to, and worth an eventual follow-up.

Chapter 11

Seminar and Newsletter Planning Guidelines

Successful seminars and newsletters do not happen by accident, but only through careful and correct planning.

WHY SHOULD ANYBODY ATTEND YOUR FREE SEMINAR?

Even a free seminar will not attract an audience if the prospects do not perceive it to be in their direct interests to attend—if, that is, they do not see how they can gain immediate benefits from attending. And persuading attendees to show up out of simple curiosity will not do the job, either; for the event to work to your own benefit, the attendees must be genuinely interested in what you promise. Ergo, you must analyze the concept from the prospect's viewpoint, not your own, and there is a simple exercise you can use: Take the general topic you have decided on and explore a universe of variants, each of which is actually an application of the basic idea. And think in terms of specific benefits, specific applications, and specific individuals.

Suppose, for example, that your specialty is that service we have hypothesized earlier of helping people quit smoking. Your basic concept may be generalized as something along the lines of "the easy way to quit smoking in 24 hours," and you might prefix that with something such as "free demonstration."

That will be regarded by almost everyone who reads it as a direct invitation or challenge to him or her to give up cigarettes. However, those individuals who either have never smoked or who have already given up cigarettes will rarely give the message a second thought because they identify as non-smokers, which means that the message is *not addressed to them* or, at least, not *perceived* so. With only rare exceptions, those prospects are lost to you immediately. But, you may say, they aren't really prospects, are they? So how could I have lost them?

You are partially right in this: As addressed in the above example, they are indeed not prospects. But perhaps something can be done to *make* prospects of them: Suppose that you brainstorm the idea of quitting smoking a bit. Who *are* your prospects? That is, to whom is your message really addressed? To the smoker only? Or to his or her friends and family? Let's try a few variants on the theme:

How to help your teenager quit smoking

Help your wife/husband give up cigarettes

Help your father/mother give up smoking

Help stamp out smoking in your family

This will enlist at least some of those non-smokers to tell their friends, children, spouses, and others about your free seminar, and some will urge others to attend.

Always think hard about who all your possible prospects are and develop sales headlines that address all of them. But remember that the first and most prominent headline is the title of your seminar. Vague and general titles deliver vague and general messages, and people do not often respond to vague and general messages. To capture a prospect's attention, the message must first make it absolutely clear to whom the message is addressed, as well as what the promised benefit is.

To do this, you must think hard about all the possible applications of your own knowledge and skills. Ask yourself the following kinds of questions, to start the ideas flowing: What are the common, serious problems of many people, in connection with this idea? Who, specifically, are these people? What is different, special, novel, or otherwise noteworthy (attention getting) about what you can do for these people? What are the *specific* benefits you offer them?

For example, let us suppose that you have a service that trains people in becoming more effective writers in their business organizations. Your basic topic, then, is along the lines of how to write more effectively or how to communicate more effectively. (As the Evelyn Wood organization has done so successfully, this kind of subject lends itself to offering a free lesson as the inducement to attend the free seminar.) And let us suppose that you intend to present these programs in businesses to help employers by training their staffs. Your principal objective is to induce business executives to attend your free seminar or, at least, to delegate someone to attend and report back. And, of course, you must first persuade the prospects that there are adequate benefits to be derived out of what you teach. Those topics suggested earlier in this paragraph will be effective in doing so only in those few cases where the prospect will extrapolate that general thought and those general words. But they will be few cases, indeed; if you want prospects to *understand* what you promise as benefits, you must be absolutely clear about it. Advertising is no place for subtleties.

Your problem, then, is to make the extrapolations yourself. To do so, give some thought to all the possible applications that will bring direct benefits. But ask yourself first what benefits the typical business proprietor usually wants. Some suggestions are increased profits, increased sales, larger sales, lower costs, business growth, greater public recognition, greater prestige, and expansion.

Of course, not all these executives are proprietors. Even vice presidents and other officers of the company usually have somewhat narrower and more specialized interests than the proprietor does. The sales manager wants more sales, above all; that's the main mission and measure of his or her success or failure. The comptroller wants to show cost reductions and better control of all matters financial, for the same reason. The purchasing agent wants to find better sources and make better buys. All want to be able to do their own jobs more effectively, according to whatever measures are used to gauge their effectiveness in their jobs. And while it is in their direct interests for their organization to prosper, they also want to shine as individual employees.

Let's try to take that very general topic of how to write more effectively and see what variants we can produce, bearing the above in mind:

How to write more effective sales proposals

How to write better annual reports

How to communicate more effectively with customers

How to write clear and unambiguous contracts

How to write more persuasive internal memos

Better brochure writing

How to prepare more powerful sales presentations

How to write clear purchase orders

How to write better financial reports

Even that is only the first step. Think also in terms of individuals in business organizations, for in many cases employers will approve the cost and time of such a program for any employee who applies to attend it (at least, if they can justify the cost and time). Who are those specific employees, then, most likely to derive personal or career benefits—improve their personal skills— while also benefiting the employer? Try the following ideas out:

More effective communication for executives

Business writing for marketing managers

Clearer writing in the law office

Writing more powerful legal briefs

Business writing for the personnel manager

Clearer correspondence for the administrator

There is also the possibility, in this case, that many individuals might attend such a program on their own time and at their own expense, so it may very well draw people who want to improve their personal skills. And in such case your message ought to address those benefits, perhaps along such lines as these:

Writing skill increases your personal value to your employer

Communication skills help you step up to a better job

Writing ability is a key to greater career success

Good communicators are in demand everywhere

Employers want people who can write clearly

Writing skill opens many new doors

It becomes clear, from such exercises as these, that (1) it is not always immediately and automatically apparent who the real prospect is, (2) there is often more than one prospect to be addressed, and (3) it often requires more than one kind of message to address all the prospects.

But there is still another point: It is not always the prospect who is the buyer. The prospect is that individual who must be persuaded by your appeal, while the buyer is that individual who must pay. If an employer sends people to a seminar or contracts for a course for employees, the employer may or may not be the prospect. In that case where the employer will accept applications from employees for company-paid training, the employee is the prospect, but the employer is the buyer. (In a sense the employee is the buyer too, inasmuch as the employee "buys" by applying to the employer for authority to take the course.) Both have to be convinced that the training is worthwhile and will be beneficial, but each must be offered a different reason (a different promised benefit and rationale, that is) for reaching that conclusion. And the sale can usually be consummated only by achieving that dual persuasion.

On the other hand, where the employer arbitrarily decides to send certain employees to the course, the employer is both prospect and the buyer. (In all references here, employer does not necessarily refer to a proprietor, of course, but refers to whomever in the organization has the authority to make the buying decision for the organization.)

USING THE COMPUTER TO HELP

Developing, framing, and phrasing the sales messages is one activity in which the computer is especially valuable. Once you become experienced and adjusted to working directly on the screen and keyboard, you will find no other way that is as satisfactory, as convenient, or as helpful in organizing ideas as this modern electronic doodling. You record thoughts as they occur, juggle ideas and wording around, try new combinations, electronically scratch out, and generally stimulate your own imagination with this unprecedented convenience.

You can print out hard copy if you wish, if you find that it helps you study words on paper, rather than on screen, but even that does not interfere with your discarding that in favor of more phosphorescent (on screen) note making. And unless you are very much the exception, you will never want to go back to pencil-and-paper methods, for the computer is not merely more efficient in doing this work; it is a great aid to original thinking and contributes directly to creative imagination.

APPLICATIONS TO NEWSLETTER PLANNING

Much of the foregoing observations about the need for thoughtful development of a seminar title is directly applicable to the planning and development of a newsletter, but in one sense even more so, for this reason: A seminar is a single event and may easily be handled as a unique event, but that is not true for the newsletter. That is, if a seminar title fails to do its job well, no one takes the slightest notice of your change in title for the next seminar. But if you once launch a newsletter and decide shortly after to change its title, you all but destroy whatever marketing and promotion you have done and must start all over. Moreover, readers want to know why the newsletter name is changed. (This is not to say that newsletter names never change; they do. But it is not easy to do so without suffering losses, despite all efforts to minimize such losses.)

In short, each seminar is itself a single and unique project, and mistakes in planning and staging are easily buried when the seminar is over. You can even forget about ever doing another, if you so choose, because the presentation of a seminar in no way implies that others will be offered, and no one has any reason to infer that there will be others. But a newsletter carries a clear implication that it is a long-term commitment, and that you will continue to publish it indefinitely. Hence the greater need for getting it right the first time, when developing a newsletter.

The title of the newsletter, like the title of a seminar, ought to say something specific, giving anyone who reads it some reasonably clear idea of what the newsletter is all about—what kind of information it contains, to whom it is addressed, what it promises to do, and other related information.

Obviously, no title can spell out all such information in any detail and remain short enough to even be qualified as a title, so it requires a fair degree of that same original thinking and creative imagination suggested as being necessary to title seminars, although there is some methodology available (to be described shortly).

To illustrate some of these points, consider the following actual newsletter titles: CRI Forecaster, The Loft Letter, Update, New Directions, AJHS Report, and CHI Dispatch.

If you were to guess what these newsletters are all about and to whom they are addressed, you would be doing just that—guessing. Probably their readers understand the implications of those titles, but to the stranger they are entirely cryptic.

On the other hand, consider whether you can surmise fairly well what the following newsletters are all about and to whom they are addressed: Marketing Professional Services, The World of Rodeo, Futures Market Service, Computer Opportunities, Solar Electric News, and Mining Newsletter.

You can easily tell what each of the second set of newsletters is generally about, at least, although you might not be absolutely clear on whom the intended readers are. They do represent a step in the right direction. But let's see if we can find some that represent another step in that direction: Executive's Personal Development Letter, Marketing for Sales Executives, On Your Own: The Newsletter for the Soon to be Self-Employed, Sharing Ideas, For Professional Speakers and Their Friends, Freelance Writer's Marketing Newsletter, and Findout: The Newsletter For People Who Use Information.

Obviously this latter class of newsletters is published by owners who are not afraid to use somewhat longer titles so that they can get a basic message across. Note that each of these titles identifies intended readers, at least generally, and implies clearly the promised benefit—help in personal development for executives, information pertinent to marketing for sales executives, ideas for speakers, and so on.

Many have to overcome the mental block against lengthy titles. This is as mistaken a bias as the one against solid text in print advertisements. (That latter has been disproved again and again by specific examples.) You may as well call your newsletter X, as to call it The Joe Smith Report.

Developing a newsletter title should be done with great care, but along the same lines as those listed earlier. Ask yourself these questions: To whom is this newsletter addressed (who will be most interested in and helped by this newsletter)? That should be someone who is your proper prospect for your main venture, of course. What can I promise to do (and deliver) for this reader? How can I make this clear without letting the title get out of hand?

The sensible way to develop the title is to begin by writing out in whatever detail and whatever number of words necessary your answer to the above. Your first draft might be, for example, "The newsletter with ideas and tips on how to win government contracts by writing winning proposals, for marketing managers and proposal specialists."

That's a beginning, and it doesn't matter how long it is; the point is to include everything about whom the intended readers are and why they should be reading the newsletter. Time enough after we have gotten all that down in writing to study it and decide how to shorten it without losing the main reader identification and message.

You might want to work that statement over several times (again, using the unmatched blessings of the word processor to do so), until you are satisfied that you have said everything that could be and should be said to identify the reader and the promised benefits.

Then comes the first step of the editing process—shortening the statement by eliminating unnecessary words that do not contribute to meanings and/or minor rephrasing that accomplishes the same thing:

"~~The~~ newsletter ~~with~~ ideas and tips ~~on how to~~ win government contracts by writing winning proposals, for marketing managers and proposal specialists."

This is then refined into, "Newsletter of ideas and tips on winning government contracts; for marketing managers and proposal specialists."

It is not necessary to call out both marketing managers and proposal specialists, since proposal writing is a marketing function. And it is not only the proposal specialists who ought to read this newsletter, but all those engineers and others who have to help with proposal writing. Hence, this is a logical next step. The word "newsletter" is not really necessary. Nor is it absolutely necessary to mention winning government contracts and proposal writing in the same breath, since they are so closely related. So in the interest of getting the title down to a more manageable size, while keeping the most important elements in the title, any of the following would accomplish that:

Proposal Writing Ideas and Tips

Ideas and Tips for Writing Winning Proposals

Ideas and Tips for Winning Government Contracts

"Ideas and tips" is a key phrase, since that is what the newsletter offers, so that appears in each of the suggested titles. The third candidate is not as specific as the second one because it does not mention nor even clearly imply that the ideas and tips are for proposals, but "winning government contracts" is a more persuasive promised benefit than "writing winning proposals" because it addresses the reader's needs more directly (i.e., the winning proposal is only the means to the prize); whereas, the government contract is the prize. "For marketers/proposal writers" can be added as a subtitle because it is quite helpful, although not absolutely essential, since winning government contracts is clearly a marketing function.

Obviously, there had to be some compromises here, and compromises other than the ones suggested here are possible, of course. However, the process is the same: Get it all articulated, and then edit it down to manageable size, while making considered judgments on what is to be kept and what discarded.

THE DIRECT-MAIL PACKAGE

There is a body of conventional wisdom in the direct-mail field as there is in all established fields. And like conventional wisdom in other fields, it is based on truth and the experience of many but is nevertheless never totally accurate or trustworthy for at least these reasons:

1. By the time anything is established long enough to have become conventional wisdom, obsolescence has begun to overtake the truth because of the ever greater rapidity of change in our modern world.

2. Conventional wisdom tends to try always to establish immutable laws without regard to the almost endless variety of conditions and circumstances, and especially the enormous number of combinations and permutations resulting.

3. Conventional wisdom invariably fails to take into account the ingenuity of resourceful individuals who are themselves the agents of change.

4. Conventional wisdom is inevitably based on probability or what is generally considered to be the average case and does not provide for the many exceptions.

5. The exceptions or the myriad conditions and circumstances that affect results are for the most part totally unpredictable and therefore tend even to invalidate the idea that there is such a thing as conventional wisdom.

This is a disclaimer. The following paragraphs will describe and report what the many experienced direct-mail specialists believe to be true enough to be regarded as the rules of the trade. But the information is offered here with a clear caution to accept it on only a tentative basis, and test the waters for yourself, as you go. Try these methods, observe and measure results carefully, and be guided accordingly. Never fear to strike out in another direction, if your experience leads you thus. Trust your own experience and judgment as much as you trust what others advise.

Some of the anecdotes that follow will clarify this.

The Obligatory Components

The minimum content of a typical direct-mail package, according to many experts, should include the following:

A sales letter

A brochure, circular, "broadside" or other such enclosure (often called "insert")

An order form (may be part of second item, but preferably a separate card or form)

A return envelope (preferably postage-paid so that respondent does not need to find a stamp)

The sales letter should have handwritten markings to stress items— marginal comments, underlines, circling of words, and other such dramatic intercessions. The circular ought to be multi-colored, if possible, especially if it is a broadside (a circular that unfolds to some huge size, such as 17×23 inches), and it is better to have more than one of these items in the mailing. The order form ought to be a separate, attention-getting card, preferably in more than one color, stressing the need for prompt action. The return envelope is a must, and it is far better to have it postage prepaid.

Many direct-mail specialists believe that special inserts, such as plastic cards that resemble credit cards, are helpful. And many believe that sales messages ought to be inscribed on the carrier (outer) envelope.

Other Immutable Truths

Many insist, too, that a firm, money-back guarantee is obligatory, and that the lack of it is the kiss of death.

Conventional wisdom says the summer, June-August, is deadly dull, when sales plummet, but things pick up sharply after Labor Day, peak at Christmas, and many forecast brisk sales activity in January.

My own experience and that of some others is not directly contrary to this but suggests that the exceptions are numerous. I once dropped my guarantee completely, to test this theory. I would make refunds, if merchandise was returned, but I did not make the offer to because I thought that that simply invited people to return merchandise. The result? Returns had never been high, but they dropped even lower, and sales did not appear to be at all affected.

An expert condemned most bitterly a piece of sales copy I wrote, declaring it utterly worthless. But I had printed it in quantity already and decided to risk the envelopes and postage. The returns were satisfactory—quite good, in fact.

I tried mailings with and without return envelopes. I could not detect a significant difference. Nor could I determine any difference between the results of using multi-colored literature and using black-and-white literature.

On the other hand, I agree that, at least in general, "the more you tell, the more you sell" is a valid idea: I did indeed find a definite increase in response when I used a letter, order card, and a brochure, where I had previously used only the letter and order card.

My own experience and that of many others I know regarding seasonal effects on direct-mail results has been that the conventional wisdom is true—sometimes. But it is as often not true. One summer is poor for sales, the next quite brisk; one fall is good for sales, the next quite slow; one January good, the next poor; etc. All that can be said, really, about this is that seasonal fluctuations are unpredictable, and the so-called exceptions are not really exceptions at all.

In all fairness, however, I should reveal that the results I report were on the basis of relatively small mailings, where a 0.05 percent difference is difficult to detect, much less measure. On the other hand, a 0.05 percent difference in orders resulting from a mailing of several hundred thousand pieces would show up sharply in dollars and cents. And even the most zealous expert counts the differences in tenths of a percent, when evaluating the impact of those items mentioned earlier.

Finally, then, it is necessary to try various items for yourself and observe results most carefully. Determine what works for you, not what is or is not true. But even then do not expect any consistency in results, for there are too many unpredictable and unfathomable circumstances that affect outcomes.

Testing

The only reliable guide is your own experience, and even that is not reliable if it is not based on specific tests and measurement. Each mailing you make should be recorded so that you know precisely what the results are. And you should not use these as any certain weather

vane, either; your next mailing may well produce totally different results.

The wise direct-mail specialists make small test mailings before each
campaign, and only when a test mailing reveals that all is well do they
"roll out"—make the complete mailing.

That is the wise way to do it.

Chapter 12

Testing

Testing should be regarded as an absolute must in direct mail. Anything done without testing is guesswork, no matter the circumstances.

WHAT SHOULD BE TESTED?

You may use any or all of the many services offered to help you with your sales, advertising, and direct-mail campaigns, and to some degree these services can even help you gather useful test data. However, it is unwise to rely on anyone but yourself (except, perhaps, for a reliable consultant you have retained, if you decide to pursue that route) to determine what data you need, how to analyze it, and how to interpret it. And the items to be tested include at least the following: the media, the timing, the offer, and the copy.

Here again we run into conventional wisdom about what ought to be tested, and again I find it necessary to disagree with much of what I have read—others' opinions—about what are the most important items to test. Let's first review that conventional wisdom.

Testing the Medium

There seems to be a prevalent idea that the medium is the first and most important item to be tested. (Some appear to believe that it is the only important item to be tested.) And that term, media, includes the broadcast media (radio and television), the print media (periodicals of all kinds), and the mailing lists.

A suggested form for collecting data was shown earlier. Typically, those who use print and broadcast media set up forms and records along the general lines of Figure 19. These formats are particularly

19.
Formats for Analyzing Advertising Results

PERIODICAL	DATE(S)	COST ($)	NO. ORDERS	COST/ORDER	PROFIT (LOSS)

PERIODICAL	DATE(S)	COST ($)	NO. RESPONSES	COST/RESPONSE

STATION	DATE(S) TIME(S)	COST ($)	NO. ORDERS	COST/ORDER	PROFIT (LOSS)

STATION	DATE(S) TIME(S)	COST ($)	NO. RESPONSES	COST/RESPONSE

useful for gathering data during initial test mailings or test advertisements, and help to select the best ones before rolling out the campaign.

The idea is, of course, to list the various periodicals, broadcast stations (both radio and television), and mailing lists used and to evaluate by actual measure which have been most useful, both in total numbers of orders and in cost per order, if you are selling something. On the other hand, if you are trying to draw attendees for a free seminar or requestors for a free newsletter, it is responses, rather than orders, that you are trying for, so you simply substitute the words and eliminate the profit/loss heading, of course, as the examples show. (For broadcast media, be sure to note whether you used radio or television, in that column, or use separate forms for each.)

These formats may be used for mailing lists also, substituting the mailing-list identification (source and key) in the first column, so that you are recording results produced by each mailing list you try out in the test mailings. However, bear in mind that there is a difference in what the cost column means. For the categories and media shown in the figure, the costs to be listed are the media costs. But if you use this format to record the results of mailings, the cost column does not refer to the cost of the list rentals but to the total cost of the mailing of each list.

Consider two factors in evaluating results here: the number of responses (whether they are orders, inquiries, or other kinds of responses) and the cost of each response. For example, if the advertisement or commercial announcement cost $1,000 and you got 200 responses, each cost you $5, of course. However, another advertisement or commercial may have brought you 25 responses, but cost you only $100, which means that these responses cost you only $4 each. Does this mean that you should roll out your campaign using the less-expensive medium?

In most cases, the answer to this would be negative, unless you are sure that you can get enough total response by expanding your $100 advertising medium coverage, and you may not be able to do that. Cost per response is a useful guide only if you can get enough responses at an acceptable rate. If you can get a much more adequate number of responses for only a little more, it is probably better to pay a little more.

This is as true for mailing lists as for media costs, of course. It is a call for judgment, a management decision. You must try to keep costs as low as possible, but you must keep your eye on the ball, too, Nothing is gained by keeping costs low if you do not achieve your objectives.

The formats shown in Figure 19 are useful for measuring any me dium to compare the various possible vehicles in any medium you choose to run your test and subsequent campaign. However, you may wish to run tests and possibly your campaign in all media; if so, you will find it useful to compare results among the media, after you have decided which is the best vehicle in each medium. That is, you first run your several tests and select the best one, the one you will use for each medium, and compare these with each other.

The format is easily adapted to this use, as shown in Figure 20. And, again, nothing is required other than changing column heads. You can use this form, as in the case of the previous figure, for measuring orders, inquiries, or any other kinds of responses. And, again, you want to study both the number of responses and the cost per response to reach a decision on whether you will use more than one medium and which you will use. The criteria are the same as before, and cost per order may or may not be highly significant, depending on how great the differential is and on how effective each medium is.

20.
Adapting the Format to Compare Media Results

MEDIUM	DATE(S) TIME(S)	COST ($)	NO. RESPONSES	COST/RESPONSE

Testing Timing

These data test both timing and vehicle. Time is tested literally, in the case of broadcast media—time of day and day of week, as well as specific station. And time is, of course, important in the case of broadcast media. In the case of periodicals it tests days, months, and/or seasons, depending on the periodical and other pertinent factors. But it tests timing, too, in a general sense, for timing does make a difference. The same vehicle, whether periodical, broadcast station, or mailing list, can produce totally different results on different occasions.

In consideration of this, you may record several different periodicals on one form to compare them, but you may wish to record different times for a given periodical or broadcast station, to determine what time produces the best results.

Practical Limits

Obviously, this can become a protracted process that requires an intolerably long time and an impossibly large budget to complete. Hence, testing must be on some practical basis. And that basis is, for many professionals in the direct-response field, continuous. That is, while they make preliminary tests and evaluations before making the major investments in rolling out the campaign, they continue to gather this data continuously, and they continue to analyze it as they conduct the campaign, making any changes and adjustments the tests and evaluation suggest.

Testing the Offer

All of this is necessary; however, one problem is that it assumes that the offer is satisfactory and will produce adequate response, once you find the right medium and right vehicles—the right mailing lists, the right periodical, or the right station. If you accept this as a premise, you can waste a great deal of time and money making an offer that everyone finds he or she can refuse. Testing media is simply not useful or even sensible until you are sure that your offer is an acceptable one. But it is necessary to review marketing briefly and be sure that we understand what that word *offer* means.

As the term is used here, an offer is the proposition you present to the prospect: the benefit you promise and the rationale you use to back up the promise. For example, when advertisements and sales literature for my newsletter, *Government Marketing News*, promised to bring prospects valuable marketing news because it came directly from the seat of government in Washington, D.C., a great many prospects yawned and turned their attention to something else. But when the literature promised to help prospects win government contracts by sharing the publisher's knowledge of how to write the winning proposals, they stopped yawning and began writing checks for subscriptions.

Note that the offer is the benefit promised—what you say you will *do* for the prospect—and the rationale or simple explanation of how you will do this. There is a great deal more to the presentation you make, of course, but if you fail to capture attention and arouse interest with the promise and follow that immediately with some rationale that at least initially appears plausible, the rest will not count: You will have lost the prospect already.

The rationale required depends on how extravagant the promise is. The more wondrous the benefit you promise, the more difficult it will be for the prospect to accept it at face value, hence, the more plausible the rationale must be.

Had I been smart enough to test my offer first, I would have saved a good bit of time and money because the difference in appeal between and results produced by the two offers was dramatic and apparent immediately upon testing of the final offer. (Actually, there had been several others tested between the two extremes cited here.) In fact, it took only a very small test mailing of 300 pieces to demonstrate the difference. The best mailing lists in the world would not have produced the degree of change in response that a different offer did.

Be sure that your offer explains to the prospect what the benefit is to be and provide at least some rationale for it—a logical argument, your personal credentials as an expert, citation of some outstanding success, or whatever you can produce that is plausible and persuasive.

You may have to test several offers to find the best one. And you may want to test different offers in some single medium, or you may want to try them out in all media. You can use the same forms as those shown, adapted for the purpose. That is, simply key (code) each offer and use it as a title for the table, printing it above the table.

Testing the Copy

Don't confuse the offer with the copy. They are not the same thing at all. The copy is the presentation of the offer—the headline, type, layout, illustration, and/or language. In fact, you might use a humorous approach in the copy or a deadly serious one, appeal to greed or fear, use a scare headline or modest one, employ lengthy copy or short copy, adopt a folksy tone or a pedantic one, or any of many other possible styles and approaches. The copy may also use any of many kinds of persuasive tactics, depending on circumstances. When Joe Karbo ran his highly successful "Lazy Man's Easy Way to Riches" campaign with full-page advertisements, he invented a new device which has since been widely imitated by others: To "prove" that his claims of wealth achieved by his unique method were true, he had his accountant swear to the truth of his statements and presented that as a signed affidavit in a small box in the copy.

Of course, the copy has a great deal to do with the success of the campaign, and many campaigns owe their success more to the quality of the copy than to any other factor. But there are exceptions; in most cases, the order of importance of the four items cited here (bearing in mind the definitions used here) is probably this: The offer, The medium, The timing, and then the copy.

The first two items are critical. Unless both are "right," the campaign will not do as well as it should and is likely to flounder or even founder. A strong offer with acceptably effective media is likely to succeed, even with some weaknesses of copy and timing, but the reverse is rarely true. Hence, my firm conviction that the major share of attention should be given to the structuring of the offer and tests to find the best media for presentation of the offer to the right prospects. Of course, if it has not been apparent before, the main objective in testing media and timing is to determine whether the appeal is reaching the desired prospects, for that is an absolute necessity. Some mailers tend to evaluate the quality of mailing lists by how up-to-date they are and how free of nixies—bad addresses—they are, but that is secondary, although not insignificant, because it does affect results. However, the first consideration is or should be the quality of the mailing list with respect to how accurately it is what it is represented to be (e.g. a list of professional engineers, of bank presidents, of book buyers, and so forth). It is impossible to gauge the effectiveness of anything else if the offer is not being made to the right prospects.

Chapter 13

Sources and Support Services

> Resources to turn to for necessary services, and support from individuals and organizations, are abundantly available.

There is no shortage of organizations and services available to help you do those things suggested to you in these pages. Quite the contrary, your problem will more often be which support service to select than how to find a suitable one. A number of such services are listed in the following pages, but these are merely representative; there are many, many more in existence.

THE NEWSLETTER ASSOCIATION

Although many of the useful services you can buy are obvious ones—like printing—many others are less so. There is today, for example, an association of newsletter publishers that holds meetings and annual conferences where you can meet other newsletter publishers, many experts in the field, and vendors of a wide variety of services. Of course, you can gather a great deal of valuable information and relevant materials, too, at this conference.

In fact, the conference is an international one, with conferees from other countries gathering for a full five days of lectures, discussions, demonstrations, exhibits, and other events of interest. As an example, here are some of the seminar and workshop titles for the 1985 conference in Washington, D.C.: raising capital; strategic planning; electronic publishing; how to increase renewals; postal rates; making PR help sell newsletters information from the government; alternative ways to market; creating direct-mail packages; and strategic planning.

Although it is an international association, there are local chapters you may join to participate in year-round activities. And membership brings you the association's guidebook to newsletter publishing, their own newsletter, group insurance, and other benefits. For more detailed information, write or call the national headquarters:

The Newsletter Association
1341 G Street, NW, Suite 700
Washington, DC 20005
(202) 347–5220

PERTINENT PERIODICALS

The *DM News*, which calls itself "The Newspaper of Direct Marketing," is a most useful weekly publication of interest to everyone in any kind of direct-response marketing, although the newspaper focuses primarily on direct mail and is heavy with advertising by prominent mailing-list brokers. Each issue presents news items and feature stories about happenings in the industry. Here, to illustrate the coverage, are a few story captions from a recent issue:

American, European Interests Try Telex as Int'l DM Medium

Toll-Free Service Pulls 10,000 Orders from Authors' Appearances on TV

Weather May Affect Response for Some Direct Marketing Firms

Doctors Who Advertise Now Have a Newsletter

Database Tips From Great Britain

How to Get Precise Printing Quotations

The publication is a controlled-circulation trade periodical, which means that it is distributed free of charge to those qualifying for free subscriptions, in this case, anyone legitimately in the direct-marketing field. The address given for applying is:

Circulation Department
DM News
19 West 21st Street
New York, NY 10010

Meetings & Conventions, also one of those controlled-circulation periodicals, is a slick-paper monthly guide to hotels, resorts, cruise ships, and other establishments that offer facilities for meetings and other such convocations. It also gives attention to airlines, is quite heavy with advertising every month, and publishes an extra-thick directory issue periodically. The address is as follows:

News Group Publications, Inc.
One Park Avenue
New York, NY 10016
(212) 503-5700

Meeting News, Facts, News, Ideas For Convention and Meeting Planners Everywhere is a monthly tabloid publication (but on slick paper, not newsprint) offering news, features, ideas, methods, and other helpful coverage of the industry. The coverage is national, but there are special issues covering Florida, Colorado, Texas, and California. It has also published special issues with extensive directories of services and service organizations useful to meeting planners, such as speakers bureaus and agents, convention managers, suppliers, and other such necessary support. The publisher's address is:

Gralla Publications
1515 Broadway
New York, NY 10010
(212) 869-1300

Meeting Planners' News, New York/New England is also a monthly tabloid publication covering the New York and New England areas only. The publisher's address follows:

McKenzie Communications, Inc.
96 N. Pleasant Street
Amherst, MA 01002
(413) 253-9441

The Newsletter on Newsletters is published twice monthly by Howard Penn Hudson, a well-known expert on newsletters and a founding force in the Newsletter Association. It is available from:

The Newsletter Clearinghouse
44 West Market Street
Rhinebeck, NY 12572
(914) 876-2081

Sharing Ideas Among Professional Speakers and Their Friends is a bimonthly periodical which is listed as a newsletter but is much more a magazine than a newsletter, running to as many as 40 pages and bound, with ample advertising, letters from readers, and many articles. The major audience is the professional speaker, but a great many of the readers are also writers, publishers, and consultants, so there is ample coverage of and material addressed to those interests. It is a chatty journal, as much an exchange among members of the relevant professions as a source of information. The publisher is the well-known Dottie Walters, herself a professional speaker, writer, and entrepreneur, as well as a publisher. Her address is as follows:

Sharing Ideas!
18825 Hicrest Road
P.O. Box 1120
Glendora, CA 91740
(818) 335–8069

The Inkling Literary Journal is a monthly publication that is also more a magazine than a newsletter, addressed to writers primarily and carrying articles and market news of interest to writers. The address of its publisher is as follows:

The Inkling Literary Journal
P.O. Box 128
Alexandria, MN 56308
(612) 762–2020

Writer's Digest is a venerable journal of freelance writers, serving us for a great many years. Virtually every freelance writer interested in writing for periodicals reads it each month for tips and news of markets for his or her work. This is the magazine in which to list your requirements if you wish to attract freelance contributions. If you explain just what you want and ask the editors to list your needs in their pages, you are certain to be offered a good many contributions for your own newsletter from freelance writers who read this journal. And "WD" also publishes an annual *Writer's Yearbook*, with many more market listings. The address follows:

Writer's Digest
9933 Alliance Road
Cincinnati, OH 45242
(513) 984–0717

SOURCES OF MAILING LISTS

There are a great many list brokers, and they are to be found throughout the United States, despite the fact that a great many of the leading list management firms are in New York City. The following list is representative and not a complete compilation by any means. But these are all active list brokers, and their addresses are current at this writing. They vary in size and nature. Most offer descriptive literature, even voluminous catalogs, describing their offerings, prices, and business arrangements in detail, and you can write or call them directly to request catalogs and other descriptive literature. The listing is in alphabetic order.

Advanced Management Systems, Inc.
9255 Sunset Boulevard, Penthouse
Los Angeles, CA 90069
(213) 858–1520

American List Counsel, Inc.
88 Orchard Road
Princeton, NJ 08540
(201) 874–4300
800–526–3973

Association for Computing Machinery
11 West 42nd Street
New York, NY 10036
(212) 869–7440

BFC Mailing Lists
1900 Quail Street
Newport Beach, CA 92660
(714) 467–1154

Boardroom Lists
330 West 42nd Street
New York, NY 10036
(212) 239–9000

Cahners Direct Marketing Service
1350 East Touhy Avenue
Des Plaines, IL 60018
(312) 635–8800

Compilers Plus
2 Penn Place
Pelham Manor, NY 10803
(914) 738–1520
800–431–2914

Dependable List Management
33 Irving Place, NY 10003
(212) 677–6760
1825 K Street, NW

Washington, DC 20006
(202) 452–1092
333 N. Michigan Avenue
Chicago, IL 60601
(312) 263–3566

Direct Media List Management Group, Inc.
70 Riverdale Avenue
Greenwich, CT 06830
(203) 531–1091

D-J Associates
Box 2048
445 Main Street
Ridgefield, CT 06877
(203) 431–0452

Ed Burnett Consultants, Inc.
2 Park Avenue
New York, NY 10016
(212) 679–0630
800–223–7777

Hayden Direct Marketing Services
10 Mulholland Drive
Hasbrouck Heights, NJ 07604
(201) 393–6384

ICO List Rental Services
9000 Keystone Crossing
P.O. Box 40946
Indianapolis, IN 46240
(317) 844–7461

The Kleid Company, Inc.
200 Park Avenue
New York, NY 10166
(212) 599–4140

List Services Corporation
890 Ethan Allen Hwy
P.O. Box 2014
Ridgefield, CT 06877
(203) 436–0327

Phillips List Management
7315 Wisconsin Avenue, Suite 1200N
Bethesda, MD 20814
(301) 986–0666

PCS Mailing List Company
125 Main Street
Peabody, MA 01960
(617) 532–1600

Qualified Lists Corp.
135 Bedford Road
Armonk, NY 10504
(212) 409–6200
(914) 273–6700

Roman Managed Lists, Inc.
101 West 31st Street
New York, NY 10001
(212) 695–3838
800–223–2195

Steve Millard, Inc.
Spring Hill Road
Peterborough, NH 03458
(603) 924–9421

Woodruff-Stevens & Associates, Inc.
345 Park Avenue South
New York, NY 10010
(212) 685–4600

ADVERTISING SERVICES

There are many firms who do all the work for you, after you have prepared your copy. Many specialize in mailing out postcard-sized advertising cards, some in the form of booklets, perforated so that the cards may be removed easily, but more popularly today simply as decks of cards encased in transparent plastic envelopes. You can have your advertising card arranged to require a postage stamp or as a prepaid card (you will pay the postage when the mail carrier delivers it). There are also some telemarketing services, firms who will telephone prospects with a sales message for you, often via computerized automatic-dialing mechanisms. And there are firms who do any kind of mailing you wish and even handle the fulfillment of orders for you. And many of these are also list managers and list brokers.

Services offered and business arrangements vary somewhat. Most charge for their services on some kind of fixed rate, such as cost per 1,000 cards. However, there are also firms who will mail cards for you, using their own return address so that the responses (inquiries or orders) come to them. They then forward the responses to you and bill you at some fixed price per response.

Here are a few such firms, with appropriate notations, again in alphabetical order:

DialAmerica Marketing, Inc.
125 Galway Place
Teaneck, NJ 07666
(201) 837–7800
  Telemarketing

Fala Direct Marketing, Inc.
70 Marcus Drive
Melville, NY 11747
(516) 694–1919
  Mailing, fulfillment, printing, data processing, telemarketing

Hahn, Crane, Inc., Advertising
114 West Illinois
Chicago, IL 60610
(312) 787–8435
  Advertising, consulting

Hughes Communications, Inc.
211 West State Street
P.O. Box 197
Rockford, IL 61105
(815) 963–7771 or 800–435–2937
  Card deck mailings

Mar-Tel Communications, Inc.
375 S. Washington Avenue
Bergen, NJ 07621
(201) 385–7171
  Telemarketing

Progressive Marketing Services
3649 W. 183rd Street
Hazel Crest, Il 60429
(312) 957–5200
  Telemarketing

Solar Press
5 South 550 Frontenac
Naperville, IL 60566
(312) 357–0100
  Card deck mailings

Tele America, Inc.
1955 Raymond Drive, Suite 112

Northbrook, IL 60062
(312) 480–1560
  Telemarketing

WorldBook Telemarketing
799 Roosevelt Road, #3
Glen Ellyn, IL 60137
(312) 858–4703

NATIONAL NETWORKS AND SERVICES

A list of those public data bases and information services referred to earlier is offered here, along with a brief idea of the kinds of information and services offered. (Write or call the firms for more details.) Again, this is not represented to be a complete list, nor is there any significance to the order in which the services are listed: They are alphabetical.

ADP Network Services, Inc.
175 Jackson Plaza
Ann Arbor, MI 48106
(313) 769–6800
  Business information—forecasts and projections; data processing services

Boeing Computer Services, Inc.
7990 Gallows Court
Vienna, VA 22180
(703) 827–4603
  Economic and financial data (securities/stock-market) quotations

Bolt Beranek and Newman, Inc.
50 Moulton Street
Cambridge, MA 02238
(617) 497–3505
  Timesharing, electronic mail, mathematical and statistical library, text processing services

Brodart Co.
500 Arch Street
Williamsport, PA 17705
800–233–8467
800–692–6211 (in PA)
  Data base, library support services, references over 1 million monographs, book orders can be placed online

Broker Services, Inc.
8745 E. Orchard Rd., #518

Englewood, CO 80111
(303) 779–8930
Over 100 stock-analysis/investment programs

BRS/Bibliographic Retrieval Services & BRS After Dark
1200 Route 7
Latham, NY 12110
(518) 783–1161
800–833–4707
Over 80 data bases in medicine, education, engineering, science, business, financial areas

BRS/Executive Information Service
John Wiley & Sons, Inc.
One Wiley Drive
Somerset, NJ 08873
(201) 469–4400
Summaries of recent major business articles from 600 periodicals; abstracts of other business articles/information

Chase Econometrics/Interactive Data
486 Totten Pond Road
Waltham, MA 02154
(617) 890–1234
Historical data and forecasts, all countries, all U.S. counties on labor, energy, savings, insurance, related topics

Chemical Abstracts Service
2540 Olentangy River Road
POB 3012
Columbus, OH 43210
(614) 421–3600
Online search service; accesses Registry File of structural information of over 6 million substances, related data

Citishare Corporation
850 Third Avenue
New York, NY 10043
(212) 572–9600
Computer support, economic-financial-securities data bases, stock quotations, other financial data and services

Commodity Information Services
327 S. LaSalle, Suite 800
Chicago, IL 60604
(312) 922–3661
Financial, agricultural, other futures, updated daily, library of programs for analysis, trading models

CompuServe
5000 Arlington Centre Blvd
Columbus, OH 43220
(614) 457–8600
800–848–8990
Data and various services for general consumer—news, stock market reports, schedules, banking and travel services, electronic mail, games, business news, other data, services

The Computer Company
POB 6987
1905 Westmoreland Street
Richmond, VA 23230
(804) 358–2171
Timesharing, access to various business data bases in banking, energy, and transportation industries

Computer Directions Advisors, Inc.
11501 Georgia Avenue
Silver Spring, MD 20902
(301) 942–1700
Profiles of 6,000 + companies, updated daily as filed with SEC; covers institutions, other organizations

Comshare, Inc.
3001 S. State Street
Ann Arbor, MI 48104
(313) 994–4800
Decision support systems for financial planning, marketing, personnel applications. Also demographic data

Connexions
55 Wheeler Street
Cambridge, MA 02138
(617) 938–9307
Employment positions online; online resume services; electronic mail

Control Data Corp.
Business Information Services
500 West Putnam Avenue
POB 7100
Greenwich, CT 06836
(203) 622–2000
Marketing, financial, other busiess data bases on variety of business topics; profiles of companies, industries, consumers, markets

Cornell Computer Services
G–02 Uris Hall

Ithaca, NY 14853

(607) 256–4981

Data base featuring 1,000 time series on various economic factors, including car sales, consumer buying, and forecasts, financial indicators, and help-wanted advertising

Customer Service Bureau

Box 36

Riverton, WY 82501

800–446–6255

800–442–0982 (in WY)

A network that offers subscribers gateways (access) to a variety of other networks and data bases

Data Resources, Inc.

1750 K Street, 9th floor

Washington, DC 20006

(202) 862–3700

Business and investment data, data on various companies, business patterns, and financial information

Delphi

3 Blackstone Street

Cambridge, MA 02139

(617) 491–3393

800–544–4005

Data bases on travel, finances, stock quotes, investments, commodities, and securites; also online brokerage games, conferencing services, that permits buying and selling via online connection

Dialog Information Services, Inc.

3460 Hillview Avenue

Palo Alto, CA 94304

800–227–1927

(415) 858–3785

Contains hundreds of data bases, including CBD Online, business, advertising, economics, politics, government, medicine, other topics

Dow Jones News/Retrieval Service

POB 300

Princeton, NJ 08540

800–257–5114

27 data bases business/economic and financial/investment services

Dun & Bradstreet Corporation

299 Park Avenue

New York, NY 10171

(212) 593–6800

Timesharing and such business services/information as D&B is already well known for

General Electric Information Services Co.
401 N. Washington Street
Rockville, MD 20850
(301) 340–4000
Teleprocessing and data processing services, access in 700 cities and 20 countries, hundreds of software programs available

GTE Telenet
8229 Boone Blvd
Vienna, VA 22180
1–800-TELENET
Electronic mail, intercomputer communincation/network service, medical, pharmaceutical, clinical practice information; stock quotes

GML Information Services
594 Marrett Road
Lexington, MA 02173
(617) 861–0515
Technical data bases on computers and related technologies

InnerLine
95 W. Algonquin Road
Arlington Heights, Il 60005
800–323–1321
News and other information for bankers: banking news, money market funds, related data bases

Interactive Market Systems, Inc.
19 West 44th Street
New York, NY 10036
(212) 869–8810
800–223–7942
Access to media and marketing-related services, timesharing services, legal-research services

ITT Dialcom, Inc.
1109 Spring Street
Silver Spring, MD 20910
(301) 588–1572
Data bases for *Fortune* 100 companies, government agencies, other large organizations; electronic mail, airlines schedules, other

Mead Data Central
POB 933

Dayton, OH 45401

(513) 865–6800

LEXIS for legal research; LEXPAT for patent information; NEXIS for general news service

NewsNet
945 Haverford Road
Bryn Mawr, PA 19010
(215) 527–8030 (in PA)
800–345–1301

Business information utility distributing variety of online business newletters and wire services and providing search services

The Source
1616 Anderson Road
McLean, VA 22102
800–336–3366

One of the, if not the, oldest online data base services for general consumers: news; schedules, TV listings, stock quotes, etc.

TRW Information Services Div.
Business Credit Services and Credit Data Service
500 City Parkway West, Suite 200
Orange, CA 92668
(714) 937–2000

Provides both business and individual consumer credit as names reveal, plus related business information

United Communications Group
4550 Montgomery Avenue, Suite 700N
Bethesda, MD 20814
(301) 656–6666

CBD On-Line (government contract bids and proposals), other general data

Westlaw
West Publishing Co.
50 West Kellog Blvd
POB 43526
St. Paul, MN 55164
800–328–9352

Legal research and related information, plus news and index coverage of several financial and general newspapers

Chapter 14

Specifications and Planning Worksheets

> Plans should be sufficiently detailed so that they are actually specifications, if you are to move decisively and firmly when you are ready to begin.

WHY SPECIFICATIONS?

Earlier (in Chapter 8) checklists were provided to help you make some preliminary decisions for seminars and newsletters. In fact, those worksheets were also designed to help you perceive the choices and alternatives available. In this chapter you will get help in going a large step beyond checking off items and begin drafting actual specifications—converting and adding to those checklists to provide the specific details. Then, when you want to make arrangements with a hotel manager for a meeting room, or with a printer for producing your newsletter, or with a list broker for ordering mailing lists or for any of the myriad other such matters you will have to make decisions about, you can virtually read out a list of specifications from your worksheet or hand over a copy of the worksheet, which represents your specifications. Thus you will not have to lose time pondering the alternatives later, when you wish to actually get started.

Most of these matters and arrangements are relatively simple, but it is quite dismaying to learn only at the last minute that you should have provided for some things that simply take planning to arrange and cannot be done very well at the last minute. Even getting a blackboard provided at the last minute, when it was not specified in advance, has been a problem in at least one seminar in my own experience and represented a rather disruptive and disconcerting element in the seminar.

In fact, the reasons for going to this device of preparing actual written specifications are twofold: one, so that you can move on efficiently with your preparations when you are ready to begin, and not waste time puzzling over decisions then; and, two, so that you do not risk making the mistakes that are so easy to make when you are forced to make decisions spontaneously or hastily.

The first portion of this chapter will be devoted to helping you draft your specifications for seminars, with specific suggestions in many cases; and the second part will be given over to preparing specifications for your newsletter. (Some items, however, are common to both.)

These specifications are final, but only in the sense that they represent decisions for your first seminar or newsletter. They are not final in the sense that they are immutable; they can be changed if your experience suggests a need for change.

You need more than one set of specifications because you must deal with more than one person or entity, and the material is so organized.

SEMINAR SPECIFICATIONS

To produce and present your seminar, you need to make arrangements with a hotel (presumably you will use a hotel meeting room, as most seminar producers do). You may choose to do everything else personally, but if not, you will probably deal with suppliers of materials you will use, possibly with individuals to help you, and possibly with others, if the hotel does not handle some of your other needs, such as projection equipment. (Most do, but you may run into one that does not, or you may prefer to handle those arrangements yourself.) For that reason, the specifications are subdivided into groups.

ARRANGEMENTS WITH THE HOTEL

You need to make a number of decisions in advance to specify to the hotel what you want. But you should be aware that in a great many cases, while the hotel will state a flat rate for the kind of meeting need you specify, it is often possible to negotiate a better rate than the one quoted. However, do not select a rundown or third-rate hotel to save money. That is a false economy, for image is important. Try to make arrangements with good-quality hotels only.

One tactic that Howard Shenson reports is that of starting by asking for a somewhat smaller room than you expect to need, estimating 10 or 15 percent below your true expectation, and only then, after getting a quotation for a relatively small room, suggesting that perhaps you need a slightly larger room and exploring that possibility. That, Shenson reports, inhibits the hotel manager somewhat in quoting for the larger room, if you negotiate capably.

21.
Basic Specifications for Meeting Room

SPECIFICATIONS FOR SEMINAR

HOTEL:_____

SEATING STYLE: SIZE OF ROOM (seating capacity):

[ ] Theater   [ ] Classroom   [ ] 25-50   [ ] 50-100   [ ] _____

WHEN: LENGTH OF USE:

Date_____ Time_____   [ ] 2 hours   [ ] All day [ ] _____

[ ] Registration table   [ ] Literature table

[ ] Speaker's table   [ ] _____

EQUIPMENT AND FURNISHINGS:

[ ] Dais   [ ] Lectern   [ ] Overhead Projector   [ ] Slide Projector

[ ] Screen   [ ] Blackboard [ ] _____

[ ] Microphone - If checked: [ ] Podium   [ ] Hand-held   [ ] Lavalier

                             [ ] Cordless [ ] _____

AMENITIES:

[ ] Coffee & tea   [ ] Danish pastries   [ ] Cold drinks

[ ] Luncheon - If checked: [ ] Table service   [ ] Buffet

[ ] _____   [ ] _____

NOTES:_____
_____

Figure 21 displays a suggested format for recording your decisions. Some of the items are self-explanatory; others require discussion.

The Meeting Room

You need to consider the size of the room, the seating arrangement, and even the length of time you will need it for all together because there is a direct relationship among the items. For example, a room arranged in theater style—rows of chairs—will accommodate many more people per unit of area than will a room arranged in classroom style—seated at tables.

It's a good idea to have a full room, so aside from the economic question of paying for more space than you need, a partially filled room is psychologically disadvantageous, especially for a free seminar, at which you are selling something (figuratively, if not literally). Moreover, this is a factor of the length of time you will use the room. If you are going to hold your session for only an hour or so, it won't hurt to crowd attendees a bit by squeezing in a few more chairs, or even have a few standees. The psychological effect of being oversubscribed is a definite plus for you.

You will probably want a registration table, and this is best situated outside the meeting room so that late arrivals do not disrupt the presentation. Even if the session is a free one, you should ask attendees to stop at the registration table and print their names and addresses in the log book or fill out a registration form. (If the size of the attendance or some other factor makes this impractical, pass out registration forms at the start of the session. You need to gather those names and addresses.)

You may wish to have a literature table at the back of the room, or you may prefer to hand out a packet to each attendee. Each method has advantages and disadvantages.

Some seminars require a speaker's table, as well as a lectern. If there is to be a panel discussion, for example, with several speakers or commentators, you usually must seat them at a table and, if the room is a large one, on a dais. But some seminar presenters, even when working alone, prefer to work seated at a table before their audience or require a table to hold models or other demonstration items and presentation aids.

Equipment and Furnishings

The items listing equipment and furnishings are self-explanatory, for the most part. However, some of the items will probably not be furnished unless you specifically request them. The dais and lectern, for example, must usually be requested, and the microphone will usually be a podium type—fastened to the lectern—if you do not specify otherwise. (And it may not even be connected to a public address system, if not called for in advance. Personally, unless I am working in a very large room, I prefer to work without the microphone and amplifier, but that is entirely my personal choice, and due to the good fortune of a large chest and sound lungs.)

You cannot be sure that the hotel will be able to furnish the precise equipment you want, and you should verify all of this verbally when

making arrangements and then furnish a copy of your record to con-
firm the verbal agreements.

ARRANGEMENTS FOR ADVERTISING AND PROMOTION

Advertising and promotion includes deciding what media you will
use, how you will use them, preparing your copy, and placing the advertisements, broadcast commercials, and/or mailings. Figure 22 is a
generalized worksheet which provides opportunities to consider and
check off a variety of items related to ordering print and broadcast
advertising. As in the case of the earlier worksheet (Figure 21), you
develop this in conjunction with discussions and verbal agreements
with the media.

This works equally for all advertising and promotion, whether you
are advertising seminars or newsletters, of course, as will other aspects of implementing your plans for both.

You must furnish the copy for advertisements and commercials, and
in both cases you can prepare the copy completely, as camera-ready
or its equivalent for broadcasting purposes, or you can have it "pub
set," which means that you have the medium prepare the advertisement or commercial from your own draft. Of course, you pay for this
service, and a great many people who have advertisements pub set
are disappointed in the result. The only way to have complete control
is to do it yourself—to have it set yourself and provide camera-ready
copy of your advertisements to publications and audiotapes or videotapes to radio and TV stations for commercials. You will probably find
the results much more satisfying if you go to this trouble and attend
to these details yourself.

Of course, you can have typeset copy made up rather easily; there
are firms who can do this for you. And if you go to a graphic arts shop
to get help, they will prepare the entire piece of copy for you. On the
other hand, if you hire a freelance copywriter or consultant to do this
for you, you can probably have the consultant attend to this matter
for you.

There are also many audiovisual studios today who will make audiotapes and videotapes for you. Some have professional narrators on
staff, but all maintain rosters of such professionals who can be hired
to do the job. But you can do the narration yourself, if you prefer, and
the studio will give you adequate guidance, editing, and any other aid
or service you need to produce a good result. In my own case, the
professional narrators suggested that I do my own narrations, since

22.
Basic Specifications for Advertising

SPECIFICATIONS FOR ADVERTISEMENTS/COMMERCIALS

RADIO/TV SPOTS:

Station:_____ Length of spot(s):_____

Dates & Times: _____

Who furnishes tape:_____

Station:_____ Length of spot(s):_____

Dates & Times: _____

Who furnishes tape:_____

Station:_____ Length of spot(s):_____

Dates & Times: _____

Who furnishes tape:_____

PRINT MEDIA:

Publication: _____

Size and placement:_____

Dates of insertion:_____

Who sets:_____

Publication: _____

Size and placement:_____

Dates of insertion:_____

Who sets:_____

Publication: _____

Size and placement:_____

Dates of insertion:_____

Who sets:_____

NOTES:_____

---

my voice appeared adequate to the task. However, you can also often hire professional radio announcers, many of whom do narrations as moonlight ventures and who can arrange all the production support needed.

If you choose to set up your advertising agency to save the 15 percent commissions and 2 percent cash discount (for a total reduction of 16.7 percent of the advertising cost), you can use a form such as that of Figure 23. Of course, you must select a different name for your advertising agency, but rarely will you be challenged; you have as much right as anyone to be an advertising agency, even if you are yourself the only client.

You can use a similar form, with appropriate modifications, for buying radio or TV time, as suggested in Figure 24.

23.
Suggested Form for Insertion Order

EXCELSIOR ADVERTISING AGENCY

5763 South Main Street

Copper City, California 97000

INSERTION ORDER

TO: The Copper City Post   Order No. 456

    83 Oxide Avenue   Date: Jan 23/87

    Copper City, CA 97000   Advertiser: Ajax Consultants, Inc.

==

INSERTION DATE(S): Jan 28-30/87   NO. INSERTIONS: 3 Times

SPACE: 6 column-inches   RATE: $785

PLACEMENT: Financial pages   POSITION: Above the fold, RH page

SPECIAL INSTRUCTIONS: None

TOTAL SPACE COST: $2,355

15% AGENCY COMMISSION: $353.25

NET DUE: $2,001.75

NOTES: Camera-ready copy enclosed.

24.
Suggested Form for Buying Air Time

EXCELSIOR ADVERTISING AGENCY

5763 South Main Street

Copper City, California 97000

INSERTION ORDER

TO: WPDQ-TV   Order No. 456

    77 Sulphate Street   Date: Jan 23/87

    Copper City, CA 97000   Advertiser: Ajax Consultants, Inc.

===

INSERTION DATE(S): Jan 28-30/87   NO. TIMES: 3 daily (9 total)

RATE: $145   LENGTH: 45 seconds   TIMES OF DAY: Late night

SPECIAL INSTRUCTIONS: Breaks in late, late show (movie)

TOTAL COST: $1,305

15% AGENCY COMMISSION: $195.75

NET DUE: $1,109.25

NOTES: Videotape supplied

NEWSLETTER SPECIFICATIONS

The development of newsletter specifications is a somewhat different proposition, although it has some common factors with developing seminar specifications. Where the main arrangements for a seminar are usually with a hotel, the main arrangements for a newsletter are usually with a printer, although the tasks associated with layout and composition are considerable too. And because not every printer can handle these latter tasks for you, the instructions and help offered here will be based on the assumption that you will either do the latter work yourself or will make separate arrangements to have it done. However, all the data are included here on a single form (Figure 25) because it is all directly interrelated. Anyone who is involved in designing the newsletter, laying it out, and otherwise preparing it for the printer must know in advance what the printing specifications are to be. For example, if you want to have your newsletter printed in two

25.
Form for Specifying Newsletter

SPECIFICATIONS FOR NEWSLETTER

TITLE:_____

FREQUENCY: [ ] Occasional   [ ] Quarterly   [ ] Bimonthly   [ ] Monthly

FORMAT SIZE: [ ] 8-1/2 x 11   [ ] Tabloid   [ ] _____

NO. PAGES: [ ] 2   [ ] 4   [ ] _____

COMPOSITION, [ ] Typewriter   [ ] Typeset   [ ] 12 point [ ] 10 point

TYPE,   [ ] _____ point [ ] Roman   [ ] Gothic   [ ] _____

& LAYOUT   [ ] Single column [ ] Two column [ ] Justified

             [ ] Ragged right [ ] Self-mailer [ ] 3-hole drill

             [ ] Routing box   [ ] _____

EDITORIAL: [ ] Paid contributions   [ ] Guest pieces

             [ ] Q & A column [ ] Editorial [ ] Letters

             [ ] News items   [ ] Features   [ ] Service articles

GRAPHICS: [ ] Photos   [ ] Charts   [ ] Cartoons

             [ ] _____

PAPER: [ ] White offset 60 lb   [ ] Colored offset 60 lb _____

             [ ] _____

COLOR INK: [ ] Black only   [ ] Other color: _____

             [ ] Two-color: _____

PRESS RUN: [ ] 1,000   [ ] 5,000   [ ] _____

SPECIAL: [ ] 3-hole drill [ ] Fold to #10 envelope size

             [ ] Deliver ____ copies flat   [ ] _____

NOTES:_____

_____

or more different colors, the copy must be separated for color registration because there must be a separate plate for each color ink. This is a task accomplished normally in production by those who lay out the newsletter and prepare camera-ready copy. Some printers can do this for you, especially if the color separations are simple ones—doing headlines in a different color, for instance—but it is far better (and usually far less expensive) to have the copy all ready for color-separation negatives or plates when you present it to the printer.

It is easy enough to make up two copies of this form, one for layout and composition, the other for printing, and thus have the interrelated specifications on the same form. You are far less likely to have confusion and foul-ups then. And if you use a purchase order to buy your printing, you simply attach this form and cite it in the purchase order. This helps prevent another problem that sometimes occurs: errors in printing.

Errors in printing create an awkward situation. In most cases the error is such that it cannot be easily corrected, at least not in a practical sense because the cost of correction is often almost as great as the cost of doing the entire job over. And printed material that is in error is usually of zero value, even as scrap. Therefore, it is important that you make your wishes known to the printer as clearly as you possibly can. Discuss them with the printer and be sure that you understand each other. Use the blank spaces provided for anything not covered in the form.

Most of the items are self-explanatory or have been discussed earlier, but it is a good idea to discuss some of them, even if they have been discussed earlier, to be sure that you understand them thoroughly:

Composition, type, and layout: If you use an ordinary electric typewriter, your typeface is probably 10 or 12 point, although in typewriters it is referred to as pitch, with 10 pitch equal to 12 point (10 characters to the inch, measured horizontally), and 12 pitch equal to 10 point or 12 characters to the inch. (In older typewriters 10 point is elite type and 12 point is pica.)

If you use typesetting, rather than typewriter or word processor composition, you have a wide choice of typefaces, but they all fall into two general classes, serif and sans serif, with roman typefaces the most popular serif typefaces, probably, and gothic the most popular sans serif typefaces. If you do use formal typesetting, your compositor or consultant/writer, if you retain one, can help you decide what typeface to use.

On the other hand, if you have a word processor and a letter-quality printer, you can do a nice job of typesetting yourself, and you can do single- or double-column composition, boldface, and even some other

Chapter 15

Miscellaneous Tips and Ideas

Here's potpourri of relevant information gathered over the years.

CROPPING PHOTOS

Most published photographs have been cropped, either to eliminate irrelevant material in the picture or to select a single person from a group photo. It's really not very difficult to do; anyone can do it with just a bit of patience. The process is illustrated by Figure 26. The photograph is mounted on a stiff piece of art board, and the crop marks (the solid lines) are drawn on the art board. The dotted lines are imaginary extensions of the solid lines, and the area within those dotted lines is the area the publisher wants the printer to make a screened copy of for printing. (In some newspaper offices photos are cropped by drawing on the glossy photograph itself with a grease pencil, but that mars the photo and is a rather messy way to do it.)

You have to screen photographs, as already pointed out, to print them. And when a page includes both text and photographs, a composite plate and negative are needed. This requires that there be a line negative made of the text and a screened negative of the photograph, which are then combined to make what is called a "composite negative" in the trade. That is simply a negative that contains both line and halftone material to be made into a printing plate.

THE COMBINATION NEGATIVE

There are two ways to combine negatives to make a composite. The classical way is by "stripping" them or actually splicing them together. An easier way is by creating a window in the line negative

26.
How to Crop a Photo

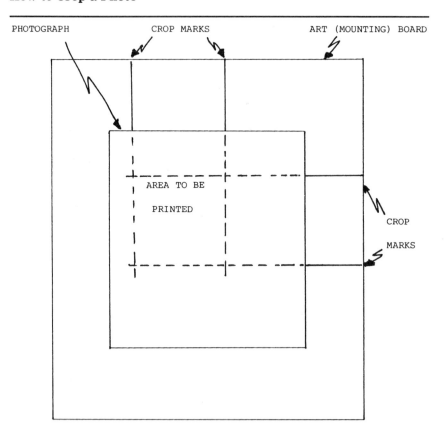

and mounting the screened negative so that the screened photograph can be seen through the window.

You can do this yourself, if you make up your own mechanicals or camera-ready copy by pasting down a "mask" in the area where the photograph is to be printed. This can be of black paper or a thin plastic film, a red material called "rubylith." Many makeup people prefer the rubylith to black paper because the camera sees red as "blacker than black."

When the page is photographed, the masked area appears as a transparent area in the negative and thus becomes a window through which the screened negative is visible. A composite negative can therefore be made without stripping the two together, which is far easier and faster.

MORTISING AND MAKEUP: VANISHING ARTS

Mortising has long been a classical publication production art—a way of making corrections to final copy by literally cutting out incorrect material and pasting corrections in. And making up two-column copy from typewritten material always required that typing be in the form of galleys, long strips of copy one column wide, which are cut to size and pasted up together on a form in two-column format. This, too, was an acquired skill that resulted from long practice.

The word processor is rapidly making these practices obsolete because it is easier to make all corrections on-screen and print out a corrected page than it is to splice or mortise corrections in. And it is far easier to compose two-column copy on-screen and print it out ready for the platemaker. (Actually, the copy is composed as galley on-screen and "pasted" up electronically in two-column format.)

It requires a certain amount of skill to do both these tasks—mortising and paste-up—which are skills acquired through long practice. It takes little skill to do this with a word processor, happily. Most people master the art after only a few tries to become familiar with it because the equipment does most of the work. All one needs to learn is the peculiarities of the system, for each word processor is different from all the others in some of its details.

Figure 27 illustrates how easily this is done. The foregoing paragraphs were copied from the original manuscript with the press of a few keys (ten keystrokes, to be exact), and then, with a few more keystrokes, made into single column, block text, right justified, and hyphenated, all automatically and spontaneously by the word processing program. And then with only a few more keystrokes, the copy was converted to two-column format. And it all was done in less time than it takes to describe it. It's a kind of electronic legerdemain, made possible by the speedy electron, which races around your computer/word-processor circuits almost as fast as light races across the universe. (And some word processors are reportedly even simpler to operate and faster than the WordStar word processor by which this was done.)

Even so, this is one of the simpler makeup and cut-and-paste chores. It is possible to carry out much more sophisticated composition tasks and special effects with a word processor, such as "run arounds," or irregular columns of type which run around an illustration or special box, such as those you see regularly in magazine and newspaper spreads.

Figure 28 illustrates the capability of word processors to do such things as run text around an illustration or to combine single-column and double-column text to run around an illustration.

27.
Electronic Cut and Paste and Other Word Processing Magic

MORTISING AND MAKEUP: VANISHING ARTS

Mortising has long been a classical publication production art, a way of making corrections to final copy by literally cutting out incorrect material and pasting corrections in. And making up two-column copy from typewritten material always required that typing be in the form of galleys, long strips of copy one column wide, which are cut to size and pasted up together.

The word processor is obsoleting these practices rapidly because it is easier to make all corrections on-screen and print out a corrected page than it is to splice or mortise corrections in. And it is far easier to compose two-column copy on-screen and print it out ready for the platemaker. (Actually, the copy is composed as galley on-screen and "pasted" up electronically in two-column format.)

It required a certain amount of skill to do these tasks, skill acquired through long practice. It takes little skill to do this with a word processor, happily. Most people master the art with only a few tries to become familiar with it because the equipment does most of the work. All one needs to learn is the peculiarities of the system, for each word processor is different from all the others in some of its details.

MORTISING AND MAKEUP: VANISHING ARTS

Mortising has long been a classical publication production art, a way of making corrections to final copy by literally cutting out incorrect material and pasting corrections in. And making up two-column copy from typewritten material always required that typing be in the form of galleys, long strips of copy one column wide, which are cut to size and pasted up together.

The word processor is obsoleting these practices rapidly because it is easier to make all corrections on-screen and print out a corrected page than it is to splice or mortise corrections in. And it is far easier to compose two-column copy on-screen and print it out ready for the platemaker. (Actually, the copy is composed as galley on-screen and "pasted" up electronically in two-column format.)

It required a certain amount of skill to do these tasks, skill acquired through long practice. It takes little skill to do this with a word processor, happily. Most people master the art with only a few tries to become familiar with it because the equipment does most of the work. All one needs to learn is the peculiarities of the system, for each word processor is different from all others in some of its details.

28.
Two Examples of Word Processing Run-Around in Text Composition

MORTISING AND MAKEUP: VANISHING ARTS

Mortising has long been a classical publication production art, a way of making corrections to final copy by literally cutting out incorrect material and pasting corrections in. And making up two-column copy from typewritten material always required that typing be in the form of galleys, long strips of copy one column wide, which are cut to size and pasted up together.

The word processor is obsoleting these practices rapidly because it is easier to make all corrections on-screen and print out a corrected page than it is to splice or mortise corrections in. And it is far easier to compose two-column copy on-screen and print it out ready for the platemaker. (Actually, the copy is composed as galley on-screen and "pasted" up electronically in two-column format.)

It required a certain amount of skill to do these tasks, skill acquired through long practice. It takes little skill to do this with a word processor, happily. Most people master the art with only a few tries to become familiar with it because the equipment does most of the work. All one needs to learn is the peculiarities of the system, for each word processor is different from all the others in some of its details.

MORTISING AND MAKEUP: VANISHING ARTS

Mortising has long been a classical publication production art, a way of making corrections to final copy by literally cutting out incorrect material and pasting corrections in. And making up two-column copy from typewritten material always required that typing be in the form of galleys, long strips of copy one column wide, which are cut to size and pasted up together.

The word processor is obsoleting these practices rapidly because it is easier to make all corrections on-screen and print out a corrected page than it is to splice or mortise corrections in. And it is far easier to compose two-column copy on-screen and print it out ready for the platemaker. (Actually, the copy is composed as galley on-screen and "pasted" up electronically in two-column format.)

It required a certain amount of skill to do these tasks, skill acquired through long practice. It takes little skill to do this with a word processor, happily. Most people master the art with only a few tries to become familiar with it because the equipment does most of the work. All one needs to learn is the peculiarities of the system, for each word processor is different from all the others in some of its details.

These are just a few simple examples of some of the things you can do to make your newsletter typographically pleasing with imaginative layouts. But the biggest advantage of the word processor is that you can experiment and you can afford to make mistakes because it is so easy to do things over. In fact, in making up this latter example I did some experimenting and managed to fumble twice, but I simply erased it all and made a fresh copy of the original each time. It took only a few minutes, in any case, even with three tries before I got it right.

A FEW TIPS ON WRITING

A great many books have been written on how to write well, and a great many more will be written, no doubt. Most explore the mechanics of usage—grammar, punctuation, rhetoric, imagery, and that nebulous subject called composition—in some depth, many suggest exercises, and many offer a variety of cliches as advice, possibly the worst of which is to write the way you speak.

That is meant to make the point that as a writer you should avoid purple prose and all other forms of verbal pomposity and circumlocution. Instead, make your point as clearly and simply as possible.

The intention is sound; the advice is not. Most of us do not speak with the precision and attention to proper grammatical forms that we must use when we write formally.

Another well-intentioned but not really valid advice is to keep sentences short and use short words. In a few moments you will see what is wrong with that particular species of advice so commonly urged on those who want to learn how to write more effectively.

There is neither space nor justification here to present a complete text on the art of writing well, and no effort will be made to do so. However, a few simple tips to help you to prepare professional copy for your newsletter and seminar presentations are not amiss here. Therefore, here are a few basic dos and don'ts of writing generally and of news writing especially, followed by a brief discussion where necessary to expand on the points:

- Use the journalistic pyramid style (as explained earlier).
- Avoid hyperbole.
- Minimize use of adjectives and adverbs, especially general and abstract ones.
- Maximize use of nouns and verbs.
- Use words, examples, and analogies that are familiar to most people.
- Be sure that you link sentences and paragraphs logically, so that each one prepares the reader or listener for the next one, and each is a natural, logical outgrowth of the one that went before it.
- Always edit your own copy and revise at least once.

It is always important in writing, whether you are writing a news-letter, a magazine article, a book, a speech, or anything else, to be *credible*. If you are not persuasive in what you say—if your reader/listener finds what you say logically unconvincing or of doubt-ful veracity—you are wasting your time and your reader's or lis-tener's time. Hence, the hazard in hyperbole—that "million" times you refer to, when you really mean a few dozen times, for example. If you said "over seventy" times, no one would challenge or doubt because that is a *believable* number. "Millions" is not.

It is for that reason that maximizing the use of nouns and verbs, and using the most specific and most concrete nouns and verbs, makes you far more believable than does text loaded with adverbs and adjec-tives.

Don't make abrupt shifts of subject. If you must go to a completely new subject, prepare your reader with a proper transition, either showing the relationship to what preceded the new material or with an introductory statement. This is largely art, and it is difficult to give you any rules or any tools for doing this, but if you are alert and watchful for this, you will soon make smooth transitions automati-cally.

Conscious effort to write short sentences and use short words often leads to two other problems. One is a dreadfully staccato and discon-certing style, resembling a child's primer. ("See Jack run.") The other is that it tends to distract the writer from the real problem this par-ticular advice is meant to address: purple, pompous prose.

Instead of focusing on keeping sentences and words short, focus on having only one central idea in a sentence and using words and im-agery familiar to us all. "The earth is an oblate spheroid" is a short sentence and has short words in it. But compare it with a longer sen-tence has somewhat longer words: "The earth is shaped somewhat like an orange, round but flattened at the ends." The problem is, of course, that "oblate" and "spheroid" are not very common words, but every-one knows what an orange looks like. (Semanticists refer to this as having a proper "referent" for the word and urge writers to use words for which readers have proper referents—a somewhat complex way of urging writers to use familiar words and familiar examples.)

If you must write lengthy sentences, learn to use stop punctua-tion—dashes, colons, and semicolons. This has the same effect as breaking the sentence into short sentences, but does not produce some of the ill effects of straining to write everything in short sentences. Unfortunately many of us do not know how and when to use these handy aids effectively, and a bit of study to learn how is likely to add greatly to your effectiveness as a writer.

Above all, do learn to edit and revise everything you write for pub-lication or presentation. Even the most gifted writers do not expect to do their best writing in their first drafts, and there is a great deal of truth and wisdom in the old writer's cliche that "all good writing is rewriting." The best writers rewrite several times, at least. That is at least partly why they are among the world's best writers.

TIPS ON PUBLIC SPEAKING

Despite the increasing incidence of public speaking, and the increasing need for many of us to mount the platform, many people would rather face a firing squad than face an audience. Even dynamic and aggressive executives who direct huge organizations and make major decisions daily sometimes fear standing before an assemblage of strangers to make even the simplest address. In fact, many well-known entertainers confess that they never get over their fear and always quail at the thought of going on stage or addressing a microphone. Fortunately, most people who speak publicly with any regularity eventually conquer this fear or at least get firm control over it.

Combating Fear

There are a number of measures that help even the neophyte speaker cope successfully with the fear, if not conquer it. And they are based on three principles or measures that many speakers who are new to the platform (and even many experienced veterans of the platform) find most helpful to understand and utilize: (1) Have a physical barrier between you and your audience; (2) Make yourself physically as comfortable as possible; and (3) Direct attention away from yourself.

Standing behind a lectern of some sort helps greatly because it does constitute a barrier, which is a protective shield psychologically. But it does more than that because it also adds to your physical comfort and it solves that problem for those uninitiated to the platform of what to do with your hands. Being seated, especially behind a table, is another way of accomplishing the same thing and is usually even more comfortable physically. Being a member of a panel seated at a table is again easier because you are not alone and you are not the sole focus of attention.

Using presentation aids—slides, transparencies, audiotapes, films, posters, models, and other such items—is also most helpful because it draws attention from you and focuses it on the presentation aid.

If you are nervous about making a seminar presentation yourself, then, at least be sure that you have a lectern and use as many presentation aids as possible.

Effective Presentation

Presentation aids help you greatly in making your points, and you should try to avoid making your seminars unbroken lectures. There are, in fact, at least two separate and distinct reasons for maximizing your use of such aids. One is, of course, that such aids help your audience understand what you are explaining. Visual aids are especially helpful: An audience ought to be able to use more than one of their senses, and abstractions are far less abstract when they are illustrated or explained by analogies that can be illustrated visually.

Forget about yourself and how you look or feel. Concentrate entirely on your audience and why they are seated there before you. Your job is to present information and to help everyone understand that information clearly. Look around and make eye contact. Some of the bad advice you may hear urges you to select some single individual as the one with whom to establish and make frequent eye contact. That would be a slight to everyone else. Do make eye contact, but make it with as many of your audience as possible, and keep moving on, maintaining eye contact with any single individual for only a minute or two, at most.

Use your hands. Make gestures, express ideas, feelings, and punctuation with your hands, eyes, face muscles, lips, and other physical body motions. But don't rehearse these gestures. Let them happen naturally, spontaneously, and they will if you are truly enthusiastic—a contagious characteristic that alone can help you become a platform success. Concern yourself only with your audience and why you are there—to serve their need. If you do that, you will not even be conscious of the gestures with which you dramatize and spice up your presentation, but your audience will love you.

This is, of course, true whether your seminars are free or attendees have paid a fee to sit in your audience, for even the free seminar exacts a fee from the audience: They must pay with their time and attention and, if at all possible, with the purchases you hope they will make. But you cannot command their time and attention unless you deliver something that is worth that price. And that is as true for the newsletter as it is for the seminar.

Glossary

We live in a world full of jargon—those special terms and idioms used within each profession and peculiar to that profession. In this case, we are dealing with the jargon of two worlds: the world of computer technologies and the world of publications and printing. Here are some of the most common of those terms—at least those which are current at the time of this writing, for they do change rapidly, especially in the dynamic computer industry. But even in publications and printing a great many new terms have evolved from the changes brought about by the effects of offset printing and by the many new office machines, including word processors. To make matters even worse, many terms have more than one meaning, depending on who is using the term and in what connection it is being used. There are several views on what the term *hacker* means, for example—and even a well-established and commonly used term such as *word processor* has two distinctly different meanings, referring to the computer itself and to the software program which does the word processing through the computer functions. But here, without further delay or equivocation, is a glossary of terms you are most likely to encounter and need to understand in the course of preparing and delivering seminars and newsletters to help you meet your marketing objectives.

address block/box: Block of white space reserved for name and address on self-mailer periodical.

alphanumeric: Adjective generally, referring to use of both letters and numerals, as in alphanumeric character set, alphanumeric codes, etc.

annotate: Practice of placing notes to explain or elaborate on text passages.

archive: Storage or backup copy of data; also verb.

automatic pagination: Word processor function of recognizing each new page and placing folio (page number) there, as ordered by program or your special command.

backup: "Insurance" copy on separate disk or tape.

baud, baud rate: In practical terms rate at which data bits are sent/received in bits per second; used especially with reference to communications via modem and telephone.

bidirectional (printing): Ability/action of printers to print in both directions.

bird-dog: To monitor, administer, and generally "stay on top" of all details of publications project, especially one with "short fuse" (pressing deadline).

bleed: Printing that runs to edge of page and bleeds off, usually a solid ink block or illustration; both noun and verb.

block: Section of text, treated as unit, for word-processing functions.

block move: Word-processor function of moving entire block of text.

blow-up: Photographic enlargement or enlarging process (both noun and verb).

boilerplate: Standard or stock information, which may be pasted up in more than one document, both physically and electronically.

boldface: Heavy typeface, available as separate font of most type families, available in many word processing programs as a special printer function.

buffer: Storage device, usually for temporary storage of data to free up computer, as in case of printer buffer, used to compensate for inability of printers to keep up with rate at which computer supplies data.

burn: Process of making metal printing plate from negative by exposing plate, through negative, to strong light in "plate burner"; also extended to refer to other ways in which printing plates are made.

byte: Group of digital bits processed as a group, currently eight bits, representing one alphanumeric character.

camera-ready: Any materials in final condition and ready to be photographed for platemaking; applied to assembled final copy, but also to any materials which are ready to be made up as part of pages, without preliminary processing; also referred to as camera copy.

cathode ray tube (CRT): Tube with screen for displaying data of all types with phosphorescent illumination; same type of tube, generally, as that used for television.

center head: Headline or caption that is centered, instead of starting flush left.

character: Individual letter, numeral, symbol, or diacritical mark; one byte in word processors.

chip: Functional electronic element consisting of entire circuit or set of circuits etched into tiny sliver or wafer of silicon.

coated paper: Paper made with coatings, such as clay, to make it dense and extra smooth, so as to present sharp, well-defined printing.

cold type: Type set by strike-on (impact) or photo-typesetting methods; nonmetal type.

color registration: Process of aligning plates to print different colors in correct positions or registration with each other.

color separation: Process of preparing camera-ready copy for printing in more than one color by providing separate copy for each color ink.

composite negative: Negative that includes both line and screened material, either spliced together or mounted together on goldenrod with a "window" in one.

comprehensive: Short form of comprehensive layout, a detailed diagram of precisely where each bit of copy and other elements will fit in final mechanical.

contributor: A freelancer who sells original material to a publication.

copy: Material for publication; generally applies to text material, although sometimes meaning is extended to cover other material, which may be rough (unedited draft), or final (edited/revised) draft, or camera-ready material.

copy fitting: Process of making copy fit space by various means, such as finding enough space for it or cutting/trimming it to fit.

crash: Refers to loss of data, collapse of program, power failure, other such disaster; similar in meaning to older term *dump,* which also referred to loss of data.

crop marks: Marks on board bearing mounted photograph to show photographer/platemaker which portion of print is to be printed and which to be omitted or cropped out.

cropping: Marking photo or other illustration to show printer which portion is to be printed.

cursor: Symbol on screen, showing where next action will take place or, conversely, moved by operator to direct computer program to site of next action.

cps: Characters per second, measure of rate at which printer operates.

daisywheel: Printing element used in many letter-quality printers.

data base: Bank of related information.

data base manager: Computer program used to manage, manipulate, process filed/stored data.

disk: Metal or plastic disk coated with magnetic oxide and serving as storage medium. *See also* floppy.

dele: Mark, comment to order deletion.

dot matrix: Method of printing wherein characters are formed by series of dots.

download: Receive files from another computer via modem and telephone connection.

dropout: Tendency of some copy to fade in photography or platemaking, especially large areas of solid blacks and fine details. Applies also to dropout of light blue, seen by camera as white and used deliberately for the purpose.

dummy: Mock-up of final product, used for study and evaluation or to guide someone, as in printer's dummy (*see* printer's dummy).

editor, text editor: Portion of word-processor program responsible for entering, correcting, manipulating text.

em, em dash: An em is the width of the capital M of any type font, and an em dash is of the same width. For typewriters and most printers, use a double hyphen for em dash.

en: One-half an em.

ENTER/RETURN: Both are used to enter commands and, usually, to start a new paragraph.

file: Set of related records in storage or in work, identified by unique name; may be of any size, at operator's choice.

floppy: Colloquial for floppy disk or diskette, a flexible plastic disk, encased in a paper sleeve, 3, 3 ½, 5-¼, or 8 inches in diameter, used to store data on its magnetic coating.

folio: Page number; also report or other brief document.

follow copy: Editorial instruction to reproduce copy exactly as shown, despite apparent misspellings or other errors.

font: Entire set of type characters, including numerals and symbols. Sometimes applied to entire type family, which includes other fonts, such as italics, boldface, small capitals, and special symbols.

foot, footing: Special copy appearing at bottom of page, such as running foot, a notice, title, or slogan appearing at foot of each page.

form: Paper form used to facilitate paste-up and layout. Usually represents a single page or two-page spread. Completed form is then camera-ready—mechanical—final copy, ready for platemaking. Term is linear descendant of metal-type days, when form was literally a metal frame to hold type.

format: Design of publication, including type style, layout, other characteristics.

formatter: Portion of word processor that permits operator to organize/reorganize copy for printer or other output peripheral device and/or issue instruction to the output device.

global search [and replace]: Refers to ability of word processors to find any/all references/uses of a word or term and, if ordered, to replace that word/term with another.

goldenrod: Yellow paper used in print shops for mounting negatives for making metal plates.

graphics: Drawings, other illustrations (although printing is itself one of the graphic arts); in word processing refers to ability of computer systems and programs to generate drawings of many kinds.

gutter: White space between columns of type in two- or three-column copy (inside margins between pages in single-column copy).

halftone: Photograph or other continuous-tone material converted to dot pattern for printing; also applied to screen used to convert copy to dot or halftone pattern and to resulting negative and plate.

hard copy: Printed copy, as distinct from screen display or soft copy.

head, heading: Abbreviation for headline as in sidehead and center head. Also title, notice, slogan appearing at top of page, as in running head (when it appears on every page).

headnote: Note appearing at top of page, usually used only with tabular data.

imprinting: Printing over surface already printed or printing in space reserved for purpose during prior printing. *See also* overprinting and surprinting.

indicia, mailing: Printed block on envelope, wrapper, or mailing label which carries permit number for bulk mailing and serves as notice of postage paid.

insert: Editorial meaning: copy to be added by insertion in text (done electronically in word processors); in direct mail: items added to basic letter in direct-mail package.

justification: Condition of left- or right-hand edges of lines or both sides in alignment, resulting in absolutely even margins; generally accomplished by adjusting spacing between words, letters, or both. Most word processors can justify automatically. Also called right justification and justified right because left justification is taken for granted.

kerning: Refers to word-processor capability of tightening spaces between characters to justify, condense type, or for other purposes.

kilobyte (Kb): 1024 bytes; each byte equals one alphanumeric character; standard page of double-spaced typed copy equals approximately 2Kb or (more commonly) 2K.

layout: Plan for organizing copy and illustrations; actual design sketch or plan for doing so; design itself; can be preliminary (rough layout) or final (comprehensive layout).

line copy: Any copy that does not require halftone screening; usually includes all text, tables, and line drawings, such as graphs, charts, and engineering sketches.

line drawing: Drawing that consists of lines and other black-and-white contrast, without shades between the two. *See also* tone.

line negative: Negative of line copy.

logo: Abbreviation for logotype, a distinctive symbol, stylized letter or word, or other unique designation of identity; usually a registered trademark.

mail merge: File-merging capability which enables operator to combine contents of files in printout, such as automatically printing form letter from one file with names and addresses (mailing list) from another file.

make-ready: Installation of printing plate and adjustment of press to begin printing; a specific task charged by most printers as a separate item.

make-up: Assembling and preparing all camera-ready material to create the mechanicals from which printing will be done.

mask: Rectangle of black or red paper or plastic pasted on camera-ready copy where photo will appear to create window in negative for making composite negative.

masthead: Column of type, in most periodicals, listing ownership and key editorial staff.

mechanical: Complete final page or multi-page spread ready for platemaking and printing.

memory: Internal circuits of computer that store information, generally on a temporary basis, usually known as RAM (random access memory) in small computers.

modem: Term derived from *mo*dulator-*dem*odulator, a device that enables computers to communicate (transfer data) over telephone lines.

monitor: Usually refers to soft copy or soft display, represented by CRT (cathode ray tube) screen, liquid crystal display, or other such presentation, as distinct from hard copy printed output.

mortise: Practice of making corrections to camera-ready copy by actually cutting defective material out and replacing it with correction copy—splicing the correction copy in; also called splicing; also used to combine screened negative with line negative to form composite negative, in which case it is called stripping.

nameplate: Headline/title block of newsletter, other periodical, usually at top of front page.

offset: Colloquialism for modern offset printing processes and related items, such as offset plates, offset presses, offset paper; also refers to undesired transfer of ink from freshly printed surface to other surface, such as back of another sheet.

online: Refers to data base/information services available via modem-telephone connection and communication and to communication process itself.

overprinting: Printing one character on top of another; printing on top of already printed surface; *see also* surprinting and imprinting; also used to create special characters not available in type font.

page display: Word processing term for displaying entire page on screen or for showing where page begins and ends to help operator fit copy.

paste-up: Act of pasting up copy, as prescibed by comprehensive; copy that has been pasted up.

photocomposition: Copy composed by photo-typesetting.

photo-direct: Platemaking by xerographic and other devices that create printing plates (usually paper or plastic, rather than metal) without the intermediate stage of a negative.

pitch: Number of characters and spaces per linear inch—e.g., 10 pitch equals 10 characters per inch.

pixel: Contraction of picture element, and measure of resolution or ability to present detail on monitor screen; analogous to halftone dots for printing photographs.

plotter: Device for making hard copy graphics from computer output; most effective way to do so.

printer: Typewriterlike machine for making hard copy printouts of computer data.

printer's dummy: Mock-up of publication to guide printer in making up small publications, such as brochure (or when special requirements must be explained); for larger publications, a running sheet is more appropriate.

process color: Color printing of continuous-tone material, such as color photos.

proportional spacing: Allotting horizontal space for each type element according to width of the element, instead of allowing the same space for each.

ragged right: Opposite of right-justified.

RAM: Random access memory; device that constitutes memory for most small computers, and is what is generally referred to by such designations as "64K computer" or "16K" memory, which denote capacity of RAM in kilobytes.

read-only memory: Designated as ROM, refers to internal device (microchip) with fixed program which cannot be changed, containing instruction set for computer.

read-write: Indicates ability of computer to read what is stored and/or write—add to or change what is written there—as in case of RAM; used as adjective to designate read-write head and other components which permit read-write functions.

reduction: Opposite of blow-up: reduction in size by photographic means.

registration: Alignment of elements on page, especially of pages which must go through the press more than once for successive printings.

registration marks: Guides on copy to help printer in getting proper registration of printed material.

resolution: Ability of monitor screen and/or printer to present detail clearly, usually as a consequence of number of pixels or dots per character block or square inch; partly dependent on hardware quality and partly on software.

roman, roman types: Whole class of typefaces, with serifs and other characteristics.

rubylith: Red plastic film used to mask photographs in camera-ready copy and so create a window for combining line and halftone negatives in a composite.

runaround: Type/text set to permit space, usually of irregular shape or different from normal column width, for tables or illustrations.

running foot: *See* foot.

running head: *See* head.

running sheet: Form instructing printer how to print the publication, especially in specifying which pages print one side only and which are backed up (printed on both sides). *See also* printer's dummy.

rough: Refers to preliminary layout and, also, to preliminary sketch.

sans serif: Without serifs, as in gothic types.

screen: Face of CRT, in word processing hardware references, and to display, in software references; also used, in publications and printing, to refer to device used to break photo up into pattern of dots and to action of so doing.

screen back: Act of using screens, even for line copy, in some cases, to create special effects of (apparent) differences in shade.

screened negative: Negative of photo made through screen; also referred to as halftone negative.

search and replace: *Same as* global search [and replace].

self-mailer: Mailing piece—brochure, newsletter, other—which has address box on outside and does not require envelope or wrapper to be mailed.

sidehead: Headline that begins flush left.

software: Programs and other computer instructions which may be changed readily.

spelling checker: Program that includes dictionary and reviews words for spelling; many are designed to permit additions by user.

splice: *See* mortise.

spooler: Buffer device, used to store information temporarily to permit computer to do other work while printer is operating. *See also* buffer.

stet: Editorial direction to "let it stand" as it was originally (before editorial change).

strip: Splicing line and halftone negatives together to form composite negative.

sulphite bond: Paper made of wood pulp, but resembling rag bond paper.

surprinting: Printing over already printed surface. *See also* overprinting and imprinting.

T/C: Common abbreviation for Table of Contents.

tint block: Technique of printing block of light color, usually by screening back and overprinting in other color.

tone: Material used by illustrators to create special effects, such as shading, somewhat resembling effects of screening back.

upload: Opposite of download; to send file to another computer via modem and telephone connection.

window: Transparent area in negative created by using mask in camera-ready copy, so that composite negative can be made up with splicing negatives.

Bibliography

There has been quite an enormous proliferation of computer books, magazines, newsletters, tabloids, and sundry other publications, although the tide has slowed somewhat in recent months. This latter trend is partly the result of an obvious surplus of popular computer literature—literature about personal computers, that is—and partly this is a reflection of the beginnings of a shakedown in the personal computer industry generally. This has been long heralded—it is not without precedent in other industries—but has only in the past year shown evidence of actually beginning to take place.

The following lists of books and other literature have been selected either because I have personally found them useful or because I believe that at least some of them will be helpful for you. However, not only computer books and periodicals offer useful information about personal computers. Many of the popular or so-called consumer publications also offer articles on the subject. For example, James Fallows, writing in *Atlantic Monthly*, provided me with most useful information that enabled me to "patch" (modify) my WordStar program and make it far more convenient to use, at least for my purposes. But the personal computer has taken hold of so many people in so many places and ways that you may encounter even fairly technical articles on the subject in popular periodicals, even in newspapers. The Monday business tabloid that is part of the *Washington Post* every week has regular articles on the subject and carries a great deal of advertising matter, often quite enlightening and useful, by local suppliers and dealers in computers and related supplies.

The books are of many categories, but in general they introduce the reader to computers, offer specific instructions in programming or some other aspect (such as maintenance), explain in (allegedly) "made simple" terms such complex subjects as various operating systems or languages, list and explain all the technical terms and jargon of computers, or furnish guidelines for buying computers and related hardware or software, and direct the reader to online systems. And there are some that fit none of these categories but are about computers or subjects closely related to computers nevertheless. Moreover, many of these books are of the advanced type—for those who are expert in computers—while others are for those who are rather inexpert and even tyros in the field.

Of course, this book is only incidentally about computers, so the books and periodicals listed here are not about computers exclusively. There are also books and periodicals about seminars, newsletters, and subjects related to those activities, although those listings are not nearly so numerous because there are not nearly as many books and periodicals devoted to those subjects as those which are devoted to computer subjects.

BOOKS

Arth, Marvin, and Helen Ashmore. *The Newsletter Editor's Desk Book*. Shawnee Mission, Kans.: Parkway Press, 1981.

Burgett, Gordon, and Mike Frank. *Speaking For Money*. Carpinteria, Calif.: Communications Unlimited, 1985.

Cane, Mike. *The Computer Phone Book*. New York: New American Library, 1983.

Edwards, Paul, and Sarah Edwards. *How to Make Money with Your Personal Computer*. Sherman Oaks, Calif.: Alfred Publishing Co., 1984.

Froehlich, Robert A. *The Free Software Catalog and Directory*. New York: Crown Publishers, Inc. 1984.

Garvin, Andrew P., and Hubert Bermont. *How to Win With Information or Lose Without it*, Glenelg, Md.: The Consultant's Library, 1983.

Glossbrenner, Alfred. *How to Get Free Software*. New York, St. Martin's Press, 1984.

GTE Telenet. *Directory of Computer-Based Services*. Vienna, Va.: Corporate Headquarters, 1984.

Haas, Lou. *Going On-Line with Your Micro*. Blue Ridge Summit, Penn.: Tab Books, 1984.

Henderson, Bill, editor. *The Publish It Yourself Handbook*, Yonkers: The Pushcart Book Press, 1973.

Holtz, Herman. *Computer Work Stations*. New York: Chapman & Hall, 1985.

———. *How to Buy the Right Personal Computer*. New York: Facts on File, 1984.

———. *How to Make Money with Your Micro*. New York: John Wiley, 1984.

———. *Successful Newsletter Publishing for the Consultant*. Glenelg, Md.: The Consultant's Library, 1983.

————. *Word Processing for Business Publications*, New York: McGraw-Hill, 1984.

Hudson, Howard Penn. *Publishing Newsletters*, New York: Charles Scribner's Sons, 1984.

————. editor. *The Newsletter Yearbook Directory*, 3rd edition, Rhinebeck, N.Y.: The Newsletter Clearinghouse, 1981.

Kuswa, Webster. *Sell Copy*. Cincinnati: Writer's Digest Books, 1979.

Lant, Jeffrey. *The Consultant's Kit: Establishing and Operating Your Successful Consulting Business*. Cambridge, Mass.: JLA Associates, 1983.

————. *Money Talks: The Complete Guide to Creating a Profitable Workshop or Seminar in Any Field*. Cambridge, Mass.: JLA Associates, 1985.

————. *The Unabashed Self-Promoter's Guide: What Every Man, Woman, Child, and Organization Needs to Know About Getting Ahead by Exploiting the Media*. Cambridge, Mass.: JLA Associates, 1984.

McWilliams, Peter A. *The Word Processing Book*. Los Angeles: Prelude Press, 1982.

National Directory of Addresses and Telephone Numbers. New York: Concord Reference Books, current edition (annual).

Ries, Al, and Jack Trout. *Positioning: The Battle for Your Mind*. New York: McGraw-Hill, 1981.

Rosen, Arnold. *Getting the Most Out of Your Word Processor*. Englewood Cliffs, N.J.: Prentice-Hall, 1983.

Shenson, Howard L. *How to Create & Market a Successful Seminar or Workshop*. Glenelg, Md.: The Consultant's Library, 1981.

von Oech, Roger. *A Whack on the Side of the Head*. New York: Warner Books, 1983.

Waite, Mitchell, and Julie Arca. *Word Processing Primer*. New York: McGraw-Hill, 1982.

Writer's Market, The. Cincinnati: Writer's Digest Books, 1985 (annual directory).

PERIODICALS

Despite the array presented here, these are only a few of the computer periodicals being produced today. Many are found commonly on newsstands, but many are found only on extremely well-stocked newsstands and so are not easy to find. And some are available by subscription only. Addresses are therefore furnished for those not readily found on newsstands.

A+, The Independent Guide to Apple Computing. Ziff-Davis, Belmont, CA 94002.

Boston Computer Society, Inc., Boston, MA 02108.

Business Computer Systems, The Magazine for Business Computer Users. Cahners Publishing Co., Boston, MA 02116.

Business Computing, The PC Magazine for Business. Penn Well Publishing Co., Littleton, MA 01460.

Business Software Magazine. Palo Alto, CA 94303.

Christian Computing. Stockridge, GA 30281.

Closing the Gap. Random Graphics, Henderson, MN 56044.

The Color Computer Magazine for TRS–80 Color Computer Users. Ziff-Davis, Camden, ME 08483.

Computer Decisions, The Management Magazine of Computing. Hayden Publishing Co., Inc., Hasbrouck Heights, NJ 07604.

Computer Graphics World. San Francisco, CA 94133.

Computer Shopper. Patch Publishing Co., Inc., Titusville, FL 32781.

Computer Trader Magazine. Lambert Publishing House, Birmingham, AL 35235.

Computer User, For the Tandy/Radio Shack System. McPheters, Wolfe & Jones, Cerritos, CA 90701.

Computerworld. Framingham, MA 01701.

Computing Canada, Canada's Bi-Weekly Data Processing Newspaper. Plesman Publications, Ltd., Ontario M2J 4P8 Canada.

Creative Computing.

The DEC Professional. Professional Press, Inc., Ambler, PA 19002.

Desktop Computing. Peterborough, NH 03458.

Digital Review, The Magazine for DEC Microcomputing.

DM News. New York, NY 10010.

80 Micro, for owners of Tandy/Radio Shack TRS–80 computers.

Hardcopy, The Magazine of Digital Equipment. Seldin Publishing Co., Placentia, CA 92670.

Hot Coco, The Magazine for TRS–80 Color Computer, and MC–10 users. Wayne Green, Inc., Peterborough, NH 03458.

ICP Series Business Review, formerly *ICP Interface Series.* Indianapolis, IN 46240.

inCider. Peterborough, NH 03458.

InfoWorld, The Newsweekly for Microcomputer Users. Menlo Park, CA 94025.

Inkling Literary Journal, The. Inkling Publications, Inc., Alexandria, MN 55308.

Interactive Computing: The Journal of the Association of Computer Users. ACU Research & Education Division, Inc., Boulder, CO 80301.

Interface Age: Computing for Business and Home. Cerritos, CA 90701.

Journal of Systems Management. Cleveland, OH 44138.

Link-Up, Communications and the Small Computer. On-Line Communications, Inc., Minneapolis, MN 55426.

LIST. Redgate Publishing Co., Vero Beach, FL 32963.

Macworld, The Macintosh Magazine. PC World Communications, Inc., San Francisco, CA 94107.

Meeting News. New York, NY 10010.

Meeting Planners' News, New York/New England. Amherst, MA 01002.

Meetings and Conventions. New York, NY 10016.

Micro: The 6502/6809 Journal. Chelmsford, MA 01824.

Micro Communications. Miller Freeman Publications, San Francisco, CA 94105.

Microcomputing, formerly *Kilobaud Microcomputing.* Wayne Green, Inc., Peterborough, NH 03458.

Micro Moonlighter Newsletter. Lewisville, TX 75028.

Microsystems, The Journal for Advanced Microcomputing. Ziff-Davis, New York, NY 10016.

Mini-Micro Systems. Boston, MA 02116.

News/34–38, For Users of IBM Systems 34/36/38. Duke Corporation, Loveland, CO 80537.

Nibble, The Reference for Apple Computing.

Office Administration and Automation. Geyer-McAllister Publications, Inc., NY 10010.

Online Today, The Computer Communications Magazine. CompuServe, Inc., Columbus, OH 43220.

PC: The Independent Guide to IBM Personal Computers.

PC World, The Comprehensive Guide to IBM Personal Computers and Compatibles.

PCM, The Magazine for Professional Computer Management. Falsoft, Inc., Prospect, KY 40059.

Personal Computer Age, The Definitive Journal for the IBM Personal Computer User. Sunland, CA 91040.

Personal Computing. Hasbrouck Heights, NJ 07604.

Popular Computing Magazine. Peterborough, NH 03458.

Portable 100, The Magazine for TRS–80 Model 100 Users. Computer Communications, Inc., Camden, ME 04843.

Rainbow Magazine. Falsoft, Inc., Prospect, KY 40059.

Sharing Ideas Among Professional Speakers and Their Friends. Glendora, CA 91740.

Softalk for the Personal Computer. Softalk Publishing, Inc., North Hollywood, CA 91601.

Softside Magazine. Softside Publications, Inc., Amherst, NH 03031.

Syntax. Syntax ZX80, Inc., POB 457, Harvard, MA 01451.

Systems User. Los Angeles, CA 90026.

Telesystems Journal. OSI Publications, Ltd., Fort Lee, NJ 07024.

UNIX/World, Your Complete Guide to the Frontiers of the Unix System. Tech Valley Publishing, Inc., Los Altos, CA 94022.

Word Processing News. Burbank, CA 91502.

Writer, The. Boston, MA 02116.

Writer's Digest. Cincinnati, OH 45242.

Writers West. San Diego, CA 92116.

Index

About the Author

HERMAN HOLTZ is a consultant, lecturer, and freelance writer. His clients include many FORTUNE 500 companies and government agencies. His experience is reflected in the many books he has written, which include *The Secrets of Practical Marketing for Small Business, How to Succeed as an Independent Consultant, The Business of Public Speaking, Successful Newsletter Publishing for the Consultant, The Advice Business,* and others.

About the Author

HERMAN HOLTZ is a consultant, lecturer, and freelance writer. His clients include many FORTUNE 500 companies and government agencies. His experience is reflected in the many books he has written, which include *The Secrets of Practical Marketing for Small Business, How to Succeed as an Independent Consultant, The Business of Public Speaking, Successful Newsletter Publishing for the Consultant, The Advice Business,* and others.